D0623024

NEW DIRECTIONS

IN

MILITARY SOCIOLOGY

N^{EW} DIRECTIONS

IN

MILITARY SOCIOLOGY

EDITED BY ERIC OUELLET

de Sitter Publications

CANADIAN CATALOGUING IN PUBLICATION DATA

New Directions in Military Sociology
Edited by Eric Ouellet

ISBN 1-897160-03-8

Copyright © 2005 de Sitter Publications, Whitby, Ontario, Canada

| Cover design: | de Sitter Publications. |
| Front cover: | Photo of Colonel Alain Tremblay, Canadian Commanding Officer of the National Command Element, looks out over Kabul from TV Hill, an observation post overlooking the Afghan capital. Photo courtesy of the Canadian Department of National Defence. |

de Sitter Publications
104 Consumers Dr.
Whitby, ON
L1N 1C4
Canada

www.desitterpublications.com

Contents

About the Authors

MORTEN **E**NDER is the Sociology Program Director and Associate Professor of Sociology in the Department of Behavioral Sciences and Leadership at the United States Military Academy at West Point, New York, U.S.A. He is an award-winning teacher at both the University of Maryland and West Point. He is the editor of two recent books *Military Brats and Other Global Nomads: Growing Up in Organization Families* (Praeger Publications 2002) and *Inequalities: Readings in Diversity and Social Life* (with Betsy Lucal, Pearson Custom Publishing 2005). His most recent published research examines the uses and treatment of core sociological knowledge in the teaching of undergraduate sociology.

ULRICH VOM **H**AGEN is a research fellow at the Bundeswehr Institute for Social Research (SOWI), Germany. He holds an M.A. in Public Administration and is currently writing a dissertation on "Military Culture" in sociology at the Humboldt University of Berlin. He gives lectures in military sociology at the Humboldt University and at Potsdam University. His current research interests include concepts of moral leadership, civil-military relations, organizational theory, and aspects of transnational security policy within European integration.

PAUL **H**IGATE is Lecturer in Social Policy at the School for Policy Studies in the University of Bristol, UK. He held a Ministry of Defence Fellowship from 2001 to 2003 exploring the experiences of veterans over a period of 2 years after leaving the British armed forces. Currently, Paul is Principal

Investigator on an Economic and Social Research Council grant to examine gendered relations between male peacekeepers and local men and women in three Peace Support Operations. Prior to embarking on an academic career, Paul served in the Royal Air Force for 8 years where he rose to the rank of Corporal.

ANNE IRWIN teaches anthropology at the University of Calgary and the University of Victoria. She received BA and M.A. degrees in anthropology from the University of Calgary and a Ph.D. in social anthropology from the University of Manchester. A former reserve officer, she is a graduate of the Canadian Land Forces Command and Staff College. She has conducted field research with a Canadian infantry unit and is working on a book about the social organization of soldiering.

LJUBICA JELUSIC is a full professor of defense studies at the Faculty of Social Sciences, University of Ljubljana, Slovenia. She teaches military sociology, polemology, peace studies and anthropology of war. She has a B.A. in International relations and a B.A. in Defense studies, a M.SC. in Defense Science, and a Ph.D. in Political Sciences from the University of Ljubljana. She also teaches at the Senior Officers Course and General Staff Course of Slovenian Army. Her research topics are civil-military relations, peacekeeping, and human resource management in the military.

RENÉ MOELKER is Associate Professor of sociology at the Royal Netherlands Military Academy. He holds a Ph.D. from the Erasmus University Rotterdam. His work in military sociology concentrates on the sociology of military families, military technology, the military profession, the military sociology of Norbert Elias, military education, conflict in Chechnya, and media.

ix

IGOR V. OBRAZTSOV, Ph.D. (Sociology), served twenty-five years as a career officer (Colonel). He is Assistant Professor of Sociology in the Department of Military-Humanitarian Sciences of the Military Academy of the General Staff and Associate Professor of Sociology in the Department of Social Policy and Administration in Social Processes of the Academy of Labor and Social Relations. Areas of interest include historical and theoretical-methodological problems of military sociology in the world. His major publications include *The Russian Army from Afghanistan up to Chechnya: A Sociological Analysis* (Moscow 1997 in cooperation with S.Solov'yov) [Russian]; "Military Sociology," in *The Sociological Encyclopedia* (Moscow 2003) [Russian]; "The Study of Military and Society in Russia," in Callaghan and Kernic, *Armed Forces and International Security: Global Trends and Issues* (Muenster: LIT 2003).

ERIC OUELLET is Director of Academics at the Canadian Forces College and Head of the Department of Defence Studies at the Royal Military College of Canada. He teaches military sociology, leadership, and command. He has an undergraduate and Master's degree in political science from Université Laval (Quebec City) and a Ph.D. in sociology from York University (Toronto). He is presently researching the social construction of military facts and knowledge in digitized command centers.

FABIAN VIRCHOW lectures at the University of Applied Sciences Kiel (Germany). He studied sociology, political science, and social history at the University of Hamburg where he also graduated as a sociologist. As a project manager at the Technology Foundation of the state of Schleswig-Holstein he worked on the European level for several years (especially in the field of Information Societies) before returning to the academic field. He recently finished his Ph.D. in Political Science at the Free University of Berlin conducting research on the far right's concepts of foreign and military policy in Germany.

CLAUDE WEBER is a professor and researcher at the French Military Academy St-Cyr in Coëtquidan, France, in the department of sociology. He teaches military sociology, intercultural relations, management in professional armies, military public communication. He has a Ph.D. in social sciences (ethnology) from the Marc Bloch University (Strasbourg, France). He is presently conducting research on joint warfare in French military operations.

C h a p t e r

NEW DIRECTIONS IN MILITARY SOCIOLOGY

Eric Ouellet
Canadian Forces College and
Royal Military College of Canada
Toronto, Canada

LEARNING OBJECTIVES

After reading this chapter, you should be able to

- recognize the functionalist nature of military sociology;
- understand how military sociology is positioned in the general field of sociology;
- appreciate the difficulty of developing a fully critical approach in military sociology;
- identify the potential applications of the interpretative approach in military sociology;
- describe the central role of organized violence in the sociology of the armed forces.

1

Military sociology, also known as sociology of the
military, is a lesser-known subfield of sociology.
Although sociologists have studied the military from
time to time in the past, only after the end of Second World
War have military affairs become a recurrent object of sociological research. Two distinct branches, or traditions, have
emerged since that time: one branch deals with civil-military
relations, and the other deals with the military as an institution. Research in these two areas was pioneered by two
American social scientists, Samuel Huntington and Morris
Janowitz respectively.

Samuel Huntington, through the publication of his
classic *The Soldier and the State* in 1957, set parameters for
the study of civil-military relations that are still standing to
this day. The study of civil-military relations attempts to
analyze how, in a given society, the armed forces interact with
the civilian authorities. Whether concerned with how a democracy like the United States can keep effective control over its
military, or how the military in South America has constituted
a modern version of the Praetorian Guards system that installs
and removes civilian leaders as it sees fit, the study of civil-
military relations can be described as a specialized form of
political sociology.

The creation of the second branch in military sociology is closely associated with the works of Morris Janowitz,
particularly his classic book *The Professional Soldier* published
in 1960. Janowitz, and many others after him, were interested
in studying the military as a social institution and as a profession. One of the key findings in the *Professional Soldier* was
that military organizations in the West were becoming increasingly professional in the attitudes, skills, and knowledge required
to functioning as a modern military. Joining the military was
less and less a matter of vocation. The importance of long-

term adherence to the institution and its values has been gradually replaced by the necessity of professional competencies. Out of this analysis, emerged the famous I/O (Institutional/Occupational) model, which analyzes a military organization in comparison to either a traditional vocational institution or, rather, any other work organization. Hence, this second branch of military sociology became, in many ways, a specialized form of sociology of the professions.

This brief overview is not intended as a history of military sociology, there are excellent historical descriptions in other works (Burk 1993; Caforio 2003c). However, it helps us to contextualize the Janowitzian branch of military sociology, which is the main focus of this collected edition. This tradition in military sociology has evolved over the years to include issues related to compulsory military service; women, visible minorities, and gays and lesbians in the armed forces; the lives of military families; military reactions to peace support operations, etc. This tradition is rich and lively. However, the production of this edited collection is motivated by both a certain disappointment with the present state of military sociology and the prospect of new opportunities for the field.

For the newcomer to military sociology, many assumptions in the field appear rather strange. For instance, some studies, although formally part of the realm of sociology, appear more germane to human resource management studies. This feeling of strangeness can also be found among some more seasoned military sociologists, particularly within the circles associated with the network of military sociologists in organizations such as the Inter-University Seminar of Armed Forces and Society (IUS) and the Research Committee 1 on Armed Forces and Conflict Resolution of the International Sociological Association (ISA RC01). Some have found military sociology to be too functionalist, too oriented toward

3

pragmatic ends, or even that it is not sociological enough. While no one is saying that most military sociologists are not doing excellent work, there is an impression among many that the field is too narrow and would benefit from expanding its horizons.

It is important to underline that, like sociology at large, military sociology has been influenced by various waves of intellectual fervor, such as feminist studies, postmodern studies, race and ethnicity studies, etc. Mady Segal (1982) was instrumental in introducing and advancing the study of women in the armed forces since the late 1970s. James Burk edited a collection in 1994 introducing postmodern analysis into military sociology. Moreover, there is the 1999 collected edition by Soeters and van der Meulen on managing diversity in the armed forces. Military sociology, understood here in its Janowitzian version, touches upon a variety of topics and borrows from many theoretical frameworks.

As it will be discussed in greater detail below, the source of dissatisfaction is not that military sociology is excluding any topics per se. One can refer to the wide array of papers presented at the Biannual IUS Conference or at the meetings of ISA RC01 to see that variety is not an issue. What *is* perceived as problematic is *how* the military institution is viewed. One of the possible directions for military sociology is to look at the military institution from the other end of the spectrum. In other words, military sociology, traditionally, takes the institution for granted when it studies the various facets of military life. What this chapter proposes, is to regard the military institution as the final outcome of military life rather than its starting point. This important complementary view about institutions is build in the interpretative paradigm in sociology, which remains clearly underused in military sociology.

The purpose of this chapter, therefore, is to explore those impressions mentioned above, put them into their specific context, and to offer some fruitful directions for military sociology to broaden some of its epistemological and ontological assumptions. Lastly, this chapter will introduce the other chapters of this edited collection, which explain, too, other directions (along with concrete illustrations) for military sociology.

How Military Sociologists View the Field

Military sociology has been described as a special sociology (Caforio 2003b; Boene 1981) as it is a subfield of the main discipline, which is especially dedicated to a particular theme (i.e., the armed forces). The description "special sociology," however, is somewhat misleading. Much of sociology is already divided into special subfields such as the sociology of gender, family, professions, culture, knowledge, etc. However, military sociology can be considered a special subfield because it draws heavily on other specific subfields in order to create its own intellectual sphere. For instance, the study of military families is very much indebted to sociology of the family; the study of minorities in the armed forces draws it is main theoretical framework from sociological studies of minorities and the workplace, and so on

This practice of borrowing from other subfields of sociology is not new in military sociology. As proposed by Morris Janowitz, "the subject of the institutional analysis of war and peace encompasses military organizations, civil-military relations, war disarmament, peace-keeping, and the management and reduction of conflict" (1975:15). In a different context, Janowitz (1979) believed there to be a threefold thematic distinction: "studies dealing with the military organization and the military profession, studies dealing with the relationships between the armed forces and society, and studies pertaining to conflicts and war in particular" (quoted in Nuciari 2003:63). One can immediately see that military sociology draws from the sociology of organization and professions, political sociology, and security studies. In a way, military sociology could be considered a "sub-subfield" of sociology, as it often constitutes a second degree of specialization. Although conceptual frameworks are borrowed, this does not lend itself to an interactive debate with the sociological community from which those concepts are borrowed. Military sociology has a strong empirical bent and concepts are used very often in an instrumental way, rather than through self-reflective inquiries. In other words, concepts are borrowed because they are useful, not because there is desire to further our understanding of the concepts themselves or to refine them. This is not to say, however, that military sociology did not develop some of its own concepts and research agendas. But they are quite specialized in nature and tend to remain confined to the study of military organizations, such as military cohesion (Shils and Janowitz 1948), the institutional/occupational model (Moskos 1977), and peacekeeping missions and related issues (Moskos 1976).

There is a tendency toward a second degree of specialization because military sociology aims at studying a specific formal institution, the armed forces, while other subfields study institutions that have far-reaching and informal boundaries such as gender, social stratification, or knowledge. The unique and special research framework of the military institution is the key to understanding the epistemological and ontological status of military sociology.

Any discussion concerning the epistemological and ontological status of military sociology invariably starts by

---

New Direction 1.1

Whether it is the growing importance of women and non-Caucasians in Western armed forces or the new demands imposed by military operations other than war, media scrutiny, etc., the institution of the armed forces remains the starting point of the analysis of change.

---

presenting the original agenda put forth by Morris Janowitz, as he was so instrumental in creating this subfield of sociology. Some key points should be highlighted. First, one has to remember that "Janowitz's central thesis is that the Military institution must be examined in its process of change because it must necessarily change with the changing conditions of the society to which it belongs" (Caforio 2003c:17). It can be argued that this primary goal remains the essence of military sociology. Whether it is the growing importance of women and non-Caucasians in Western armed forces or the new demands imposed by military operations other than war, media scrutiny, etc., the institution of the armed forces remains the starting point of the analysis of change.

Janowitz believed that the influence of military sociology on policy was of paramount importance and the Inter-University Seminar (IUS), as an academic organization, was to play a critical role. Burk, a colleague of Janowitz, explained this perspective:

> The idea of the IUS as a "bridging institution" was not simply a reenactment of Janowitz's wartime experience, but an idea justified by the political requirements of the postwar era. As Janowitz wrote in 1971 [in a letter to William Bader], "A new intellectual, critical,

7

and truly academic relation between the universities and the military will have to be created—since such contacts will be essential for effective civilian control and a meaningful military policy." (Burk 1993:178)

Janowitz clearly believed that military sociologists should seek a balance between having access to the military institution and creating enough distance from the military institution to criticize it. He was particularly worried about the rise of "unanticipated militarism" (Burk 1993:180) in the United States (which is very much a current issue in the context of the so-called War on Terror). This pragmatic and prescriptive epistemology was certainly in concordance with the ontological primacy given to the military institution as the starting point of any analysis. Yet, it is important to note that Janowitz also had concerns about this situation. For him, "'military sociology' places excessive emphasis on the boundaries—the formal boundaries—of the military. In effect, it tends to remove the military as an object of research from the societal environment" (Janowitz 1975:15).

The combination of both of these ontological and epistemological conditions is the well-known hallmark of the functionalist paradigm in sociology, which, like Comte's approach to the social, is dedicated to "human and social unity" (Aron 1965:59). Military sociologists trained by Janowitz have subsequently agreed that military sociology is dominated by functionalism (Segal, Wechsler Segal, and Eyre 1992:123).

Military sociology, in its proximity to the military institution, is also limited by it. As a result, some military sociologists conclude that "military sociology issues in general are not of broad national interest, outside the military organization. This is of course reflected in little support for research"

(Caforio and Nuciari 2003:33-34). Furthermore, because most research funds are coming from the military institution, "researchers sometimes complain about restrictions in the choice of research topics, pressure in order to get fast and ready-to-use results (at the expense of a deeper and cautious scientific outlook), or even about the perceived underestimation and final uselessness of their work" (Caforio and Nuciari 2003:38). Again, Janowitz saw this as being a serious problem for military sociology:

> While the distinction between basic and applied research is an elusive one in the social sciences, it is clear that the pressure of day-to-day problems and the elaborate organization of research support lead the military to subsidize 'operational' research which does not necessarily contribute either to a deeper understanding of military institutions or to the development of the social sciences. (Janowitz 1974:20)

Even within the parameters of the functionalist paradigm, it is possible to conclude that "one of the issues that the sociology of the military is called to deal with in the near future is therefore that of more complete freedom of research, freedom that is in the very interest of the potential commissioner, as only in this way can data of sure reliability be provided" (Caforio 2003d:443). Janowitz envisioned and attempted to produce the appropriate mechanisms (and analytical tools) for effectively criticizing the military institution (for its own good) and for developing a genuine intellectual debate with the military. This vision, also shared by many others, has yet to be fulfilled.

Another problem caused by the strong functionalist bent in military sociology is that it tends to isolate the researcher

9

from the rest of the discipline, particularly from sociological subfields that reject outright the functionalist paradigm. This isolation, as stated above, is certainly compounded by a simple lack of interest for military matters by sociologists in general. Yet, military sociology also suffers from the problem of guilt by association. As stated by Burk, historically "there were concerns that obtaining data from the military required political contacts and the image that one was a 'friend' of the military. And there was a general reluctance to identify oneself too closely with military studies" (Burk 1993:177).

Sociologists understand that studying military matters from a sociological perspective can provide, *de facto,* certain legitimacy to the military in the eyes of the sociological community. Within many sociologists' worldview, military matters are usually associated with capitalism, patriarchy, and authoritarian decision-making structures, which are part of the worst "ills" of Western civilization. In other words, many sociologists, with regard to their professional context, would prefer to leave military matters for others to study.

This reluctance to be associated with the military is a defensible perspective, especially in view of the growing importance of the critical paradigm in sociology since the 1960s. Proximity to, and familiarity with, powerful institutions is a very delicate matter in sociology. This is clearly illustrated by one of the key points of contention in the well-known

---

New Direction 1.2

Sociologists understand that studying military matters from a sociological perspective can provide, *de facto,* certain legitimacy to the military in the eyes of the sociological community.

---

rivalry between sociology and psychology. Indeed, sociologists nowadays talk about psychology in the following terms:

> No matter how benevolent one as a psychologist may
> be towards those one studies, no matter how concerned
> with "their" liberation, with "their" betterment, with
> preventing "their" victimization, etc., the fact is that
> "their" lives are made sense of in terms which do not
> in fact make sense to "them." They only make sense, as
> Smith (1988) points out, within the "ruling appara-
> tuses" of the State, e.g. within schools, universities,
> polytechnics, the law and the police, health care, social
> welfare policy, etc. (Parker and Shotter 1990:3)

To draw another parallel, this kind of criticism, leveled
against psychology, is not unique and is also echoed within the
discipline of history toward military history. Traditional historians are often accused by social and cultural historians, who
now form the dominant historical paradigms, of replicating
myths and narratives that justify oppression, colonialism,
sexism, racism, etc. Academic military historians are often
perceived as being more traditional and too integrated into the
military institution (such as faculty in military academies,
staff and war colleges, etc). The greatest consequence of these
perceptions is that they frequently find themselves isolated
from the rest of their discipline and apparently facing the serious danger of disappearing as a subfield of history (Lynn 1997).
If guilt by association is often an outcome of perceived
proximity to powerful institutions or military matters, then
military sociologists may have reason to be concerned about
the future of their discipline. Hence, it is possible that military
sociology, from the perspective of social epistemology, is
doubly limited by its functionalist approach to the military

institution. Not only are certain approaches to military life not studied because they are not "useful" to the military decision-makers (who often provide the financial and material resources to conduct research), but also interesting sociological perspectives from other subfields are not applied to military objects out of principle.

It is in this context that the broadening the epistemological horizons of military sociology becomes critical. Not only would other dimensions of armed forces and society be studied, but this would also allow for the building of bridges with the other branches of sociology. The following section explores one possible way of building those bridges.

A New Direction in Military Sociology

C. Wright Mills (1959), in his classic work *The Sociological Imagination*, underlined that sociology should serve, first and foremost, as an eye opener and a mind opener. Sociology, according to Mills, should be called upon to look beyond the obvious and the familiar ways of doing things and should be innovative in making sense of possible choices and perspectives. Military sociology, evaluated under this light, does not fare too well, as it is relatively unknown in the broader sociological community and is even less known in most Western societies in general.

Those who follow Mills' advice consider sociological imagination as essentially a capacity to criticize and are, for the most part, doing their work from the perspective of critical sociology. Given the critical turn that many sociologists have embraced since the 1960s, could the creation of a critical military sociology be enough to establish bridges between traditional military sociology and other sociological approaches, and make it more imaginative overall? Some have already

12

accomplished this. For instance, feminists have already written extensively on the military from a critical perspective. Similarly, there is a small but growing literature on gays and lesbians in the military that employs a critical perspective. Although those studies have their own merit, given their specialized nature, they do not truly engage the larger discipline of sociology.

In itself, the critical tradition has not been very successful in expanding horizons in military sociology. Could it be otherwise in the future? If the present trend continues, the answer appears to be unlikely. Unless one wants to merge military sociology with peace studies or the "new" security studies, access to empirical material from the armed forces remains crucial, and going to military decision-makers for access with a critical epistemology is not an easy sale. As clearly stated by military sociologists,

> when speaking with sociologists and social scientists in general dealing with the armed forces, a common trait arises, about a more or less explicit and more or less widespread mood of "suspicion" and "reticence" on the part of military institutions toward sociology and social scientists in general; such a mood has to be overcome and turned into trust by means of an accurate and somewhat continuous action of explanation, clarification, and reassurance that the research is necessary and that its outcome will be fruitful and the intentions are positively bound to the well-being of the institution. (Caforio and Nuciari 2003:38)

Another more likely possibility is to re-energize the use of the interpretative tradition in military sociology. Again, as with the critical tradition, the interpretative tradition is not completely new in military sociology. One can cite the discussions on the military mind (Abrahamsson 1972; Garb 2000; Jelusic 2003), the study of initiation rituals from an anthropological perspective (Winslow 1997), and studies on masculinities and the warrior ethos (Dunivin 1994). There is a growing literature on military culture, but one has to be aware that it is mostly produced from a managerial and functionalist perspective (Winslow 2000). Among the studies using the concept of culture from an interpretative approach, there are the flight decks studies of Weick and Roberts (1993), the Winslow (1998) study of misplaced loyalties, and the Ricks (1997) study on the Marines Corps.

It is important, before going any further, to clarify what is meant by the interpretative tradition, because it is often misunderstood. The interpretative tradition is "informed by a concern to understand the world as it is; to understand the fundamental nature of the social world at the subjective level of experience. It seeks explanation within the realm of individual consciousness and subjectivity, within the frame of reference of the participant, as opposed to the observer of action" (Burrell and Morgan 1979:28). This tradition is also referred to as the constructionist perspective and "the conceptual center of the perspective, which some constructionist might argue does not exist, lies in the proposition that constructs (definitions, ideas, values, beliefs) are inseparable from and mutually constitutive of social conditions (categories, 'facts', forms, structures)" (Maines 2000:578). The interpretative tradition, therefore, is first and foremost concerned with how our preconceived ideas and perceptions shape social life, rather than attempting to change society (critical tradition). This is not say that the sociological research inspired by the interpretative tradition cannot participate in social change, it has done just that for a long time now, but it is not the primary objective of the approach.

14

The interpretative tradition in sociology is often associated with the works of Max Weber (1864-1920). However, this tradition has older and broader roots. The German philosopher Immanuel Kant (1724-1803) is probably the most important source of this tradition. For Kant, the universe is made up of *a priori* truths, which implies that we have a rather complex relationship with our surrounding environment. *A priori* truths are derived by reasoning from self-evident propositions and help us decipher our experience in the empirical world. Otherwise, we would not be able to comprehend what we observe and experience. This phenomenon is often illustrated by philosophers of science through this short dialogue: "Just observe," says the scientist. "Observe what?" replies the student. In other words, we need to know what we are looking for in order to see it clearly. This does not mean that we can make and structure reality the way we want, or that our knowledge will not change once we look attentively, or that we will not find anything new; this simply means that we need to discover the starting points and know that any relationship with reality occurs only through the mediation of our preexisting ideas. For both scientific research and ordinary daily activities, these starting points are deeply embedded in our social and cultural constructs, norms, and values. This position, lately, has been referred to as scientific realism (Bhaskar 1978; Harré 1986), which is a form of epistemological relativism (i.e., our relationship with the world can only occur in a mediated way through our preconceptions) combined with ontological positivism (i.e., the independent existence of world around us is accepted as such).

Other philosophers such as Wilhelm Dilthey (1833-1911) and Edmund Husserl (1859-1938) have pushed Kant's ideas further. Dilthey, in particular, developed the concept of *verstehen,* which means understanding by trying to see the

15

world from the point of view of the social actor. Max Weber, then, took this concept to develop an understanding of the social group, particularly institutions, by seeing the world from the point of view of the people that are a part of them; focusing on their *a priori* knowledge. This led him to develop his well-known concept of ideal-type. It is for this reason that this tradition is often referred to as being "interpretative," because sociologists try to interpret how others see the world. This tradition has flourished ever since with the ethno-methodological work of Harold Garfinkle (1967), the symbolic interactionist perspective developed by George Herbert Mead (1934) and continued by scholars such as Herbert Blumer (1969) and Norman Denzin (1989), the well-known work on the social construction of reality by Peter Berger and Thomas Luckmann (1966), and, more recently, the actor-network theory developed by social scientists such as Bruno Latour (1986) and Michel Callon et al. (1986) in the science studies.

As one can see, the interpretative tradition in sociology is a rich one and has a lot to offer for military sociology. Not only can old and new topics be studied and analyzed under a different light, but it also allows military sociology to engage the rest of sociology on a common ground. To follow are a few examples of how the interpretative tradition can bring additional sociological imagination to military sociology.

Western armed forces are facing a greater variety of missions with less-than-clear objectives. Troops are thrown into complex and violent intra-state conflicts for which they are too often not well-prepared (Winslow 1997, Thiéblemont 1999). Simultaneously, there is a shrinking recruiting pool combined with a diminishing interest in military life. These new realities are very much a matter of how social constructs are formed about war and about the military in general. Thus,

16

an interpretative approach is certainly a well-suited approach to understanding how new preconceptions and constructs will lead to an evolution of the military institution. For instance, beyond the functionalist studies geared toward understanding why people join the military and how human resources policies should adapt, the mutation of the ideal-type of the military person needs to be better understood. The interpretative approach reverses the angle of questioning. In the context of the increasing importance of military missions other than war, some have already asked whether soldiers should see themselves as social workers, diplomats, police officers, general laborers, etc. But if they do, then it is not only a matter of managing human resources, it is also a matter of defining how those preconceptions modify the institution in the long run, *in spite of any human resources policy*. These new social realities, therefore, are both challenges and opportunities for military sociology to renew its utilitarian dimension while engaging the broader sociological community about wider societal changes and their associated conceptual assessments.

If one looks at the specific social construct making the military institution possible, many issues can be added to military sociology. Since the end of the Cold War, armed forces have evolved quite rapidly. Such evolution occurs at many levels. First, in the Western world there has been a "general demilitarization of society" (Scott 2001:190). Not only have defense budgets been reduced in the post-Cold War era, but also the willingness to make sacrifices appears weaker.

Fighting at a distance, particularly from high in the sky as well as the limited involvement of ground forces, and a fear of showing casualties in the media are emerging as central features of Western armed forces' approach to war. The first Gulf War and operations in Bosnia, Kosovo, and Afghanistan are clear illustrations of such tendencies. On the other hand, since the events of September 11, 2001, one can observe in the

17

United States a relative remilitarization of the American society. Yet, the willingness to fight a prolonged conflict in Iraq appears unclear at the present time. Again, beyond the known tensions that the post-Cold War era creates in civil-military relations, the implications of the new ways of looking at war (e.g., fighting at a distance) have been enunciated by some, but not thoroughly explored. In other words, there are a lot of general discussions on the "Nintendo Wars," but rarely do they reach enough depth to explain how the soldiers' self-concept is affected, which, in turn, might affect the kind of military institution that will emerge. By using an interpretative perspective, military sociologists can engage their fellow sociologists in critical debates on important issues such as the emerging forms of social organization (e.g., Western armed forces as indirect security provider, particularly the demilitarization and digital remilitarization of societies; the role of the mass media in shaping new institutional ideal-types; etc.) In other words, what the military institution will become also has to be assessed from the point of view of the forces that shape its existence in the first place.

Along the same lines, it is possible to expand upon Martin van Creveld's (1991) *Transformation of War*, one of the best-known works on the changing nature of armed conflicts. According to Van Creveld,

> If no nuclear holocaust takes place, then conventional war appears to be in the final stages of abolishing itself; if one does take place, then it will already have abolished itself. This dilemma does not mean that perpetual peace is on the way, much less that organized violence is coming to an end. As war between states exits through one side of history's revolving door, low-intensity conflict among different organizations will enter through the other (1991: 224).

18

In other words, we are "moving away from the Clausewitezian trinity of the state, the army, and the people. Wars between nations…will be replaced by intra-state warfare in which national boundaries will no longer hold a central place" (Moskos and Burk 1994:149). Although some might consider van Creveld's position as somewhat extreme, most analysts agree that Western armed forces are increasingly involved in conflicts where traditional constructs (e.g., state-controlled forces, regular formations, uniforms, etc.) are absent or disappearing fast. The various wars of liberation and the Vietnam War, Rwanda, Somalia, and the former Yugoslavia are good examples of such a tendency. In this context, to be a military person, strictly speaking, requires more than just being involved in military operations. Military leaders, particularly, now have the responsibility of giving meaning to conflicts that appear to be foreign to their troops' expectations and preparations. Social constructs, such as patriotism, courage, gallantry, liberation, and oppression, are increasingly open to new interpretations by the very people on the ground facing violence and conflicts. Additional common research interests with other sociologists can be built. For instance, the issue of power-knowledge within evolving institutions, as described by Foucault and those who followed him, can be used to raise serious questions about how institutions truly dominate through knowledge in a world where information and educa-

---

New Direction 1.3

Militias, paramilitary forces, irregular forces, and private security forces are fully a part of military reality and, therefore, should be full-fledged topics of interests to military sociologists.

19

tion are so abundant and where official knowledge and reality on the ground appear so disconnected. Conflicts outside the Western world obviously lead to serious questions about the meaning of modernity and tradition, the right to intervene to defend human security, and neocolonialism, which are topics of interest to many sociologists. These issues also have a tremendous impact on conceptions of identity for the "military person" and what they "ought to do." Lastly, many usual social constructs surrounding the armed forces are challenged. Militias, paramilitary forces, irregular forces, and private security forces are fully a part of military reality and, therefore, should be full-fledged topics of interests to military sociologists. In doing so, they can engage criminologists and political sociologists in interesting sociological debates. The Western military institutions are experiencing profound transformations, but such transformations are the outcomes of the mutation of key social frames of reference.

Military operations other than war (MOOTW), including peacekeeping, peace support operations, and peacemaking, are well known for their intense exposure to media coverage, far-reaching political and civilian control, and their associated requests for new military capabilities to support the reconstruction of devastated civil societies. Yet, not only do they involve "a growing complexity" of tasks, they also place military personnel in situations where mission goals are facing constant political "interference" (Shamir and Ben-Ari 2000:49). This issue goes beyond studying civil-military relations in a given country. This has immediate implications for those directly involved in conflicts and facing violence. One of the immediate implications is "our young officers are routinely thrust into volatile, uncertain, complex, and ambiguous situations in which more is demanded of them in terms of intellect, initiative, and leadership than was normally seen during the

Cold War" (McCausland and Martin 2001:19). Not only do they have to provide meaning to what is to be accomplished by their troops, as stated above, but military officers also become, more than ever, integrated into the political realm. The very idea that the military constitutes a profession distinct from the profession of the politician is rapidly eroding. The self-concept of a military person is also in a process of mutation in this respect. In this context, military sociologists can enter into interesting debates with other sociologists who use Bourdieu's concept of *habitus* to understand institutional life. How long is it possible for the military to maintain a self-concept that is becoming increasingly out-of-phase with its social conditions? How does this happen, and can this change?

The various transformations described above are accompanied by other transformations occurring in the larger society. One of them is the increasing importance of techno-logical knowledge and apparatus. As early as 1982, Kellett argued "technological change increased the interdependence of military society and civilian society and altered the mili-tary's internal social structure. New roles—the 'military manager' and the 'military technologist'—developed and sometimes supplanted the earlier staple of the heroic leader. In turn, these roles resulted in different and more consensual leadership patterns" (Kellett 1982:61). With a few exceptions, such as René Moelker's (2003) analysis of technological deter-minism in a military context, military sociologists have an almost untapped field in which to engage sociologists of knowledge and technology and proponents of the Actor-Network Theory in order to understand military affairs. Since the beginning of the industrialization of war in the nineteenth century, a large portion of the military personnel has been spending a lot of their time attending to various machines and pieces of equipment. Today, those machines are more present

21

than ever and include objects such as ships' armament systems, digital command systems, truck spare parts inventory, etc. As in the world of science and technology, those machines, also named actants (Latour 1988), participate in constructing social relations and networks to shape institutions. Again, this offers the possibility of creating interesting debates with sociologists of science and knowledge.

The examples provided above illustrate how much military sociology can expand the nature of its epistemological reach, establish linkages with the other subfields of sociology, inform the military institution on a variety of issues that have not been thoroughly studied, while being able to criticize the institution in view of those new realities. This is not to say that no sociologists have touched upon those topics. There is a small but growing literature pertaining to the examples provided above. However, the expansion of military sociology needs to occur within its own boundaries to include other perspectives and paradigms.

Discussion

Another important opportunity for military sociology, in the expansion of its epistemological reach, is the possibility of defining a specific social realm for study, rather than a specific formal institution. In the previous section, it was briefly shown that many concepts related to war and war-fighting are becoming much less clear-cut since the end of the Cold War. Similarly, the expression "armed forces" is certainly a useful construct, but as the existing parameters seem to blur in the post-modern world, it would be important to reflect on the possibilities of a broader and more flexible construct. For instance, if it is true that military might in the West is the exclusive domain of nation-states, it is clear that elsewhere this is not the case. Furthermore, the present expansion of the so-called "War on Terror" has brought a new emphasis on private armed security apparatus sponsored by Western states. Clearly, the very idea of "armed forces" is becoming less attached to the traditional conceptions found in the West.

It is in this context that an interpretative sociological approach to the military can be particularly useful. After all, it is our understanding and perceptions of war, war-fighting, and armed forces that have evolved. The brutality of armed violence might change from a technological point of view, e.g., increased firepower, but otherwise human suffering has not. This section, therefore, proposes a short discussion on a possible central construct that would be helpful both to understand the present change of perspective about armed forces and provide a useful conceptual framework for military sociologists.

The central construct, which appears to me as already latent in military sociology, is violence or, more accurately, organized violence. Military sociology is the sociology of organized violence. This might appear unusual to some, but violence is the object of study of military sociologists. What needs to be clarified, here, is that violence, as a social reality, does not necessarily have to be enacted: the potential or the threat of violence is a real social object, too, in that it influences perceptions and behaviors. Violence can be found in various forms and through many channels: *actually* present, such as in times of conflicts; *symbolically* ritualized through training, exercise, uniforms, rank systems, etc.; or as *potential* through the military institution as the ultimate guarantor of the political order. In this context, the interpretative tradition as described above is well-suited to developing a better understanding of our relationship with organized violence. The reality of violence, actual, potential, or symbolic, is not questioned (ontological positivism), but the way we construct violence is never set once and for all (epistemological relativism). Along similar lines, Sir John Hackett is well-known for reinforcing the idea that military people, and especially the officers, are managers of violence, emphasizing that violence can be managed in a professional way (hence, the expression "the profession of arms") or, perhaps, not so professionally (Hackett 1983:103).

Some authors, such as Michel Maffesoli, have written about the foundational character of violence establishing symbolic order. Similarly, von Bredow (2003) presents an interesting analysis about how violence, order, and the military interact as social constructs in civil-military relations and in the international system. These, and other interesting studies (such as the various studies about peacekeeping missions where troops have to be "mentally refocused" in how they use violence) provide interesting examples of how violence, although real, is also a social construct because of our precon- ceptions, our understanding, and our acceptance/rejection of violence. In turn, those social constructs will define the forms of violent actions.

The idea of a sociology of violence is not a new one, but for various reasons has historically been subsumed to either criminology when violence does not have political ends and to political sociology when it does have a political purpose. Yet, both criminology and political sociology have emphasized the study of violence on the "receiving end" of it, so to speak, i.e., the impact on the victims of violence. Military sociology, however, emphasizes the study of violence at the other end of the spectrum, i.e., those who use violence in an organized way (it must be noted that military personnel are also victims of violence whether in its actual or symbolic form). In this light, it is easy to understand why most military

---

New Direction 1.4

Military sociology, however, emphasizes the study of violence at the other end of the spectrum, i.e., those who use violence in an organized way...

---

sociologists have focused their research on regular armed forces, which are expected to respect certain rules of ethics and the laws of armed conflict, or at very least the "good guys" in partisan warfare (for instance, Malinowski 1944). However, some studies, like Bartov's well-known (1991) research on the nazification of the German Army during the Second World War, show that it is indeed possible to create a sociology of violence emphasizing the bad guys too.

Other issues, analyzed through the lenses of violence, understood in its social construction, shed a new light on older questions. It is possible to clarify certain research agendas, for instance the internalization of violence by veterans, military women, and their primary and secondary socialization to violence; military education as a form socialization to organized violence; military family and its relationship with violence at large; military leadership framing the meaning of organized violence; the social construction of terrorist violence in the military institution, etc.

As one can see, the potential of expanding the use of the interpretative approach within military sociology is substantial, particularly if organized violence is used as a central operating concept. If, indeed, violence exists within a web of social conditions, then the present Western military institutions are only one possible type of outcome, based on our socially mediated relationship with violence. This proposed direction for military sociology, however, is one out of several that are proposed by the contributors of this edited collection.

Other Directions in Military Sociology

The contributors to this collected edition present other avenues and directions for military sociology that encompass a wide variety of fields and perspectives. The range of possibilities is much greater than what can be written in a volume like this one, and it is not our pretension to set a specific research agenda through these pages. However, it is our hope that by providing specific examples of other directions for military sociology, other researchers and students will be stimulated and encouraged in exploring lesser-known perspectives concerning military affairs.

The book is divided into three sections. The first section aims at providing a context as to why military sociology would benefit from expanding its horizons. Beyond this introductory chapter, Fabian Virchow (Germany) presents and explains the need for military sociology to become more in tune with other military constructs (or military ways of thinking) that are situated beyond the military institution itself. Virchow then offers some examples of military habitus and thus introduces Bourdieu's concept into military sociology through an analysis of the importance of sport in the German armed forces and how "militainment" is used to foster certain social representations for the armed forces. Igor Obraztsov (Russia) presents the evolution of military sociology in the former Soviet Union and present-day Russia to illustrate the course that discipline took in the West is in no way a mandatory one. In Russia, as Obraztsov shows, in the nineteenth century there was already a significant interest in developing a scientific study of military affairs. Some key historical events (First World War, creation of the Soviet Union and the imposition of socialism, the end of Stalinism, etc.) had a significant impact on the evolution of the discipline in Russia. The Russian experience, thus, is very helpful in contextualizing military sociology in view of the emerging postmodernity and postmodern military in the West.

In the second section of the book, the authors illustrate how the interpretative tradition in sociology can inform military sociology. Anne Irwin (Canada) presents an original study using an ethno-methodological approach to highlight the problems of how reality is constructed and perceived in the context of military training. Using participant observation with a rifle company in Canada, Irwin analyzes the contrast between "game-playing" and being ready for the "real stuff," which is found in the heart of military exercise and as perceived from the participants' point of view. Uli vom Hagen (Germany) borrows from Max Weber's study on Protestantism and the rise of capitalism to study how religious constructs were so important in the German Army. Particularly, the ascetic nature of the German Army's military culture is analyzed as an extension of the Lutheran ascetic ethics to understand the importance of discipline, austerity, vocationalism, and the service ethics found in German military institutions.

René Moelker (Netherlands) innovatively employs the figurational approach, based on the work of Norbert Elias, to explain how the military institution has evolved. The figuration approach is a potent, but underused, sociological tool to understand conflicts between ways of being and relating to others and how those conflicting relationships reshape military cultures and military constructs as lived by the social actors. Finally, Claude Weber (France) presents a study on the importance of the symbolic representation of the military service and its impact on the officer corps since the abolition of the draft system in France. The army-nation relationship is analyzed here as a social construct, but emphasizes that multiple discourses and evaluations about the status of this relationship co-exist both parallel and independently from the formal institutional representations.

In the last section, interdisciplinary research is used to illustrate that outside the other subfields of sociology, military sociology can greatly benefit from cross-discipline exchanges. Ljubica Jelusic (Slovenia) proposes an analysis of emotions to show how they are ritualized in a military context, bringing together concepts from anthropology, social psychology, and the sociology of emotions. Particularly, the management of one's emotions in a military organization is analyzed as an attempt to maintain the institutional emotions that are expected from the soldiers. Morten Ender (United States) studies how various means of communication impact the soldiers' lives, relationships, and families, bringing together concepts from communication studies and sociology of the family. Concern for the family has been known for a long time as one of the key pressures on military cohesion in times of conflict. Modern communication technologies present both opportunities and challenges in alleviating soldiers' concern for their families and the nature of the media can inform and affect the nature of the relationship with the family. Lastly, Paul Higate (United Kingdom) analyzes the issue of homelessness among veterans, bringing together concepts from social work and sociology of the body. Particularly, the socialization of physical discomfort, and the associated curious pride that emerges from being "roughed up," is used to illustrate the need for more analyses that start from the human experience of the internalization of violence and disserving self-concepts. Hence, the idea of institutional socialization should not be seen as an explanation but rather as an outcome.

New Direction 1.5

Given that the world is going through a rapid rate of change and toward greater international anarchy, and as many assumptions are questioned more than ever, it appears timely that military sociologists embrace new approaches to old and new questions.

Conclusions

This chapter does not pretend to be launching a new paradigm for military sociology. As shown, there are already several authors using, directly or indirectly, the interpretative tradition in military sociology. As well, the call for greater interdisciplinary approaches can be heard from several quarters. Hence, this chapter should not be construed as a "revelation" but rather as a manifesto of sorts, a rallying cry for those interested in expanding the limits of military sociology. Given that the world is going through a rapid rate of change and toward greater international anarchy, and as many assumptions are questioned more than ever, it appears timely that military sociologists embrace new approaches to old and new questions. In the final analysis, it is the realization that a latent new paradigm is ready to emerge within military sociology, and this remains our key purpose.

This being said, one should not construe this as an attempt to promote a true Kuhnian (1970) revolution by replacing one paradigm by another (which, in any case, never occurs in social sciences; they are simply added and continue to exist in parallel). The functionalist perspective has proven itself a useful perspective for the military institution; other perspectives should be considered complementary to it rather than opposition.

SUMMARY

This chapter examined the way in which military sociologists are constrained by the functionalist and pragmatic nature of military sociology. Among the possible directions that might be taken to remove such constraints, it was proposed that efforts should be made to re-energize the interpretative tradition in military sociology. The interpretative tradition is often misconstrued, however, and it should first and foremost be concerned with how our preconceived ideas and perceptions shape social life. In the case of the military institution, it means that military sociologists would benefit from assessing what makes its existence possible in the first place, instead of viewing the military institution as an assumed starting point. A central construct useful for achieving such a task is to focus research on the organized violence of armed groups; whether this violence is actual, potential, or symbolic. Hence, military sociology could become a sociology of organized violence. This chapter also outlined some prospective directions for military sociology.

KEY TERMS AND CONCEPTS

- Epistemology
- Ontology
- Functionalism
- Interpretative tradition
- Constructivism
- Organized violence
- Pragmatism

STUDY AND DISCUSSION QUESTIONS

1. If a sociologist focuses on social constructs within the military institution, is he/she at risk of missing the prag-

matic nature of the military affairs? If so, how could this be avoided?

2. Given the pragmatic orientation of military decision-makers, how could sociological research using an interpretative approach be useful to them?

3. What are the other potential applications of studying the armed forces through the lenses of the sociology of organized violence?

4. What are the ethical implications of studying paramilitary and guerilla groups from the perspective of military sociology?

5. Does interpretative military sociology lead to perspectives that could be truly critical of the military institution? If so, give some potential examples.

REFERENCES

Abrahamsson, B. 1972. *Military Professionalization and Political Power*. Beverly Hills: Sage.

Aron, R. 1965. *Main Currents in Sociological Thought - 1*. London: Weidenfeld and Nicolson.

Bartov, O. 1991. *Hitler's Army*. Oxford: Oxford University Press.

Bhaskar, R. 1978. *A Realist Theory of Science*. Hassocks: Harvester Press.

Blumer, H. 1969. *Symbolic Interactionism*. Englewood Cliffs: Prentice-Hall.

Boene, B. 1981. "Quatre décennies de sociologie militaire aux États-Unis: bilan et perspectives" (Four Decades of Military Sociology in the United States: Updates and Perspectives) *Stratégique* 12.

Berger, P. and T. Luckmann. 1966. *The Social Construction of Reality*. Garden City: Doubleday.

Burk, J. 1993. "Morris Janowitz and the Origins of Sociological Research on Armed Forces and Society." *Armed Forces and Society* 19(2):167-185.

Burk, J, ed. 1994. *The Military in New Times: Adapting Armed Forces to a Turbulent World*. Boulder: Westview Press.

Burrell, G. and G. Morgan. 1979. *Sociological Paradigm and Organizational Analysis*. Portsmouth: Heinemann.

Caforio, G., ed. 2003a. *Handbook of Sociology of the Military*. New York: Kluwer Academic.

_____. 2003b. "Introduction." Pp. 1-6 in *Handbook of Sociology of the Military,* edited by G. Caforio. New York: Kluwer Academic.

_____. 2003c. "Some Historical Notes." Pp. 7-26 in *Handbook of Sociology of the Military,* edited by G. Caforio. New York: Kluwer Academic.

_____. 2003d. "Conclusion: Themes and issues of the Sociology of the Military." Pp. 437-444 in *Handbook of Sociology of the Military,* edited by G. Caforio. New York: Kluwer Academic.

Caforio, G. and M. Nuciari. 2003. "Social Research and the Military: A Cross-National Expert Survey." Pp. 27-58 in *Handbook of Sociology of the Military,* edited by G. Caforio. New York: Kluwer Academic.

Callon, M., J. Law, and A. Rip. 1986. *Mapping the Dynamics of Science and Technology*. Basingstoke: Macmillan.

Denzin, N. K. 1989. *Interpretive Interactionism*. Newbury Park: Sage Publications.

Dilthey, W. 1976. *Selected Writings*. Edited by H. P. Rickman. London: Cambridge University Press.

Dunivin, K. O. 1994. "Military Culture: Change and Continuity." *Armed Forces and Society* 20:531-547.

Garb, M. 2000. "The Role of the Military Identity in Demobilization and Reintegration." Pp. 25-27 in *War Force to Work Force, Global Perspective on Demobilization and Reintegration,* edited by N. Pauwels. Nomos Verlagsgesellschaft: Baden-Baden.

Garfinkle, H. 1967. *Studies in Ethnomethodology.* Englewood Cliffs: Prentice-Hall.

Hackett, J. 1983. *The Profession of Arms.* London: Sidgwick and Jackson.

Harré, R. 1986. *Varieties of Realism: A Rationale for the Natural Sciences.* Oxford: Basil Blackwell.

Huntington, S. 1957. *The Soldier and the State: The Theory and Practice of Civil-Military Relations.* Cambridge: Harvard University Press.

Janowitz, M. 1960. *The Professional Soldier: A Social and Political Portrait.* New York: Free Press.

_____. 1974. *Sociology and the Military Establishment.* Beverly Hills: Sage.

_____. 1975. *Military Conflict.* Beverly Hills: Sage.

_____. 1979. "On the Current State of the Sociology of Military Institution," *SOWI-Forum* no. 17, Munich.

Jelusic, L. 2003. "Conversion of the Military: Resource-Reuse Perspective after the End of the Cold War." Pp. 345-359 in *Handbook of Sociology of the Military*, edited by G. Caforio, New York: Kluwer Academic.

Kellett, A. 1982. *Combat Motivation: The Behavior of Soldiers in Battle.* Boston: Kluwer/Nijhoff.

Kuhn, T. 1970. *The Structure of Scientific Revolution.* Chicago: University of Chicago Press.

Latour, B. 1986. *Laboratory Life: The Construction of Scientific Facts.* Princeton: Princeton University Press.

_____. 1988. *The Pasteurisation of France.* Harvard: Harvard University Press.

Latour, B and M. Callon. 1986. *Mapping the Dynamics of Science and Technology: Sociology of Science in the Real World*. Basingstoke: Macmillan.

Lynn, J. A. 1997. "The Embattled Future of Academic Military History." *The Journal of Military History* 61(4):777-789.

Maines, D. R. 2000. "The Social Construction of Meaning." *Contemporary Sociology* 29(4):577-584.

Malinowski, Wladyslaw R. 1944. "The Pattern of Underground Resistance." *Annals of the American Academy of Political and Social Science* 232:126-133.

McCausland, J. and G. Martin. 2001. "Transforming Strategic Leader Education for the 21st Century Army." *Parameters* 31(3):17-33.

Mead, George Herbert. 1934. *Mind, Self and Society from the Standpoint of a Social Behaviorist*. Chicago: University of Chicago Press.

Mills, C. W. 1959. *The Sociological Imagination*. New York: Oxford University Press.

Moelker, R. 2003. "Technology, Organization, and Power." Pp. 385-402 in *Handbook of Sociology of the Military*, edited by G. Caforio. New York: Kluwer Academic.

Moskos, C. 1976. *Peace Soldiers: The Sociology of a United Nations Military Force*. Chicago: Chicago University Press.

_____. 1977. "From Institution to Occupation: Trends in Military Organizations." *Armed Forces and Society* 4(4):41-50.

Moskos, C. and J. Burk. 1994. "The Postmodern Military." Pp. 141-162 in *The Military in New Times: Adapting Armed Forces to a Turbulent World*, edited by James Burk. Boulder: Westview Press.

Nuciari, M. 2003. "Model and Explanations for Military Organization: An Updated Reconsideration." Pp. 61-85 in *Handbook of Sociology of the Military*, edited by G. Caforio. New York: Kluwer Academic.

Parker, I. and J. Shotter. 1990. "Introduction." Pp. 1-14 in *Deconstructing Social Psychology,* edited by I. Parker and J. Shotter. New York: Routledge.

Ricks, T. 1997. *Making the Corps.* New York: Scribner.

Segal, D. R., M. Wechsler Segal, and D. P. Eyre. 1992. "The Social Construction of Peacekeeping in America." *Sociological Forum* 7(1):121-136.

Segal, M. 1982. "The Argument for Female Combatants." Pp. 267-290 in *Female Soldiers—Combatants or Noncombatants?* Edited by Nancy Loring Goldman. Westport: Greenwood.

Scott, A. 2001. "The Political Sociology of War." Pp. 183-194 in *The Blackwell Companion to Political Sociology,* edited by Kate Nash and Alan Scott. Oxford: Blackwell.

Shamir, B. and E. Ben-Ari. 2000. "Challenges of Military Leadership in Changing Armies." *Journal of Political and Military Sociology* 28(1):43-59.

Shils, E. and M. Janowitz. 1948. "Cohesion and Disintegration in the Wehrmacht in World War II." *Public Opinion Quarterly* 12:280-310.

Soeters, J. and J. van der Meulen, eds. 1999. *Managing Diversity in the Armed Forces: Experiences from Nine Countries.* Tilburg: Tilburg University Press.

Thiéblemont, A. 1999. *Cultures et Logiques Militaires* (Military Culture and Logics). Paris: Presses universitaires de France.

van Creveld, M. 1991. *The Transformation of War.* New York: Free Press.

von Bredow, W. 2003. "The Order of Violence: Norms, Rules, and Taboos of Organized Violence and the De-legitimization of the Military." Pp. 87-98 in *Handbook of Sociology of the Military,* edited by G. Caforio. New York: Kluwer Academic.

35

Weber, M. 1949. *The Methodology of the Social Sciences.* Glencoe: Free Press.

Weick, K. E. and K. H. Roberts. 1993. "Collective Minds in Organizations: Heedful Interrelating on Flight Decks." *Administrative Science Quarterly* 38:357-381.

Winslow, D. 1997. *The Canadian Airborne in Somalia: A Socio-Cultural Inquiry.* Ottawa: Canadian Government Publishing Center.

_____. 1998. "Misplaced Loyalties: The Role of Military Culture in the Breakdown of Discipline in Peace Operations." *Canadian Review of Sociology and Anthropology* 35:345-367.

_____. 2000. *Army Culture.* Virginia: Army Research Institute.

C h a p t e r

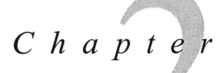

FAVORING A SOCIETAL TURN IN MILITARY SOCIOLOGY

Fabian Virchow
University of Applied Sciences Kiel
Kiel, Germany

LEARNING OBJECTIVES

After reading this chapter, you should be able to

* understand how military sociology can broaden its scope to include various societal sectors through an analysis of military ways of thinking;
* understand how the military institution in Germany gets closely involved with sports;
* understand the relationships between organized sports and military ways of thinking;
* recognize the importance of the entertainment industry for the military institution;
* understand how "militainment" contributes to the maintenance and reproduction of banal militarism.

Military sociology has gone through decades of development as an academic discipline. Since its starting point in the early 1940s, when survey research was used inside the U.S. armed forces for the first time, it has systematically produced large numbers of essays and research reports. While military sociology in the United States has had a respectable foundation and considerable resources and, therefore, has dominated the discipline in the first decades of its existence, sound military sociological work has emerged in quite a number of countries (Kümmel and Prüfert 2000).

Military sociology—which can be pursued in its most prominent journal (*Armed Forces and Society*) as well as in its conference programs (*IUS, Ergomas, ISA-RC 01*)—has focused heavily on the social nature of the armed forces as a social system or as an organization thereby referring to, *inter alia*, the rich empirical knowledge of organizational sociology. The morale of soldiers, the causes and manifestations of battle stress, careerism, as well as the growing diversity in many armies around the world have been, and still are, important fields of research. Also, the changes in security policies in the context of recently emerging or newly assessed threats are discussed, as they are closely interlinked with the standards and requirements that the military and the soldiers are expected to meet. Finally, the question of civil-military relations receives permanent attention from military sociologists, many focusing on the democratic control of armed forces (*Geneva Centre for the Democratic Control of Armed Forces* 2003). While in the last decade much of the research done on the matter of democratic control has referred to the transformation process of the armed forces as it continues in new, market-oriented democracies created in the wake of the dissolution of the Soviet Union, and has referred to the development of armed forces in countries of the southern

---

New Direction 2.1

The patterns of military habitus and the interrelated dimensions of feeling, thinking, and doing may become an important topic of investigation and research.

---

hemisphere, comparably little (critical) research is done on civil-military relations within the highly industrialized capitalist countries (Kümmel and Prüfert 2000; Kuhlmann and Callaghan 2000; Caforio 2003).

This becomes even more applicable—as I would like to emphasize—if one looks not only at the relationship between the military and the political sector (mostly government, parliament, parties, and politicians) but broadens the field of vision. This broadening should include, firstly, societal sectors such as culture and arts, science or sport. Further, military sociology should not only focus on the military as an institution or as a social system, but also take into consideration the existence of military ways of thinking that do not necessarily have to be directly linked to, or created by, military institutions.

Indeed, an expanded approach will consider the patterns of military habitus and the interrelated dimensions of feeling, thinking, and doing, which may become an important topic of investigation and research. These are probably less attractive for military sociologists at the moment, as little research in the field of military sociology is done independently from the military, its financial and organizational resources, or its requests. This close collaboration has quite often resulted in an instrumental orientation that Vogt has characterized as "Pentagonism" of military sociology (Vogt 1991:126-148). Close personnel, financial, and institutional

39

relations and amalgamations between military sociology and the military as an institution, as well as the concentration on questions of military fitness and readiness for action, may block the awareness for societal developments and changes that may be of little direct relevance for the armed forces and the improvement of its fighting ability. Such changes, however, are possibly of great importance for the society, some of its sectors, or the political culture of a society.

Below, I will identify areas to which military sociology does not pay enough attention because it is a discipline too acutely focused on issues like social cohesion, battle stress, careerism, or on developments like MOOTW. First, I will outline the pertinent role of the German Armed Forces in sport affairs, resulting in a far-reaching dependence of top-class athletes on sponsorship from the armed forces. Some other examples will deal with the growing cooperation of artists, musicians, and the toy industry with the military collectively known as "militainment." Of course, these remarks can give only a first impression of these areas and of approaches that arise from a "societal turn" of military sociology.

Sports and Armed Forces

In mid-January 2004, the German Minister of Defense (MoD), Peter Struck, demanded that not only should company logos be visible on the sportswear of successful athletes, but also the logo of the German Federal Armed Forces (Förderung des Spitzensports bleibt 2004). This is, perhaps, surprising to many observers upon first glance, but is not without logic; the German Department of Defense (DoD) is the biggest single sponsor of sport in Germany, allocating an estimated 25 million Euros each year (Buse 2004:3).

New Direction 2.2

The German Department of Defense is the biggest single sponsor of sport in Germany, allocating an estimated 25 million Euro each year.

Since the 1960s, the German Armed Forces have—partly in reaction to the military sponsored support of top-class sportsman in the former GDR—provided for athletes in order to allow them to take part in special training courses (Balbier 2004:16-21). Despite some reservations by lieutenant colonel Dr. Hugo Bach, the then expert for sports affairs of the German Armed Forces who feared a violation of the amateur status of the Olympics and who was worried about undermining those sports activities done in a spirit of comradeship by focusing on top athletes, the competition of political systems set the course. It was especially the decision to hold the Olympics in Munich in 1972 that spawned the establishment of cooperation between the military and the sports associations (Bundesministerium der Verteidigung 1998). The lively demand from athletes, the favorable repercussions on the reputation of the German Armed Forces, as well as the successful participation of German soldier-athletes at the international competitions organized by the *Conseil International du Sport Militaire* (CISM), were seen as a confirmation of the efficacy of the decisions that have been made.

In the years following the late 1960s, both German states saw systematic development and institutionalization of financial support of sport by the military. In the GDR, these activities at the beginning had been centered on the Army Sport Clubs (*Armeesportclub*), which in the 1970s developed Training Centers (*Trainingszentren*); in the FRG, the Sport

41

Support Groups (*Sportfördergruppen*) became the most important instrument for leading German soldier-athletes to win medals at the Olympics. After 1990, the Army Sport Clubs of the former GDR's army in Frankfurt/Oder, Oberhof, Potsdam, and Rostock have been transitioned to Sport Support Groups of the Federal Armed Forces (Becker 2004:60-63). At the end of the year 2003, a total of 744 athletes were backed (Biewald 2003:106-107). The kinds of sports sponsored and supported ranged from American Football and billiards to bowling and rugby.

The Armed Forces' sponsorship of sport had notable results in terms of medals. 16 out of the 29 medals German athletes gained at the Winter Olympics in Nagano, Japan, in 1998 were won by members of the German Armed Forces, roughly 55 percent (Bundesministerium der Verteidigung 1998:6). Four years later, in Salt Lake City, United States, the percentage of medals won by soldiers rose to 71 percent (Buse 2004:3). In many sports, German soldier-athletes are world-class. Several times, for example, the world championship in bobsled racing has been won by German soldier-athletes, as was proudly reported by the weekly magazine of the German Armed Forces (Kleinheyer 2004:13).

Indeed, the publications of the German Armed Forces regularly report on, and extol, the abilities of the soldier-athletes (Mitrevska 2002:3; Biewald 2003:106-107; Becker 2004:60-63) and often have personal feature articles on the

---

New Direction 2.3

The world championship in bobsled racing has been won severtal times by German soldier-athletes, as was proudly reported by the weekly magazine of the German Armed Forces.

---

more successful cases (Bergmann 2004:13; Bauer 2004). In addition, larger events, such as the world's biathlon championship in Oberhof (Thuringia/Germany) in February 2004, are transmitted by the army's radio station, *Radio Andernach*, to the German soldiers deployed abroad in the Balkans and in Afghanistan. Meanwhile, the official Internet presentation of the German Armed Forces has also improved the topicality and scope of news about the soldier-athletes and the efforts to support them (Bundeswehr 2004).

Since the Olympic Games in Sydney, athletes from Germany who are supported by the DoD's sports program have received orders to identify themselves as soldiers when being presented at receptions or official ceremonies. Therefore, the female biathletes of the German Skiing Association, for example, add the word *Bundeswehr* (German Armed Forces) to the association's sign on their tracksuit and casual clothes. In general, there is close cooperation between the German Armed Forces and the German Sport Association in deciding whose sporting performance is worthy of admission to the support program.

Despite the enormous significance of the Armed Forces support program in terms of medals won at international competitions, and in spite of the efforts of the Armed Forces to use the attractiveness of sport for recruiting (Bundeswehr Olympix 2004), there is neither public debate nor scientific research on the symbiosis between the German Armed Forces and the sponsoring of top-class athletes.

From a sociological perspective, there are many questions and research topics that may be derived from this situation that have not been considered by military sociology sufficiently. One point, for example, is that throughout European history sport has prepared men and women for war:

Classical Greek games included martial sports—useful preparations for war in a world that saw city-states destroyed, men put to the sword and women and children taken into slavery. Rome used sport as a brutal adjunct of imperial wars. Medieval jousts were preparation for often un-chivalric battle. Renaissance Italy had its games of *ponte* and *pligna* to bring foot soldiers up to scratch. Later, the *Turnen* movement was a means of ensuring readiness for patriotic struggle. Late Victorian Britain prepared its middle-class schoolboys on games fields for "civilizing" warfare throughout its empire. Prussia used sport to harden its efficient officer class. Fascism gave sport a high priority as means of making cold ideological warriors. (Mangan 2003:281-286).

Of course, the specific combination of sport and the military through the ages have changed depending on several factors. That there are close relations between the military and sporting activities in many countries today, should encourage a closer analytical look at this relationship in order to clarify the interests of all participants, the mechanisms of this kind of collaboration, as well as its broader context.

Remember, for example, that sporting events, especially the bigger ones, have always played a prominent role in the memories of a nation. So have wars. What does it mean to the memory of a nation, when the successful competitors are simultaneously athletes and soldiers? Will the people—and will the nation—not only identify themselves with the sporting aspect, but with the soldierly or militarily aspect as well, since the military had been contributing to the success through sponsorship? This idea has guided at least one comment in one of the most respected German daily newspapers. The paper

44

pointed to the relevance of the successes of soldier-athletes to the process of "nation building" and for the creation of "national identity" (Reinsch 2004). In addition, the official magazine of the German Armed Forces, which is titled *Y* (its name referring to the first character on the license plate of the army's vehicles), states that the German Army, as well as the "nation," profit from the sporting successes of soldier-athletes (Becker 2004:60-63).

Altogether, cooperation between the military, on the one side, and athletes or their associations, on the other, needs a much closer examination from sociology of sport as well as from military sociology, in order to discover the motives of the cooperating partners involved, what mechanisms are at work in these relationships, what level of awareness does society have for these interactions, and how do they effect the society and its political culture at large?

Entertainment and Armed Forces

In general, the same can be said about the cooperation between the military as an institution, or members (and former members) of the military, with the entertainment industry. This cooperation, which presumably is most advanced in the United States, covers several kinds of entertainment, such as music, video games, television, and motion pictures. Not all of these areas can be examined here. Some (for example the cooperation between the Pentagon and some movie directors and producers from Hollywood) are even researched, albeit meagerly, by military sociologists (Suid 1996, 2002). The most recent developments, like the *Military Diaries*—which are produced by the U.S. cable company VH1 with support from the Pentagon—have not yet been considered. In *Military Diaries*, GIs were provided digital cameras and their filming

45

resulted in visual "diaries" about how they "fulfil their patriotic duty." These are offered to the audience via TV or the
Internet.

Restricting the analysis to two spheres of collaboration, between the military and the entertainment sector (video
games and entertaining the troops), nonetheless elucidates the
wide variety of interactions and the volume of customers and
users of products that result from the collaboration (to illustrate, consider the millions of players of war games on
computers). The analysis also demonstrates that the level and
the intensity of cooperation, as well as its dynamic, may vary
from one country to the other, as well as over time. This is
easily comprehensible if one looks at the activities of armed
forces that aim at keeping the morale of soldiers high while in
action, by organizing visits and concerts from well-known pop
singers.

In the United States, because of the existence of its
many bases around the globe and its decades of military intervention, there are specialized branches called *U.S.O.* and
Armed Forces Entertainment that organize the entertainment
of the soldiers. Moreover, there exists a strong tradition of
artists visiting U.S. soldiers abroad. German Armed Forces are
now reinventing this kind of entertainment after many years of
absence as an active military force.

In the Federal Republic of Germany, these kinds of
activities have been limited to low-level entertainment in the
barracks for a long time. Only since larger contingents of the
Armed Forces have been deployed to the Balkans,
Afghanistan, and Africa, has the growth and diversification of
entertainment measures proliferated. Nowadays, entertainment for the German military units abroad includes satellite
TV, movie theatres, sports equipment, telephone links to
Germany, and special radio programs by the German Army's

own radio station. While these are permanent offers, visits and performances by artists and actors constitute a very special event for the soldiers. *DJ Bobo*, the rock band *Asshole*, the *Berlin Thunder Cheerleaders,* and the *Bremer Musical Company* demonstrate the broad range of styles. Some of the artists, for example the well known country-singer *Gunter Gabriel* or the *Heart & Soul Blues Brother Cover Band,* have visited the troops several times. *When the Heart & Soul Blues Brother Cover Band* did their gig in Pristina in April 2003, German MoD Struck took a microphone and performed as one of the Blues Brothers wearing a black hat and sun glasses.

"What Gerri Harriwell and Britney Spears can do, I can do easily," declared young female radio presenter "Freddy" from the city of Leipzig when the German Armed Forces invited her to visit German soldiers in Kosovo. The 23-year-old woman explained her motivation for taking the stage in front of the soldiers in Raijlovac to present the celebration each contingent had before returning to Germany: "This is service to my country." The looks of the soldiers had been "well, quite masculine, hm, very animal" she admitted, but she still keeps contact with the army (Thomas 2002).

The military leadership is well aware of the usefulness of these types of "cultural acts." Accordingly, the media edited by the German Armed Forces itself publish illustrated reports about them in combination with comments from soldiers and interviews with the artists and singers. At the same time, the cultural protagonists use their concerts and performances as a method of image building. In this sense, Friederike "Freddy" Lippold looked at her visit in Raijlovac as a service to the listeners of the radio station she is working for. Gunter Gabriel shows appreciation for the work of the German soldiers by giving concerts in front of them. He performs a song entitled *There is a House in Kosovo,* which is a reworking of *House of*

47

New Direction 2.4

Militainment of this kind contributes not only to the reputation of the armed forces and supports recruitment, but also, as a form of cooperation between the military on the one hand and protagonists from the cultural sector on the other, has repercussions within the political culture of a country or society.

---

the Rising Sun. He says he composed this number during one of his visits to Kosovo; meanwhile, it is a regular part of the concerts he gives in Germany. This way, songs written for soldiers infiltrate the society.

The *Bundeswehr* tries hard to deepen relations to musicians. Therefore, a nationwide contest called "BW-Musix '03" was organized in autumn 2003 to attract young people. More than 2,000 DJs, music groups, and youth orchestras took part in order to win prizes, ranging from the production of a CD, to concerts with the German Army's big band. The composition of the jury, to which several journalists had been invited, ensured that the Armed Forces got positive media coverage.

Entertainment for the troops is surely one of the most developed, perhaps even the most genuine, form of "militainment." Militainment of this kind contributes not only to the reputation of the armed forces and supports recruitment, but also, as a form of cooperation between the military on the one hand and protagonists from the cultural sector on the other, has repercussions within the political culture of a country or society. Although there have been some smaller studies on the historical relationship between music and the military (Witt-Stahl 1999), these recent developments have not been addressed by military sociology.

Though there is quite a limited number of people who are directly involved in the armed forces entertainment mentioned above, computer games are one of the most popular leisure activities in many countries, and war games have a significant share of the market. Companies doing their business in this market segment try hard to make their games credible. They try to create believable theatres of war (desert, jungle, urban areas, etc.); offer sufficient availability and use of "weaponry"; as well as suitable, war-like missions for the players, which are as realistic as possible. In addition, they often try to put new games on the market that reflect the recent wars fought in reality. Accordingly, the company *Kuma Reality Games* announced a new episodic game in February 2004 that incorporates scenes of film of real war from Afghanistan, Iraq, and Liberia in order to enhance authenticity. Even the killing of the sons of Saddam Hussein can be copied virtually using the same kind of ammunition the U.S. forces used in reality.

As in many other cases, military veterans gave advice to the development of this game. The armed forces of the United States systematically makes use of computer games and has entered into cooperation with several computer game companies and university departments (Derian 2001). The growing relevance of computer games for the military goes back to the rising status of simulation as part of training exercises, especially since the middle of the 1980s. Games like *Counterstrike*, which is played by more than ten million players around the world, lead to a heightened level of visual attentiveness, as neuro-scientific research has shown (Green and Bavelier 2003:534-537). Even newcomers are able to perceive various objects on the screen simultaneously after just ten days of playing the game. Of course, this is interesting for Special Forces that are trained with action videos in order to enhance their capability to survey unknown territory very fast.

49

Many of the computer war games are about the battles of World War II. *Medal of Honor* and *Battlefield 1942*, to name just two of them, are regularly updated and promoted as "a must for every front-line soldier." Among these are, not surprisingly, numerous people from the extreme political right. The possibility of experiencing WW II battles, virtually, in the form of an officer of the Wehrmacht or of the Waffen-SS attracts these individuals. As one can see from the German speaking fan page (http://www.bf42.de), they share enthusiasm for weaponry and soldiership with militarists and non-political players. The real-time computer game *Sudden Strike 2* simulates the attack of the Waffen-SS on the Russian city of Charkov, which had been the place of murder of 20,000 Jews in mid-December 1941 by members of the Wehrmacht and the Waffen-SS. In the game, the soldiers of the Waffen-SS are depicted as courageous fighters with soldierly virtues such as honor, patriotism, pluck, and propriety. Because *Sudden Strike 2* had been such a commercial success, the production company CDV-Verlag launched *Blitzkrieg* as its successor. These games, in general, leave it to personal choice whether players identify more with the Waffen-SS or their Allied counterparts, as though it were only a matter of taste, similar to the preference for a certain baseball club in a sports game.

The U.S. armed forces spent $7 million to develop *America's Army*, which is "the official U.S. army game" (*America's Army* 2004). In mid-April, 2004, there had been more than 3,290,000 registered users playing either the single-player version or the squad-based, multiplayer variant. In the first option, the player guides a soldier from enlistee to high ranking officer, periodically adapting the soldier's values and goals to shape his final outcome. Through these career stages, according to the U.S. Army, you can "see for yourself what a rich life experience the U.S. Army offers." The game espouses values that are central to the Armed Forces: duty, respect, loyalty, selfless service, personal courage, and honor. One of the main matters of concern in the game is the training of obedience. Firing is allowed only on command. The violator of these rules is threatened with detention. The course has to be completed under continuous verbal threats from the drill instructors: "Don't mess up my freshly raked sand pit!" (*America's Army* 2004).

The multiplayer version may be much more attractive with its multiple environments like swamp, desert, indoor, and forest. Missions range from sneaking into a terrorist camp as a group of U.S. elite soldiers retrieving important intelligence from the enemy's computers, to guarding sensitive government intelligence from an invading gang of terrorists. For the "realistic" experience of being a fighting soldier, it is generally important that many dimensions of the game appear to be as authentic as possible. To ensure this, the producers of the game visited dozens of Army bases and interviewed hundreds of soldiers. Game designers were taken on simulated missions and each development was approved for realism and accuracy. In *America's Army*, therefore, weapon reload times are true to life, grenades have an explosion radius of up to 250 feet, necessitating strong teamwork to avoid incidents of friendly fire. And "aiming a sniper rifle is affected by your breathing— and it's much more accurate if you take the shot from a crouched or prone position or take the time to set up your tripod...Teamwork is emphasized, especially through communication—via speech, radio messages, or actual military hand and arm signals" (Nvidia 2004).

While *America's Army* puts more emphasis on soldiers' teamwork than other games of this kind, conflict scenarios (and the missions) deal with military dimensions only, leaving aside economic, political, and social factors.

51

Conflict Desert Storm, developed and produced by *Pivotal Games* with the advice of a former SAS member (*Conflict Desert Storm* 2004), sold more than a million times within six months of entering the market. The plot of this game is about three members of an elite unit intent on liberating Iraq from Saddam Hussein. House-to-house fighting, sniper's fire, and the militarily ambience are shaped as realistically as possible, but the societal situation in (virtual) Iraq is not addressed. No civilians ever show up.

Such computer war games, which have become increasingly more war-like and, yet, which simplify complex social settings and societal developments, have found an ever-growing number of mostly young users over the last ten years. As the average starting age has significantly decreased, these war games have become an important factor of socialization. Here, once again, as with many other measures of the armed forces, the aim is to make (young) people familiar with the situation of soldiers in training and battle circumstances. They endeavor to have the viewers get involved in military thinking and behavior and minimize the distance from weapons and the force of arms. To what extent this really takes place, and how it affects society, should be a matter of interest for military sociologists, not least of all because the military is an important active subject in this context.

Society and Armed Forces

Indeed, there are a myriad of forms in which military, militaristic, or war-like attitudes are (re)produced in a society. From camouflaged clothing, books and booklets on armament available at kiosks at railway stations, to a wide selection of war toys in department stores, and numerous video games in which players can pick from roles as a military strategist, a special agent, a fighter, or a killer. In capitalist societies, hege-monic ideas spread more effectively, and are sustainable, the more they are shaped as an offer of an emotionalizing experi-ence and transformed into products that circulate in the marketplace for news, games, music, arts, and literature.

The diverse and increasing activities of militainment are not only relevant in their function of improving the reputa-tion of armed forces and enhancing the recruitment procedures, but also have to be considered in relation to the changes they can effect in the political culture of a society. The level of acceptance and agreement with regard to the existence and general task of the military, as well as the normalization of the use of violence by the military, is established, to a substantial extent, by the multiple forms of everyday media communica-tion about the military as an institution, and the dissemination of militarily attitudes, values, and patterns of behavior.

At the same time, new leisure activities, like playing paint-ball or computer war games, have their relevance on a micro-sociological level, in the sense that by taking part in such games, certain dimensions of military behavior are performed by the participants. What dimensions these are, of course, depend on the game that is played. But in such

---

New Direction 2.5

The term "banal militarism" seems most appropriate for describing the wide range of public discourses, media activities, and political events that take the exis-tence of the armed forces, its public manifestations, the spending of relevant sums of money for military purposes, and the acceptance of war as a matter of conflict resolution, (nearly) for granted.

53

processes of mimetic learning, not only mental activities are required to play such games successfully; the body is also involved in multiple ways. Therefore, referring to Bordieu's concept of *habitus*, it can be assumed that "doing military while playing" will gradually change the *habitus* of the persons involved.

Michael Billig has chosen the term "banal nationalism" in order to describe the daily and ordinary routines by which the nation-state, and the "nation," is reproduced as the often unconscious, doxic point of reference in the feelings, thoughts, and actions of people (Billig 1995). Accordingly, the term "banal militarism" seems most appropriate for describing the wide range of public discourses, media activities, and political events that take the existence of the armed forces, its public manifestations, the spending of relevant sums of money for military purposes, and the acceptance of war as a matter of conflict resolution, (nearly) for granted. In addition, the term includes the activities by which military affined and war-like attitudes and behaviors are "performed." "Banal militarism" also comprises the wide range of "privatized militarization" that can be observed as "gun culture" in several countries.

The adjectival addition helps to delimit the term "banal militarism" from the discourse on militarism that is associated with the historical forms of militarism and militarized societies, like Prussian and fascist Germany, and Japan until the end of the first half of the twentieth century. At the same time, it aims at a productive connection to the scientific debate about "militarism" (Vagts 1959; Berghahn 1981; Bredow 1983; Shaw 1991; Krippendorff 1993; Regan 1994; Berger 1998). Therefore, research on "banal militarism" is not about the extremes of militarism like military dictatorships or stereotypes, for example spiked helmets or soldierly exhibitionism. Banal militarism is instead a matter of militarily ritualizations, performances in military style in leisure time, and the dissemination of military/war-like modes through the media or the entertainment sector.

Even if one finds the term "banal militarism" inappropriate for the phenomena described above, military sociology should widen its perspective in order to not only look at the military as an institution (whether its internal state of affairs or its relations to the society), but also to search the various forms of interaction between the military and other societal spheres and institutional bodies. In addition military sociology should examine, in much greater detail, the relevance and acceptance of military values in the society (whether connected to the military as an institution or not). This "societal turn" of military sociology will benefit from, and contribute to, the research of political culture, to the sociology of leisure, to media research (consider the media of the military), to the sociology of sport, and many more and will allow military sociology to be more aware of military procedures and mechanisms as phenomena that are deeply embedded in the everyday routines of societies.

ACKNOWLEDGEMENT

I would like to devote this chapter to Tanja Thomas, with whom I have been working on the issue of militainment.

SUMMARY

This article discussed the need for military sociology to take a "societal turn" in order to achieve a more complete understanding of how the military institution intersects with various segments of society. Not only is the military institution influenced by its mother society and by its members, but there are also military ways of thinking that exist beyond the military institution itself that need to be better understood. The article offered two specific examples of those military ways of thinking to illustrate a "societal" approach. The first one explored the relationships between the German Armed Forces (Bundeswehr) and organized sports. It explored how direct support to organized sport creates "soldier-athlete" representations and how such constructs are part of the nation-state construct. The second illustration was based on an analysis of "militainment," which covers a wide variety of military cultural artifacts (such as movies, computer games, and paraphernalia). Such "militainment" contributes to a way of thinking that can characterized as "banal militarism," which is a matter of militarily ritualizations, performances of military style in leisure time, and the dissemination of military/warlike modes through the media or the entertainment sector.

KEY TERMS AND CONCEPTS

- Societal Turn
- Habitus
- Soldier-Athlete
- Elite Sport
- Militainment
- Simulation
- Banal Militarism

STUDY AND DISCUSSION QUESTIONS

1. Do you think that military sociology could be more critical by taking the "societal turn"? Explain how.

2. Should the military institution get involved in supporting elite-level athletes? Why or why not?

3. Do you believe governmental support for elite-level athletes contributes to nation building? What could be the negative impacts?

4. Discuss how pervasive "militainment" is. How does it favor the growth of militarism?

5. Do you think that "militainment" also has an influence on violence in general? Explain.

REFERENCES

America's Army. 2004. Retrieved April 15, 2004. (http://www.americasarmy.com).

Balbier, Uta Andrea. 2004. "Kampf um Gold. Spitzensportförderung in der Nationalen Volksarmee und in der Bundeswehr" (Fighting for Gold. Supporting Top-Class Sports in the National People's Army and the German Federal Armed Forces). *Militärgeschichte* 14(4):16-21.

Bauer, Markus. 2004. "Hoffen auf die Staffel" (Hoping for the Relay Team). *Aktuell* 40(5):13.

Becker, Susanne. 2004. "Die Medaillenmacher" (The Medal-Makers). *Y* 4(3):60-63.

Berger, Thomas U. 1998. *Cultures of Antimilitarism: National Security in Germany and Japan*. Baltimore, MD: John Hopkins University Press.

Berghahn, Volker. 1981. *Militarism: The History of an International Debate 1861-1979*. Cambridge: Cambridge University Press.

Bergmann, Olaf. 2004. "Gute Ausbeute" (Good Results). *Aktuell* 40(12):13.

Biewald, Nicole. 2003. "Weit hinaus" (Far Out). *Y* 3(12):106-107.

Billig, Michael. 1995. *Banal Nationalism*. London: Sage.

Bredow, Wilfried Von. 1983. *Moderner Militarismus. Analyse und Kritik* (Modern Militarism: Analysis and Critique). Stuttgart: Kohlhammer.

Bundesministerium der Verteidigung. 1998. *Sport*. Bonn: BMVg.

Bundeswehr. 2004. Retrieved April 3, 2004 (http://www.bundeswehr.de/sport/).

Bundeswehr Olympix. 2004. "BW-Olympix' 04." Retrieved April 3, 2004 (http://www.bw-olympix.de/).

Buse, Dietmar. 2004. "Konzentration" (Concentration). *Aktuell* 40(8):3.

Caforio, Giuseppe, ed. 2003. *Handbook of the Sociology of the Military*. New York: Kluwer Academic.

Conflict Desert Storm. 2004. Retrieved October 3, 2003 (http://www.pivotalgames.com/games/desertstorm/cds_spence.htm).

Derian, James der. 2001. *Virtuous War. Mapping the Military-Industrial-Media-Entertainment Network*. Boulder: Westview.

Geneva Centre for the Democratic Control of Armed Forces. 2003. Retrieved May 22, 2004 (http://www.dcaf.ch/).

Green, Shawn and Daphne Bavelier. 2003. "Action Video Game Modifies Visual Selective Attention." *Nature* 423 (29 May):534-537.

Kleinheyer, Adrian. 2004. "Ich habe mehr vor" (I am ambitiuos). *Aktuell* 40(7):13.

_____. 2004. "Dominiert und deklassiert" (Dominated and Outclassed). *Aktuell* 40(8):13.

Krippendorff, Elkhart. 1993. *Militärkritik* (Critique of the Military). Frankfurt/Main: Suhrkamp.

Kuhlmann, Jürgen and Jean Callaghan, eds. 2000. *Military and Society in 21st Century Europe*. Münster: LIT-Verlag.

Kümmel, Gerhard and Andreas D. Prüfert, eds. 2000. *Military Sociology. The Richness of a Discipline.* Baden-Baden: Nomos-Verlag.

Mangan, J. A. 2003. "Epilogue: Many Mansions and Many Architectural Styles." In *Militarism, Sport, Europe. War Without Weapons,* edited by J. A. Mangan. London: Cass.

Mitrevska, Monika. 2002. "Olympisches Edelmetall" (Olympic Precious Metal). *Info-Post* 26(1):3.

Nvidia. 2004. "Games: America's Army: Operations and Soldiers." Retrieved October 3, 2003 (http://www.nvidia.com/view.asp?IO=games_army).

Regan, Patrick M. 1994. *Organizing Societies for War: The Process and Consequences of Societal Militarization.* Westport: Praeger.

Reinsch, Michael. 2004. "Medaillen auf Befehl" (Medals to Order). *Frankfurter Allgemeine Zeitung,* January 14.

Reinsch, Michael. 2004. "Förderung des Spitzensports bleibt. Bundeswehr möchte das Logo sehen" (Support of Top Sport Continues. Armed Forces want to see the logo). *Frankfurter Allgemeine Zeitung,* January 14.

Shaw, Martin. 1991. *Post-Military Society: Militarism, Demilitarization and War at the End of the Twentieth Century.* Cambridge: Polity.

Suid, Lawrence H. 1996. *Sailing on the Silver Screen.* Annapolis: Naval Institute Press.

_____. 2002. *Guts & Glory.* Louisville: University Press of Kentucky.

Thomas, Tanja. 2002. Interview with Friederike "Freddy" Lippold (September 11, 2002).

Vagts, Alfred. 1959. *A History of Militarism: Civilian and Military.* New York: Free Press.

Vogt, Wolfgang R. 1991. "Soziologie ohne Frieden?" (Sociology without Peace?). In *Friedensforschung, Eine Handlungsorientierung zwischen Politik und Wissenschaft* (*Peace Research, A Framework of Action between Politics and Science*), edited by C. Ulrike Wasmuht. Darmstadt: Wissenschaftliche Buchgesellschaft.

Witt-Stahl, Susann. 1999. *...But the Soul goes Marching On. Musik zur Ästhetisierung und Inszenierung des Krieges* (Music Serving the Aestheticization and Production of War). Karben: Coda.

C h a p t e r

3

MILITARY SOCIOLOGY IN RUSSIA: ORIGINS, TRADITIONS, AND PROSPECTS

Igor V. Obraztsov
Military Academy of the General Staff of Armed Forces of Russian Federation, Moscow, Russia

LEARNING OBJECTIVES

After reading this chapter, you should be able to

* understand that military sociology, like other social sciences, is very much influenced by historical and political events from its parent society;
* describe the importance of other traditions in military sociology;
* identify how military sociology can become an instrument of domination;
* outline how military sociology, as an applied discipline, can become a tool to promote military effectiveness;
* describe how military sociology, even within strict guidelines, can become a critical and "inconvenient" discipline for the authorities.

Military sociology, when compared to other subfields of sociology, is less popular and confined to a relatively limited circle of researchers. The number of social scientists devoting their time to the study of issues related to both armed forces and society is limited to a few dozen individuals at best, even in those countries where military sociology is institutionalized (Armor 1992; von Bredow 1996). Furthermore, there are usually only a few such social scientists in each of those countries. Even within international associations that have a military sociology section, such as the International Sociological Association Research Committee 01 on "Armed Forces and Conflict Resolution" (ISA RC01), or those dedicated to the study of topics germane to military sociology, such as the European Research Group on Military and Society (ERGOMAS), and the Inter-University Seminar on Armed Forces and Society (IUS), the total number of participants barely exceeds 500 people. It is only in the United States that a stable and significant number of military sociologists exist. Not surprisingly, American military sociologists have made the most significant and well-known contributions to the discipline since the middle of the twentieth century.

It is important to know, however, that the actual origins of military sociology are located in Europe, at the turn of the nineteenth to the twentieth century (see, for instance, the work of Du Pic 1880; Vaccaro 1886; Novicow 1894; Berndt 1897; Korf 1897; Steinmetz 1899; Constantin 1907; Bodart 1908; Rezhepo 1903, 1905, 1909; Oberuchev 1909, 1910; Djubjuk and Zakharov 1915). It also important to note that the shock of the First World War was a significant catalyst for the development of military sociology in Europe and interesting theoretical works appeared in many European countries during the inter-war period (see Schumpeter 1919; Sorokin 1922a, 1922b, 1928; Shpil'rejn 1928; Cru 1929; Steinmetz 1929;

New Direction 3.1

Russian sociology is certainly as old as sociology itself. The appearance of the first Russian sociological publication was as early as 1845.

Golovin 1931, 1938; Salomon 1938; Demetr 1930, 1935; Lewis 1939). Some of them still have theoretical and practical significance to the present sociological study of armed forces. In my opinion, to ignore these works would impoverish military sociology from a wealth of available knowledge.

It is therefore important to understand that military sociology has a history of its own, which is often forgotten, and its future trends are far from being set. The present chapter aims to provide a historical perspective and show how themes and approaches are relative, historically, within military sociology. The chapter is intended as a history of the Russian tradition of military sociology.[1]

Origin of Military Sociology in Russia

In each country, the history of the development of sociology tends to contain elements that are specific to the national reality. This, indeed, holds true for Russia. However, it is important first to clarify a possible misconception and underline that Russian sociology is certainly as old as sociology itself. One of the founders of Russian sociology, Nikolay Kareev (1850-1931), noted the appearance of the first Russian publication of sociological character as early as 1845. According to Kareev:

> Valerian Maykov (1823-1847), in his work "Social Studies in Russia," (in 1845)...shows his knowledge of

"Cours de Philosophie Positive" and that he incorporated Auguste Comte's basic concepts...[Hence]
Russian sociology is not younger than sociology of
other countries. (Kareev 1996:28-29)

Interests in sociological matters is therefore quite old
in Russia but, as will be shown below, its later development is
closely associated with historical events such as the Bolshevik
Revolution and the rise of Stalinism. The linkages between
historical events and military sociology are even greater given
that the shape, nature, and role of the armed forces closely
intertwine with the political situation of a country. For the
purpose of this chapter, the history of Russian military sociology has been divided into five basic periods: (1) from the early
days to the revolutions of 1917; (2) from the revolutions of
1917 to the Stalin Purges of the 1930s; (3) from the Stalin
Purges of the 1930s to the post-Stalin era of the 1960s; (4)
from the post-Stalin era of the 1960s to the end of the Soviet
Union in 1991; (5) from the end of the Soviet Union to the
present.

From the Early Days to the Revolutions of 1917

In the nineteenth century and early twentieth century, a tradition of military sociology was created within the officer corps
of the Imperial Russian Army. This military origin of the discipline had a profound impact on its later stages of development
in Russia. In fact, until very recently, military sociology was
essentially practiced by people in uniform or by civilians
working directly for the military. There have been several
intellectual influences that have contributed to the creation of
military sociology, but one of the most profound was the rise
of military science in Russia.

64

A few key thinkers believed that military science had to go beyond simple tactics and strategy and had to incorporate other elements such as philosophical analysis about human nature in the context of war. One of those early thinkers was General Genrih Antonovich Leer (1829-1904), Chief of Staff at Nikolaevsky Academy[2] between 1889 and 1896. His work *Strategy* is subdivided into a section on *knowledge by the strategy-art ("a science about conducting war")* and a section on the *strategy-science ("a science about war")* (Leer 1893). The second section is especially of interest, as it discusses the philosophy of military science to reveal the laws and general principles of war. Implicit is the idea that military strategy includes much more than military matters, strictly speaking; it includes human affairs as well. The publication of this work was an important step in expanding the horizons of strategic thinking in Russia.

Another important early theorist was General Nikolay Petrovich Mihnevich (1849-1927), who was also based at the Nikolaevsky Academy of the General Staff. He studied war from two sides: as a social phenomenon and as a military phenomenon, where both sides connect by the use of military force to gain a victory over the enemy. Mihnevich, therefore, went further than his contemporaries in military science by developing a "synthetic" (i.e., social-military) science of strategy. This synthetic approach was also a methodological innovation as military science was mostly attempting to replicate the exact sciences (mathematics, mechanics, geography, etc.). Mihnevich's works gradually led the study of strategy to include philosophical and sociological approaches. By the beginning of twentieth century, their works provided the methodological basis for the sociology of war (military sociology).

The Russian sociology of war that was emerging acquired another important development through the work of

Nikolay Andreevich Korf (1866-1924), who was a disciple and follower of Leer and Mihnevich. Korf was preoccupied with "connecting military sciences with social studies," in a way that was even more synthetic at the theoretical level. In his main theoretical work, he continued to develop the views of his predecessors of strategy as a "philosophy." He offered a new definition of war for military science as "an armed struggle between social forces" (Korf 1897). He also, for the first time, raised the question of the necessity of creating a new branch of scientific knowledge: military sociology. However, most significant, and which had a lasting influence in Russia, was that he investigated the study of social phenomena in the armed forces from a military point of view. Hence, what he proposed to call *military sociology* (Korf 1897:66) was essentially a science at the service of military effectiveness.

A second important intellectual tradition in Russia that influenced the development of military sociology was what was known by the end of the nineteenth century as *military statistics*. This area of interest was already institutionalized as an independent scientific branch within the Imperial Army. In 1847, the *Department of Military Statistics* (the first in the world) was created at the Nikolaevsky Academy of the

---

New Direction 3.2

Nikolay Andreevich Korf raised the question of the necessity of creating a new branch of scientific knowledge: military sociology. He investigated social phenomena in the armed forces from a military point of view. What he proposed to call *military sociology* was essentially a science at the service of military effectiveness.

General Staff. By 1903, its teachings and methodologies were extended to the entire General Staff of the Imperial Army with the creation of several military-statistical departments. It must be noted, however, that the military statistics of that time were, in many respects, subsumed under military geography (the geographical component dominated over military-statistical research), but based on methodologies and theories of statistical analysis.

Military statistics evolved over time to include research topics beyond geography and pure military strategy. The statistical works of Colonel Peter Aleksandrovich Rezhepo (1873-1918) and Colonel Konstantin Mihajlovich Oberuchev (1864-1929) are quite interesting as they analyze the qualitative structure of the military elite and the officer corps of the Imperial Russian Army (Rezhepo 1903, 1905, 1909; Oberuchev 1909, 1910). Using personnel files, they studied the socio-demographic characteristics and career paths of senior officers (more than 1,300 generals and more than 3,000 colonels were studied) and the causes of socio-demographic fluctuation among the officers.

In spite of those scientific developments within the Imperial Russian armed forces, it was only with the acid test of military battle that a major impetus to rethink the military institution was put in motion. The Russian-Japanese war exposed major weaknesses in the Imperial Russian Army and especially within its command structure. To find the true reasons for such serious ineffectiveness by the Russian military, a survey was mailed in early 1906 to the officers who participated in the war and who graduated from the General Staff academy from 1880-1903. The respondents were asked two questions: (1) what defects were revealed in the areas of the special training and practical skills of officers? (2) What changes should be made within the academic portion of education to take into consideration the experience of war? By September 1906, only 20 percent of the dispatched question-naires were returned, however this quantity was recognized as sufficient for summarizing. The data received were used by the Defense Ministry to carry out the military reform of 1906-1912 (Obraztsov 2004).

It is also interesting that applied qualitative analysis became a reality during the First World War. For instance, it was used to study the troops morale based on soldiers' letters sent from the frontlines. In February 1916, the correspondence sent from the Western front was interpreted as follows: 2.15 percent of letters show signs of depression; 30.25 percent of letters are considered as showing vigorous morale; 67.6 percent of letters show a steady morale but also contain doubts about the Russian Army's capability to win the war (Golovin 1939:158).

It is important to note that during this period, the majority of studies were initiated and done directly by military bodies (particularly the Nikolaevsky Academy, which became the center of military sociology research). Even if military sociology, in those days, was mostly an internal affair to the armed forces, as a scientific discipline it was acknowledged by the Russian military as having value and warranted further development as a discipline. Unfortunately, much that was gained during that period, from both a theoretical and empiri-cal perspective, was to be lost or practically forgotten for a long time.

From the Revolutions of 1917 to the
Stalin's Purges of the 1930s

The revolutions of 1917 brought profound changes to the Russian society. Not only was the monarchy abolished and a

---

New Direction 3.3

Sociological research became geared toward ideological development rather than dealing with empirical
research. Military sociology also followed this trend.
As a result, the empirical findings of the previous
period were soon forgotten.

---

communist regime forcefully put in place after a bitter civil
war, but the role and composition of the armed forces was seriously modified. Reforming the officer corps from an
aristocratic entity into a proletarian and subservient force
remained a key preoccupation of the new regime put in place
by Lenin. The development of military sociology was therefore stunted by historical events.

In the first part of that period, social sciences in
general in the new Soviet Union saw a significant decline. For
instance, the number of sociological publications during the
period from 1898 to 1902 in Russia was 267 books, brochures,
and articles; during the period from 1903-1907, the number of
sociological publications was 346; during 1908-1912, the
number of sociological publications was 408; even during the
war the number of publications continued to rise as in 1913-
1917, the number was 485; then, in 1918-1922, there were
only 107 (Golosenko 1995).

There are many reasons for this decline, which include
the social and economic consequences of the civil war and the
post-war efforts concentrated on reconstruction. However, it
was the development of the communist ideology as the sole
acceptable ideology that would have the most profound
impact. Individuals representing "bourgeois" sciences, and
literature supporting "bourgeois" concepts and analyses, had

to be replaced. For instance, it was declared that there was no "pure" social science—all of them have a *class character* and are either *bourgeois* or *proletarian*. Of course, in line with the new regime's ideology, the proletarian sciences were deemed superior to bourgeois ones (Buharin 1921:7-8).

Sociological research became mostly geared toward ideological development rather than dealing with empirical research. This tendency was felt also in the development of military sociology. As a consequence, the empirical findings of the previous period were rapidly forgotten. Some former officers of the Imperial Army who joined the Red Army, like General Alexander Svechin (1878-1938), tried to save some of the previous advances in military sociology. Svechin's works share some similarities to Mihnevich's pre-revolutionary views, particularly on the close relationship that military sociology has to strategy. However, he departed completely with the methodological attitude of emulating natural sciences found in military science. He considered the theory of military strategy a *branch of sociology*, in line with the new ideological requirement that any science cannot be "pure" and should be based on a proletarian perspective. Svechin constantly emphasized the connection between military science and politics, the economy, and social conditions.

However, to be an intellectual, even a "military" one, was a dangerous affair in Stalin's era. Svechin became one of the many victims of Stalin's purges of the 1930s, which decimated the Red Army's officer corps. The purges often targeted the most able officers, as they were perceived as threats to Stalin's totalitarian rule. In 1938, Svechin was sentenced by the military court to execution as an "enemy of the people." His works, and the works of many others, were removed from circulation. His "excommunication" and death actually interrupted the theoretical development of military sociology in Russia until Stalin's death.

If theoretical development came to a standstill, applied research had a different fate. Applied research, as long as it was serving the purposes of the proletariat, as defined by the new rulers in Moscow, was allowed to develop. Thus, some applied research in military sociology started to emerge during the 1920s in the Red Army. For instance, large-scale empirical research and social-statistical inspection of the armed forces was undertaken. In line with the creation of proletarian armed forces, this research was mainly concerned with finding the social class structure of the command and political staff to deal with practical questions such as how to implement political training, education, and how to strengthen the party and military discipline. In 1923, the Political Directorate of the Red Army surveyed personnel and command staff among 12 regiments and 1,266 garrisons. In 1928, 14 territorial divisions in 7 military districts were surveyed in a similar manner (Shtejngart 1924; Sergeev 1990).

One unusual innovative project was the "Language of Red Army Man," which surveyed troops in the Moscow military district in 1924-1925. The project was led by the scientists of the Industrial Psychotechnics Laboratory of Narkomtrud and by The Section of Applied Psychology of the State Institute of Experimental Psychology (Shpil'rejn, Reeitynbarg, and Netsky 1928). A group of 13 scientists, under the leadership of psychologist Isaak Naftulovich Shpil'rejn (1891-1937), received the task from the Political Directorate of the Red Army to "determine the dictionary of Red Army Man and map the dictionary of political works: oral and written" (Shpil'rejn, Reeitynbarg, and Netsky 1928:18). By using formalized analysis of documents and questionnaires, the scientists experimentally surveyed 1,241 Red Army troops (the vocabulary of Red Army Man was made of 11,223 words); analyzed 12 stenograms on various themes (the language of political leaders

71

was made of 12,806 words); studied 141 letters of Red Army members to the editor of the district newspaper *The Red Soldier* (found 20,456 words); and covered 2 complete issues of *The Red Soldier* of 1924 (found 54,338 words). The report was submitted to the military-political staff of the Red Army and contained some of the richest statistical and illustrative material of the period.

In spite of some interesting developments in the empirical realm, the era is marked by a great degree of conformism. At the end of the 1920s and early 1930s, the appearance of some theoretical collections (*War and Military Art of a Historical Materialism*, 1927; *Sketches of the Marxist-Leninist Doctrine About War*, 1933; etc.) marked the end of the period of alternative theoretical approaches to the analysis of war and armed forces. With the exception of the Marxist theories of war, all other theories were deemed either "antiscientific," "bourgeois," or even "fascist." By the end of 1930s, applied research began to be curtailed also, and theoretical results in the field of military sociology were replaced by simplified Marxist dogmas.

From the Stalin Purges of the 1930s
to the Post-Stalin Era of the 1960s

This period can be called the *institutional prohibition era* for sociology (including military sociology), and it lasted three decades: from the middle of the 1930s until to the beginning of the 1960s. Again, new political developments in the Soviet society halted the development of military sociology and led to the obliteration of all previous expertise. However, it is important to underline that the work of some Russian military scientists was continued abroad during that period (particularly in France and Yugoslavia).[3]

New Direction 3.4

The object of sociological research, according to Golovin, is to understand the processes and the phenomena of war from the point of view of existence, coexistences, existential similarities, and their consequences. In other words, war is construed first and foremost as a human experience.

Among them, it is necessary to note the former professor of the Nikolaevsky Academy, Lieutenant-General Nikolay Nikolaevich Golovin (1875-1944), whose scientific work obtained international recognition. Golovin, who lived the last 25 years of his life in France, continued the pre-revolutionary scientific research of his compatriots. In the 1930s, he developed a comprehensive approach to the "sociology of war" (Golovin 1931, 1937, 1938, 1939) and, in every possible way, promoted the institutionalization of this discipline.

Golovin considered war a social phenomenon, which could be understood from many different perspectives—from the symbiosis of psychologism and social Darwinism, all the way to positivism and vulgar materialism. For Golovin, the sociology of war was worthy of the status of an independent discipline, and he worked at developing its key issues, structure, tasks, and limits, as well as its role in informing concrete social practices. He offered some key concepts (for example, the degree of "military tension within a country" and the "moral elasticity of the troops") and indicators necessary for researching war. He also reflected on the usefulness of various methodologies, whether they be historical, psychological, or statistical. According to Golovin, the object of sociological research was to understand the processes and the phenomena of war from the point of view of existence, coexistences, existential similarities, and their consequences. In other words, war was construed first and foremost as a human experience and, therefore, a science about war could only be the *sociology of war* (Golovin 1937:7).

Within the borders of the Soviet Union, the revival of military sociology was directly connected to the process of institutionalization of Soviet sociology as a whole. Thus, it was only after the death of Joseph Stalin, and the stabilization of the new regime under Khrushchev, that the intellectual work could resume. The revival of wider theoretical ideas was specifically connected with the twentieth Congress of the Communist Party (1956), which condemned the cult of the personality of Joseph Stalin; ideological flexibility was reintroduced in the Soviet regime. It is necessary to note that during this period, however, sociology was still not considered an official discipline, and only applied sociological research was officially recognized. Therefore, in the Soviet Union of those days, *concrete social research* was necessary for any project to be considered sociological. Not surprisingly, state support was given to applied sociology, while its theoretical foundations remained anchored in the official Marxist-Leninist doctrine of historical materialism.

In line with the developments of sociology in the USSR, the military sociology revival began with the renewal of applied military-sociological research. However, given the lack of theoretical work produced domestically, it seems that many approaches to practical problems were indirectly borrowed from foreign military sociologists. However, Soviet military sociologists could not officially agree with, and support, the theoretical positions and conclusions of American authors, as they were alien concepts to the official communist ideology (Savinkin 1988). Nevertheless, many personal relationships were forged.

74

The first serious sociological research in the Soviet armed forces was devoted to studying interpersonal relations in subdivisions of military towns (1966-1967); the ways and means of increasing the performance of the sergeant staff of submarines and strengthening military discipline in the Northern and Baltic fleet (1966-1967); the problems of the military and patriotic education of youth in the Kursk and Donetsk regions, and the associated organizations geared toward their training for military service (1969), and so on.

Changes in the Soviet society allowed for an expansion of military sociology and the improvement of methodological procedures. As well, sociological research started to attract the attention of the senior leadership of the armed forces (mainly the Main Political Directorate of Soviet Army and the Navy). By the middle of the 1960s, the main publication of the USSR Ministry of Defense, *The Red Star*, started to publish texts supporting sociological research in the armed forces.

The first large-scale sociological research of this period was authorized and organized by the Main Political Directorate in July 1966. It was organized to investigate specific issues raised in the Odessa and Belarus Military Districts concerning methods of perfecting officers' training of subordinates and strengthening military discipline (over 1000 military troops were interviewed). Its results were reported to the Minister of Defense and were received with high praises.

It is important to note, however, that in the Soviet Union of those days, no decision on any significant problem could be made without the supervision and direction of the Communist Party. Therefore, it was necessary for the armed forces to obtain the approval of the Central Committee of the Party to create regular sociological research branches. Such approval was granted on the premise that sociological work

75

had to be about measures intended to improve of political work (i.e., political conformity) in the Soviet Army and Navy fleet. The political staff was particularly interested in research about the political affairs in military units and subdivisions, as these were areas in which it was believed not enough information existed within the armed forces.[4] To this end, on 13 November 1967, the Main Political Directorate of the armed forces created a *Department of Military-Sociological Research*[5] (Chief, DPh Major-General Victor Kirillovich Konopliev) in accordance with the instructions of the Minister of Defense.

Its personnel size was, at first, insignificant (5 military personnel and 1 employee of the Soviet Army). During this period, because of a lack of professional sociologists, the representatives of various disciplines were included in the department: philosophers, historians, psychologists, jurists, journalists, and computer experts.

The department, through its very existence, increased the status and intellectual authority of sociological research done on the troops, but by being a military entity, it had a restrictive effect as the research results were distributed only within military circles. The main research topics were on issues such as "unauthorized mutual relations," suicide incidents, the lack of social life in military garrisons and small towns, concealment of crime and infringements to military discipline, the low efficiency of younger commanders, and the absence of effective mechanisms to protect personnel from the arbitrariness of commanders.

Many of these issues, as one can see, were about infringement of rules and the official line. Among the armed forces senior leadership, it was believed that those infringements were committed by a few careless and inefficient individuals. The sociological research, however, showed that those problems were of a systemic nature rather than about individual carelessness. These results caused some irritations and displeasure among the senior leaders. In the context of a military organization that was under the spell of the "zero-defect" mentality, it is not surprising that military sociology came to be considered by the authorities as an *"inconvenient science,"* and research results were often stamped "classified."

Beyond the "inconvenience" caused by the research results, there was also a certain *critical attitude* and *mistrust* toward social sciences in general, and sociology in particular, among the senior leadership. Ironically, such negative perception was a by-product of the Soviet education system where social sciences were dominated by Marxist-Leninist philosophy (dialectic and historical materialism) and by scientific communism. Thus, the prevalent dogmatism in educational institutions undermined any trust that one might have toward the ability of social science to handle concrete problems in a meaningful way.

This difficult situation for military sociology led some to question the connection between sociological research and the official dogma taught in higher learning institutions. However, it was not until the end of 1960s that discussions

---

New Direction 3.5

Senior leadership in the armed forces mistakenly believed that infringements were being committed by a few careless and inefficient individuals. However, sociological research showed that those problems were of a systemic nature rather than about individual carelessness.

---

emerged about the need to "separate" sociology from philosophy, so it could become an independent scientific discipline. Specifically, there was an interest in isolating the sociological components of the Marxist-Leninist doctrine about war and army from the rest of the Marxist-Leninist teachings to make it a topic of study in its own right. Various names for such a discipline were offered, including *sociology of the army*.

Here, again, the work of a few key military social scientists was instrumental in guiding the emerging discipline. They were also able to prove the legitimacy of the term "military sociology" in opposition to those who wanted to create a sociology of the army. One of them was Colonel Nikolay Dmitrievich Tabunov. Through his doctoral dissertation, he played a key role in developing the argument that the Marxist-Leninist sociology could not be limited to studying social relations inside the armed forces and between the armed forces and society. For him, the most important topic was to understand military personnel during armed conflicts. The Russian tradition of "military sociology" (regarding society from a military perspective in order to increase military effectiveness), was revived once again. Thus, after more than 70 years (since 1897 when the expression was offered by N. A. Korf for the first time) the term "military sociology" was again used by Russian sociology. This recognition became an important step in institutionalizing military sociology as special sociological subfield.

One must also note that during that period, Soviet scientists began to take part in international sociological congresses, starting with the 3rd World Sociological Congress in Amsterdam, in August 1956. However, military sociologists were allowed to take part in international forums only with the 7th World Sociological Congress in Varna, in September 1970. The dialogue with foreign colleagues allowed Soviet military sociologists to expand their outlook on the discipline and promote military sociology in the Soviet Union. There was also a high level of cooperation between Soviet scientists and their colleagues from Eastern Europe—members of the Warsaw Treaty Organization (particularly with Poland, Czechoslovakia, East Germany and Bulgaria).

From the Post-Stalin Era of the 1960s to the End of the Soviet Union

During the first part of this period, military sociology experienced a greater degree of institutionalization under the stabilizing effect of the Brejnevian era. For instance, there were a number of fundamental texts devoted to the philosophical-sociological analysis of war and armed forces produced (Puzik 1971; Volkogonov, Milovidov, and Tjushkevich 1977; Kovaliev 1980; Sredin, Volkogonov, and Korobejnikov 1981, Borodin and Chepurov 1987). In 1979, in the *Military Encyclopedia*, the entry "sociological research in the Soviet armed forces" was included for the first time (Konopliev 1979).

In line with the applied research mandate and the tradition of military sociology in the Soviet Union, the bulk of the research in that period remained concentrated toward the practical problems of the armed forces. Including among them:

* Morale, political, and psychological support to the troops in actions during large-scale military exercises
* The political, morale, and psychological stability of the personnel in extreme conditions of fighting (during the Soviet invasion of Czechoslovakia in 1968, the aftermath of the Chernobyl disaster in 1986, and during the Afghanistan War in 1979-1989)
* Efficiency of political and ideological work among the troops

- Problems related to the military press (interests of the personnel in reading, rating of periodicals, how military mass-media portray troops in action, etc.)
- Family relations in officers' families including the influence of psychological atmosphere within the family on accomplishing service tasks
- The educational system was also integrating military sociology. The Military-Political Academy V. I. Lenin started to offer a degree in sociological research in 1982, with its first graduate in 1985. In connection with this, sociology was, for the first time, officially recognized within the military education system in September 1982.

With the arrival of Gorbatchev at head of the Soviet state, and the introduction of perestroika, military sociology experienced greater recognition. In June 1988, the Political Bureau of the Central Committee of the Party provided a powerful push toward the institutionalization of sociology in the USSR by declaring there was a need for an increased the role of Marxist-Leninist sociology to inform decisions about key social problems of the Soviet society. Sociology, at last, received all the rights and privileges of an independent discipline for the first time in the whole history of the Soviet social sciences. In the same vein, military sociology began to experience an institutional renewal where research subdivisions became more autonomous in their research mandates and organizational structures. As well, in August 1990, the Military-Political Academy created the *Department of Military Sociology*.

From the End of the Soviet Union to the Present

After the collapse of the USSR, military sociology saw new prospects for development, as ideological restrictions were removed and the necessity to correlate research results with official estimations had disappeared. The withdrawal of official ideology as a topic from curriculums in military schools strengthened the credibility of the social sciences in general, but institutions remained populated by military sociologists who specialized in teaching Marxist-Leninist doctrine about war and the army. Some of them tried to adapt their previous conceptual frameworks to a more "sociological" military sociology. However, the issue of how to move from the old ways toward a renewed discipline still remains unsettled.

Now, the main research center in military sociology is the Sociological Center of the Armed Forces. The basic directions of applied research are determined by the following issues: the value structure of military personnel; moral and psychological support for the troops in action to increase of their efficiency; the development of a contractual attitude toward the service (problems of professionalism); turnover rates among the staff officers and increasing the prestige of the military career; monitoring the social and economic conditions of military personnel and their families; and examining the psychological stability of military men in fighting conditions (through the operations conducted in the Chechen Republic during 1994-1996 and 1999-2003).

In recent years, a significant number of publications in military sociology were produced: Chaldymov and Cherkasenko 1990; Slesarev 1990; Vorob'iev 1991; Andreev 1992, 1994; Vedernikov 1994; Serebriannikov and Deriugin 1996; Solov'yov 1996; Solov'yov and Obraztsov 1997; Serebriannikov 1998; Smirnov 1998, 2000; Dobren'kov 2002; Beljaev 2002; Obraztsov 2004.

Similarly, there are a growing number of publications in military sociology in scientific periodicals. For instance, in 1993 a special issue of the magazine *Sociological Researches*

81

(Moscow) was completely devoted to military sociology (22 texts). Since 1994, in the same magazine, there is a permanent section on military sociology, which publishes 5 to 6 texts annually. In 1998, a similar section was created in the *Journal of Sociology and Social Anthropology* (Saint Petersburg) and, in 2004, in the magazine *Sociology* (Moscow).

The greatest change since the beginning of 1990s is that military sociology is no longer the sole purview of sociologists who are a part of the military structures. The Institute of Sociopolitical Researches of the Russian Academy of Science, where the Center of Sociology of National Security is located, does serious work on the histories and theories of military sociology. As well, military sociology is developing in other higher learning institutions. In December 2002, the faculty of sociology at the Moscow State University created a Department of the Sociology of Security.

Conclusion

This brief introduction to the history of Russian military sociology shows that where there is a strong sociological tradition, there are also some sociologists interested in military affairs. It is important to expand the intellectual and geographic horizons of any field of research and to remember its respective history. Otherwise, we are at risk of falling into what can be called *professional solipsism,* i.e., whatever is not known is presumed to not exist. Military sociology has been very much affected by this phenomenon.

Military sociology, however, in its present state is dependent on its customers (i.e., those who finance research). Those customers tend to be senior military leaders or state bureaucracies, which are interested in the current state of affairs of the armed forces. It is hard to find customers who are interested in researching non-contemporary issues related to the military. Therefore, the choice of topics in the field appears narrow at times. This is not an excuse, however, to ignore comprehensive research that has been done elsewhere and prior to the Second World War.

In our opinion, among sections of the ISA RC01, ERGOMAS, and IUS there should be room for sections on the history of military sociology. There is a huge amount of material in military sociology, particularly in the non-English speaking world, which is almost completely unknown, or at least unexplored, by present-day military sociologists. It is awaiting its researchers. The history of military sociology is truly international and it is now necessary to start writing that history. People are gone, the material results of their research activities may disappear, many events and facts are simply forgotten or fade into the background. As time passes, it is more difficult to restore them.

Military sociology, as well as any other subfields of sociology, should have a history, a history written objectively and impartially. The diffusion of its brightest pages can attract new researchers, strengthen our traditions, and expand cooperation. Let us hope this article will help promote these achievements and purposes.

SUMMARY

This chapter presented a brief history of military sociology in Russia. The discipline has been significantly influenced by the social and political events that have occurred in Russia. During the days of the Soviet Union, military sociology became an applied science with limited theoretical development of its own, as it was restricted to following the official

Marxist-Leninist ideology dominating the country. Nevertheless, there are some traditions in military sociology that have survived through the various regimes. One fundamental tradition is that of military sociology being a method of regarding social issues from a military perspective in order to improve military effectiveness. Currently, military sociology in Russia is in transition and becomes more open to non-prescriptive approaches.

KEY TERMS AND CONCEPTS

- Military effectiveness
- "Inconvenient science"
- Applied research
- Sociology of war
- Marxist-Leninist ideology

STUDY AND DISCUSSION QUESTIONS

1. Do you think that military sociology could be an instrument of domination in your country?

2. Does military sociology has the potential of becoming an "inconvenient science" in your country?

3. Do you believe that the "War on Terrorism" and the rise of asymmetric conflicts require military sociology to modify its approach?

4. Should military effectiveness be an issue of concern for military sociology?

NOTES

1. For a more complete description of the development of military sociology in Russia, please refer to Obraztsov 2002, 2003a, 2003b, 2003c, 2004.
2. Nikolaevsky Academy of the General Staff was founded in Russia in 1832, and it aimed at educating officers for high-level assignments.
3. According to incomplete data, by the beginning of 1930s, 472 Russian scientists emigrated including 5 academicians and about 140 professors from higher learning institutions. The bibliography of works done by Russian scientists abroad during the period between 1920 and 1940 contains 13,371 entries. This number does not include a significant amount of texts that remained unpublished because of economic difficulties.
4. The issue was raised after the promulgation of the 1967 law on universal military service, which reconfirmed the politically binding character of military service for all citizens but reduced its duration by one year: from 4 to 3 years in the Navy, and from 3 to 2 years in the other services.
5. *"Military-Sociological research"*—the term used in Russia to designate sociological research conducted in the army and other military institutions.

REFERENCES

Andreev, Gennadij, ed. 1992. *Introduction to the Profession: Training Handbook for the Military Psychologists and Sociologists* (in Russian). Moscow: Centre for Military-Sociological, Psychological and Legal Research of the Armed Forces.

Igor V. Obraztsov

Andreev, Gennadij, ed. 1994. *How to Organize and Carry out Military-Sociological Research: Training Handbook* (in Russian). Moscow: Centre for Military-Sociological, Psychological, and Legal Research of the Armed Forces.

Armor, David. 1992. "Military Sociology." Pp. 1291-1299 in *Encyclopedia of Sociology* Volume 3, edited by Edgar and Marie Borgatta. New York: MacMillan.

Beljaev, Alexander. 2002. *Genesis of a Method of Military Sociology at the Turn of the 19th and 20th Centuries* (in Russian). Moscow: Military University.

Berndt, Otto. 1897. *Der Zahl im Kriege. Statistishe Daten aus der neueren Kriegsgeshishte in graphischer Darstellung* (Numbers on War. Statistical Research of the Newest Military History in Graphic Representation). Wien: Verlag von G. Freintag und Berndt.

Bodart, Gaston. 1908. *Militer-Historisches Kriegs-Lexicon (1618-1905)* (The Military-Historical Dictionary of Wars (1618-1905)). Wien und Leipzig: Verlag C. W. Stern.

Borodin, Nikolay and Vasily Chepurov, eds. 1987. *Military Sociological Research: The Methodical Training Handbook on Organization and Realization* (in Russian). Moscow: Institute of a Military History of Ministry of Defense of the USSR.

Buharin, Nikolay. 1921. *The Theory of a Historical Materialism: The Popular Textbook of Marxist Sociology* (in Russian). Moscow: The State Publishing House.

Callaghan, Jean and Franz Kernic, eds. 2003. *Armed Forces and International Security: Global Trends and Issues*. Muenster: LIT.

Chaldymov, Nikita and Alexander Cherkasenko, eds. 1990. *Army and Society* (in Russian). Moscow: Progress.

Constantin, A. 1907. *Le rôle sociologique de la guerre* (The Sociological Role of War). Paris: Félix Alcan.

Cru, Jean Norton, 1929. *Témoins: Essai d'analyse et de critique des souvenirs de combattants édités en français de 1915 à 1928* (Certificates: Analytical and Critical Research Memoirs of Participants of the Fights, Issued in French in the Period from 1915 to 1928). Paris: Les Étincelles.

Demetr, Karl. 1935. *Das Deutsche Heer und Seine Offizier* (The German State and its Officers). Berlin: Verlag von Reimar Hobbing.

_____. 1930. *Das Deutsche Offizierskorps in seihem Historisch-soziologischen Grundlagen* (The German Officer Corps in its Historical Sociological Basis). Berlin: D. Hobbeng.

Djubjuk, Eugeny and Alexander Zakharov, eds. 1915. *War and Kostroma's Village: On Sectional the Questionnaire of Statistical Branch* (in Russian). Kostroma: H. A. Gelish.

Dobren'kov, Vladimir, ed. 2002. *Sociology in Russia in the 19th and 20th Centuries. Military Sociology: Collection of Texts* (in Russian). Moscow: International University of Business and Management.

Du Pic, Ardant. 1880. *Études sur le combat* (Studies on Fighting). Paris: Hachette.

Golosenko, Igor. 1995. *The Sociological Literature of Russia 1850–early 20th Century* (in Russian). Moscov: Onega.

Golovin, Nicolay. 1907. *Study of Fight: Research of Activity and Properties of the Person as Soldier* (in Russian). Saint-Petersburg: The Economic Printing House.

_____. 1931. *The Russian Army in the World War—A Sociological Study*. New Haven: Yale University Press.

_____. 1937. "About the Sociological Study of War." *Osvedomitel (Belgrade)* (in Russian). 4:7-12.

_____. 1938. *A Science about War. The Sociological Study of War* (in Russian). Paris: Publishing House of the Newspaper "Signal."

_____. 1939. *Military Efforts of Russia during the World War* (in Russian). Paris: Company of the Incorporated Publishers.

Kareev, Nikolay. 1996. *Introduction to Russian Sociology* (in Russian). Saint Petersburg: Ivan Limbaha.

Konopliev, Victor. 1979. "Sociological Researches in the Soviet Armed Forces." Pp. 457 in *The Soviet Military Encyclopedia* (in Russian). Moscow: Military Publishing House.

Korf, Nikolay. 1897. *A General Introduction to Strategy Understood in a Broad Sense: Study of Military Science* (in Russian). Saint-Petersburg: Printing House of the Staff of the Separate Corps of Gendarme.

Kovaliev, Vladimir. 1980. *Socialist Military Collective: A Sociological Essay* (in Russian). Moscow: Military Publishing House.

Leer, Genrih. 1893. *Strategy: Tactics for the Battlefield* (in Russian). Saint-Petersburg: S. N. Hudekova.

Lewis, M. 1939. *England's Sea Officer: Study of the Naval Profession*. London: Allen and Unwin.

Mihnevich, Nikolay. 1899. *Strategy* (in Russian). Saint-Petersburg: A. E. Landau.

_____. 1921. "Evolution of Military Science in Connection with the Evolution of the Structures of the State." *Bulletin of Milition Army* (in Russian) 4-5, 8-16.

Novicow, Jacob. 1894. *La guerre et ses prétendu bienfaits* (War and its Alleged Benefits). Paris: Félix Alcan.

Oberuchev, Konstantin. 1909. *Our Military Leaders* (in Russian). Moscow: Trud.

_____. 1910. *Our Commanders: Experience of Statistical Research* (in Russian). Kiev: R. K. Lubkovskiei.

Obraztsov, Igor. 2002. "Military Sociology in Russia: A History and Modern State (Introduction)." Pp. 7-56 in *Sociology in Russia in the 19th and 20th Centuries. Military Sociology. A Collection of Texts* (in Russian), edited by Vladimir Dobren'kov. Moscow: International University of Business and Management.

_____. 2003a. "The Study of Military and Society in Russia." Pp. 121-125 in *Armed Forces and International Security: Global Trends and Issues,* edited by Jean Callaghan and Franz Kernic. Muenster: LIT.

_____. 2003b. "The Soviet Military Sociology: Past and Present." *Sociological Studies* (in Russian) 12:40-50.

_____. 2003c."Sociology of Military." Pp. 511-517 in *The Sociological Encyclopedia* Volume 2 (in Russian), edited by Gennadij Semigin. Moscow: Mysl.

_____. 2004. "Military Sociology in Russia." Pp. 353-374 in *Sociology in Russia From Inception to the End of the 20th Century* (in Russian), edited by Elena Kukushkina. Moscow: Vysshaya Shkola.

Puzik, Vasiliei. 1971. *Subject and Methods of Concrete Military Sociological Researches: Training Handbook* (in Russian). Moscow: Lenin Military Political Academy.

Rezhepo, Peter. 1903. *Statistics of the Generals* (in Russian). Saint-Petersburg: Trenke and Fiusko.

_____. 1905. *Statistics of the Colonels* (in Russian). Saint-Petersburg: S.H. Zolotarik.

_____. 1909. *An Officer's Question* (in Russian). Saint-Petersburg: Russian Velocity.

Salomon, Gaston. 1938. "A propos des sociologies de la guerre" (About the Sociologies of War). *Revue Internationale de Sociologie* 9-10:423-442.

Savinkin, Alexander, ed. 1988. *Criticism of Modern Bourgeois Sociology: A Handbook* (in Russian). Moscow: Lenin Military Political Academy.

Schumpeter, Joseph. 1919. "Zur Soziologie der Imperialismen" (Sociology of Imperialism). *Archiv fur Sozialwissenschaft und ozialpolitik* 44:1-29 and 275-310.

Serebriannikov, Vladimir. 1998. *Sociology of War* (in Russian). Moscow: Axis 89.

Serebriannikov, Vladimir and Iuriei Deriugin. 1996. *Sociology of the Army* (in Russian). Moscow: Institute of Social-Political Research.

Sergeev, Victor. 1990. "Empirical Sociological Researches in Red Army and Red Fleet in the 1920s: Conditions, Problems, and Experience." Pp. 134-154 in *V.I. Lenin and Actual Problems of Military Construction: The Collection of Scientific Articles* (in Russian). Moscow: Military Political Academy.

Shpil'rejn, Isaak, David Reeitynbarg, and George Netsky. 1928. *Language of the Red Army Man: Research on the Language of the Red Army Man of the Moscow Garrison* (in Russian). Moscow: State Publishing House.

Shtejngart, Alexander. 1924. "Commanders of Red Army under 1266 Questionnaires." *The Political Worker* 2-3:15-16 (in Russian).

Slesarev, Nicolay, ed. 1990. *Actual Problems of Development of Military Sociology in Requirements of Reorganization of Army and Fleet: Materials of a Scientific Conference* (in Russian). Moscow: Lenin Military Political Academy.

Smirnov, Alexander. 1998. *Russia on the Path Towards a Professional Army: Experience, Problems, and Prospects* (in Russian). Moscow: Institute of Sociology of the Centre of Universal Values.

_____. 2000. *Women in Military Service: New Opportunities and Social Rights* (in Russian). Moscow: Institute of Sociology of the Centre of Universal Values.

Snesarev, Andrey. 1924. *Introduction to Military Geography* (in Russian). Moscow: Military Academy of RKKA.

Solov'yov, Sergey. 1996. *Fundamentals of Practical Military Sociology*. Moscow: Ankil-Voin.

Solov'yov, Sergey and Igor Obraztsov. 1997. *The Russian Army from Afghanistan to Chechnya: A Sociological Analysis* (in Russian). Moscow: Katherine the Great Institute.

Sorokin, Pitirim. 1922a. "Influence of War on Population Structure: Its Property and Public Information." *Economist* (in Russian) 1:77-107.

_____. 1922b. "War and Militarization of Society." *Artel'noe delo* (in Russian) 1-4:3-10.

_____. 1928. "Sociological Interpretation of the 'Struggle for Existence' and 'Sociology of War.'" In *Contemporary Sociological Theories,* edited by Pitirim Sorokin. London: Harper and Row Publishers.

Sredin, Gennadij, Dmitriy Volkogonov, Mikhail Korobejnikov. 1981. *The Individual in Modern War* (in Russian). Moscow: Military Publishing House.

Steinmetz, Rudolf S. 1899. *Der Krieg als sociologisches Problem* (War as a Sociological Problem). Amsterdam: Versluys.

_____. 1929. *Die Soziologie des Krieges* (Sociology of War). Leipzig: Barth.

Svechin, Alexander. 1927. "Evolution of Strategic Theories." In *War and Military Art of a Historical Materialism* (in Russian). Moscow: State Military Publishing House.

Tabunov, Nicolay. 1969. *The Person and Military Collective* (in Russian). Doctoral Dissertation. Moscow: Lenin Military Political Academy.

Vaccaro, Michelangelo. 1886. *La Lotta per l'Esistenza e Suoi Effetti Nell'humanita* (Struggle for Existence and its Consequences for Mankind). Rome: Laterza.

Vedernikov, Vladimir. 1994. *Military Sociology: Questions of Theory, Methodology, History and Practice* (in Russian). Moscow: Humanitarian Academy of Armed Forces.

Volkogonov, Dmitry, Alexander Milovidov, and Stepan Tjushkevich, eds. 1977. *War and Army. A Philosophical-Sociological Essay* (in Russian). Moscow: Military Publishing House.

Von Bredow, Wilfried. 1996. "Military Sociology." Pp. 541-542 in *The Social Science Encyclopedia*, edited by A. Kuper and J. Kuper. London: Routledge.

Vorob'iev, V. 1991. "Military Sociology." Pp. 379-380 in *Sociological Dictionary* (in Russian). Minsk: Minsk University Press.

C h a p t e r

THE PROBLEM OF REALISM AND REALITY IN MILITARY TRAINING EXERCISES

Anne Irwin
University of Calgary and University of Victoria
Victoria, Canada

LEARNING OBJECTIVES

After reading this chapter, you should be able to

- understand the complexity of the word "reality" in a military context;
- explain how reality is constructed during military exercises;
- identify how the ethnomethodological approach can be used to study the military;
- understand the inner dynamics of military exercises from the point of view of the participants;
- describe how the interpretation of reality remains a key issue even in military organizations.

One of the significant characteristics of militaries as organizations is that they can be described as "contingent" organizations; organizations that are designed to perform certain tasks but may seldom or even never be called upon to perform these tasks. Militaries, as contingent organizations, spend the bulk of their time engaged in preparation and training, not in fighting battles. Training often takes the form of simulations or exercises, which are designed to instruct, practice, and evaluate individual and group performance in military skills. Simulations vary in scale and complexity and can range from a mock section attack involving no more than fifteen men, lasting a half hour or less, to full-blown, two-sided war games involving thousands of soldiers; vehicles, materiel, and ammunition worth millions of dollars; and lasting for several weeks at a time. Regardless of the scale, the real world constantly impinges on the simulated world of this exercise, posing problems for both planners and participants. In this analysis, the use of the term the "real world" refers to the mundane world that is not part of the simulation. Similarly, "reality" refers to physical and environmental factors that confront soldiers and affect their experience of the simulation, for example, the weather conditions, fatigue, hunger, injury. In contrast, the term "realism," refers to soldiers' evaluations of how closely a particular simulation accords with how they imagine wartime conditions.

Reality is a problem for planners who must decide how to achieve desired levels of realism within the constraints of safety, logistics, and various economic and political limitations. For example, there are limits to the number of training casualties that are considered acceptable in a peacetime army; however, in order for training to have value, a certain level of realism and authenticity is required which necessarily includes an element of risk for participants. Thus, there is constant, dynamic tension between the competing imperatives of authenticity and safety.

Reality is a problem for participants, when such things as real accidents and real casualties interfere with the conduct of an exercise, and when the logistical requirements for feeding and supplying troops affects the conduct of the exercise and influences the activities of participants. Soldiers must eat real food, (sometimes) practice with real equipment, and (sometimes) are supplied with real ammunition. Despite precautions, real casualties do occur, both to people and vehicles. Sometimes these casualties occur in the midst of a simulation in which medical evacuation and vehicle repair are being practiced. Realism is also a problem for participants, because what constitutes appropriate realism is often a subject of debate. Despite the problems that both realism and reality pose for planners and participants, they are essential elements in the lives of soldiers and their commanders. In this paper, I adopt an ethnomethodological approach to analyze how soldiers in a Canadian infantry battalion routinely manage the problems posed by reality and realism during military exercises.[1]

Military organizations are, of course, not the only organizations that use simulations as a pedagogical tool. Some of the literature devoted to simulations and gaming can shed light on the problem of reality in war games (see, for example: Anderson, Hughes, and Sharrock 1987; Crookall et al. 1987; Crookall and Oxford 1990; Watson and Sharrock 1990). However, most of the relevant literature examines business games or games used in primary and secondary schools, and these differ in significant ways from military simulations. Business games typically are treated as a "time-out" from the "real" business of an organization. Executives are removed from their normal work setting for a day or two, and play the game. They are then sent back to their "normal, regular" business with the expectation that they have learned lessons in the game that can be applied in the "real" world.

Simulations and games are exceptional and extra-ordinary rather than a part of everyday life. In the army, however, games and simulations are part of the normal routine of everyday life and are, therefore, not exceptional. The "real" business of the army—fighting wars—is, in fact, not routine, but exceptional and extra-ordinary, so the relationship between the game and "real" life can be seen as a reversal of the process of business games. The vast majority of any soldier's or officer's time, during peacetime and to a lesser degree even in wartime, is spent participating in a simulation of one type or another, including preparing for one or cleaning up and debriefing after one.

Another difference is that in both business games and educational games, the participants normally take on roles that are different from those of their business identities. A personnel manager may play a purchasing agent, a school child may play a shop assistant. In the military, it is more often the case that participants play their own role throughout the game or simulation. As a result, in military simulations, there is much more of an overlap between the "real world" and the simulation. The relationship, then, between reality and the simulation is particularly problematic and complex in the case of the military.

Most theorists who have studied simulations and gaming have examined how realistic a simulation is by measuring it against their own notions of realism, adopting a "correspondance" theory of reality or epistemology (Anderson et al. 1987). Using an ethnomethodological approach entails a "congruence" epistemology; that is, suspending our judgment about whether the simulation corresponds to some objective reality and, rather, attending to participants' assessments of whether a particular game or simulation is a realistic event.

Watson and Sharrock (both ethnomethodologists) acknowledge the importance of the participants' perspectives:

> We must not ask whether any given simulation maps or reflects some real-world situation, but instead we should ask how, and to what extent, do students and other parties to the simulation *treat* it as simulating reality: What are their practices in changing the "constitutive accent" so that the simulation is collaboratively taken by participants as realistic-for-all-practical purposes? Obversely, what are participants' practices in jointly sustaining an understanding that this simulation is not realistic or real-worldly? What is the communicative work which contributes to both the suspending and the sustaining of disbelief in simulations and games? (Watson and Sharrock 1990: 231-238).

This approach means adopting the "native's point of view," as Malinowski urged anthropologists to do (1984:25). It means entering the native's world, but it does not imply entering the native's mind. The distinctions between reality and simulation, and assessments of the reality of simulations, are interactively accomplished by members and are thus as available to us as analysts as they are to members of the military.

A short description of one event I participated in will illustrate the problems mundane reality can cause for exercise participants. During an exercise, the rifle company was conducting a "mounted advance to contact," which meant that the whole company, including its support elements of medics and mechanics, was moving forward expecting to meet and engage a notional enemy. The support elements were being exercised as well as the fighting elements, so that, after engage-

97

ments, the proper casualty (both human and vehicle) treatment and evacuation procedures were to be practiced. During one attack, however, the vehicle in which I was traveling hit a trench that had been hidden by snow and several soldiers were injured when the vehicle came to a sudden stop, throwing them forward. Thus, in the middle of this exercise practicing medical evacuation, we actually had several real casualties.

These types of events are common during military exercises, creating a necessity for the development of methods for distinguishing between real events and exercise events. The radio codeword used to identify real events, which is also used in everyday speech to distinguish between exercise events and real events, is "no-duff." In other words, exercise events are simply "exercise events," while real events are "no-duff" events. "No-duff" is called over the radio by the unit reporting the event and all hearers of the message know to treat the event with the seriousness that a real injury entails. I have, many times, been on an exercise with other participants excited and tense, during which there was a very strong sense of realism when a no-duff call was passed over the radio. It was remarkable how quickly the atmosphere changed. What seemed real before the call was recognized clearly as game-playing and pretence, and everyone attended to the radio in a new, more serious fashion.

New Direction 4.1

These types of events are common during military exercises, creating a necessity for the development of methods for distinguishing between real events and exercise events.

The ongoing interplay between reality and simulation is such that soldiers become adept at switching back and forth between the two frames of reference. One question to consider, then, is how is the status of a present situation constituted and communicated? Defining any situation is an ongoing process, constantly subject to renegotiation and reconstitution. The definition of a situation as "simulated" or "no-duff" is accomplished by the participants who make current definitions of the situation available to each other on an ongoing basis so that they know what sort of behavior is expected and appropriate.

The impossibility, if not the undesirability, of replicating an authentic war experience in training is acknowledged by members of the military. The literature produced by soldiers who have participated in combat is replete with accounts of how field training did not prepare them for the "real thing," and a number of NCOs informed me during my research that they have no idea whether or not the tactics they practice during field exercises will work in an actual wartime situation. Caputo, in his memoirs of the Vietnam War, emphasizes the complex relationship between training and reality. After serving in combat in Vietnam, he describes his Marine Corps officer training:

> Our Hollywood fantasies were given some outlet in the field exercises that took up about half the training schedule. These were supposed to simulate battlefield conditions, teach us to apply classroom lessons, and develop the 'spirit of aggressiveness'...It was easy to do in the bloodless make-believe of field problems, in which every operation went according to plan and the only danger was the remote one of falling and breaking an ankle. We took these stage-managed exercises

99

seriously, thinking they resembled actual combat. We couldn't know then that they bore about as much similarity to the real thing as shadowboxing does to street-fighting...[we] made frontal assaults against the sun-browned hills the [the fictitious enemy] defended, yelling battle cries as we charged through storms of blank cartridge fire. (1996:15-16)

Early in his first tour of duty in Vietnam, the reality of war is confused with the make-believe of field exercises:

I was careful to do everything by the book, setting up interlocking fields of fire, emplacing machine guns to cover the platoon frontage—in brief, all that I had learned at Quantico in Rifle Company Defensive Tactics. I was now plying my trade in earnest, but I had a difficult time convincing myself that that was the case. So far, the operation had the playact quality of an exercise. (1996:53-54)

As Caputo becomes more experienced, the lack of fit between training and war is evident:

Standing up in front of a stunted tree—it was the only tree in the paddy and a stupid place to expose myself— I crooked my arm and pumped it up and down. This was the hand-and-arm signal to move out on the double...Something slapped into the branches not six inches above my head; a fillip from Charlie...that one had been addressed to me; and so, for the first time in my life, I had the experience of being shot at by some- one who was trying to kill me specifically...[The company commander] came up on the radio...he calmly asked me what the hell I was doing waving my arms around under fire. I explained that I was using a hand-and-arm signal they had taught us in Quantico. "You're not at Quantico any more. You'll draw fire doing that." I told him that the VC had just given me the same message in more emphatic terms. (1996:93-94)

And later yet, he learns from experience what cannot be taught in simulated war:

We saw enough to learn those lessons that could not be taught in training camps: what fear feels like and what death looks like, and the smell of death, the experience of killing, of enduring pain and inflicting it, the loss of friends and the sight of wounds. (Caputo 1996:95)

Similar feelings were expressed to me in an interview with a sergeant who had never been in combat:

The platoon commander is here to be trained by the platoon warrant officer how to lead a platoon. He learned how on his course, but that doesn't mean shit here, Okay? because those are textbook attacks, textbook everything. And we all know that just doesn't apply. We learn that when we go through our battle school. We come to the battalion, everything is changed, and you see it every day…It's different from what they learned…they make everything simple for teaching so you do these attacks as if you were on a parade square doing drill. And that just doesn't apply when you're out in the field. I mean none of us have ever been—well, the odd guy's been shot at and stuff like that, in peacekeeping roles and stuff, but we've

101

never been in combat. And, hopefully, we never will be
in combat, you know; only an idiot wants to go to war.
But uh…so we don't know if any of this stuff works,
but we have to take what we can and try and, I don't
know, the best we can, you know. We train for what we
can and we do it. (MacPhail 1991)

In this case, training in the "real" world of the battalion is contrasted with what is taught on courses, yet there is an
acknowledgement that even battalion training is not the "real"
thing. Moreover, what constitutes realism is by no means
universally agreed upon, as the following transcript of a post-
exercise discussion among a group of sergeants illustrates:

Sgt. M: Get this, the OC [Company Commander] said
in order for the troops to get the full effect they have to
walk at least 40 kilometers.
Sgt. C: What?
Sgt. M: So we said okay, so far we've practiced lying
on the ground, being cold, now we're going to practice
walking. What the fuck? What did he say last night?
Seven platoon didn't get any contact until the early
morning? He said "uh…well, at least you know they
got two lessons learned out of it. One was how to make
up like shifts the other was endurance."
Sgt. C: Ah, fuck.
Sgt. D: Unbelievable.
Sgt. M: Where does this stuff come from?
Sgt. S: Anne, there's got to be a book of stupid ideas
'cause they must look it up okay?
Sgt. M: They learned endurance [laughter]…long time
figuring that one out—what ya talking about "learning
endurance." You learn to lie in the rain.

Sgt. D: Maybe a little tolerance there, but that's about it...tolerance and stupidity of the hierarchy.
Sgt. M: Well, they learned not to sleep on fucking ambush. (Irwin 1996c)[2]

It would seem, in this case, the sergeants do not agree with the Company Commander's estimation of the importance of walking 40 kilometers as a way of achieving an authentic experience. The evaluation of the level of realism of war games is never decided once and for all but is constantly shifting throughout the course of the game. And, it could be argued that leadership in a peacetime volunteer military consists of convincing soldiers that the training they are undertaking is realistic.

There are two frames, then, in which soldiers situate their activities: the frame of the reality of everyday life, which is the world of eating, injuries, fatigue, and equipment failure that we can identify (as do soldiers) as "no-duff"; and the frame of the make-believe world of the simulation, which we can identify as "exercise" or "tactical." These frames are not mutually exclusive, and they do overlap, so that they mutually constitute each other. Overarching these two frames is the

---

New Direction 4.2

There are two frames in which soldiers situate their activities: the frame of the reality of everyday life, which is the world of eating, injuries, fatigue, and equipment failure that we can identify (as do soldiers) as "no-duff"; and the frame of the make-believe world of the simulation, which we can identify as "exercise" or "tactical."

concern for realism, which is constantly being assessed and evaluated.

There are many different types of exercises used in the Canadian army including Command Post Exercises (CPXs), Tactical Exercises Without Troops (TEWTs), and Field Training Exercises (FTXs). Each of these exercises entail different dynamics between the frames of reference identified above as well as the different types of realism that can be achieved.

All exercises differ from real life in the sense that they are scripted in advance. Superiors have available to them a scenario prepared by the planners, which they use to control the play of the exercise. This scenario is not available to participants except as a fairly general outline sketch. Within the scenario, there is scope for independent action, even though the extent of this scope varies from exercise to exercise. But, just as in real life, participants try to interpret what is going on as a guide for their choice of action and to predict what will happen next.

Another important difference between exercises and real life, and real war, is that exercises, although they are meant to be as authentic as possible within the constraints mentioned above, are always designed with a training goal in mind, including explicit "*lessons to be taught* and procedures to be practiced…Training objectives…[for] a combat team FTX might include a long night approach march, a move to blocking positions, a counter-attack, occupation of a hide, or resupply in a leaguer" (CLFCSC 1986; emphasis in the original). While the exercise planners try to achieve these objectives as naturally as possible, the fact that the exercise always has training objectives precludes it from following the natural flow of real war.

All exercises are organized temporally; they all have a start time and a finish time (END EX). And, while the start time is communicated to participants, the participants are frequently unaware of the exact time of END EX (although they may know the day). Between these start and finish times are moments when the exercise may be stopped for a period of time by the controllers for any number of logistical or tactical reasons. There are also pockets of time in which the situation is defined by *participants* as no-duff rather than simulated: for instance, during debriefings after engagements or during real emergencies, such as vehicle accidents.

Exercises are also organized and bounded spatially, with certain geographical areas devoted to the exercise and others used as staging areas for logistical, medical, and maintenance concerns. Another form of organization is the structural level at which the exercise is to be played. Initial instructions issued by the exercise planner specify which units will be involved as participants, and whether these units are an infantry rifle company of approximately 100 officers and other ranks, or a division of thousands of soldiers. Groups and individuals are assigned roles as combatants (both ally and enemy), directing staff (evaluators), safety staff, and umpires. Nevertheless, at the same time, administrative tasks must be performed, and in any given interaction an individual may invoke either a real role or an exercise role. All of these factors are discussed in greater depth below. For now, having sketched out some of the basic characteristics of exercises, we can turn to a more detailed discussion of particular styles of exercise.

Command Post Exercises (CPXs) and Tactical Exercises Without Troops (TEWTS) are both exercises that do not involve the use of soldiers except in a peripheral capacity. Although CPXs and TEWTs are quite different in organization and in design, they share the common function of training offi-

105

cers and command elements relatively cheaply. Command Post Exercises (CPXs) are designed to exercise the command and control elements of a military unit, whereas the aim of TEWTs is to teach tactics and doctrine to officers. TEWTs and CPXs are often used prior to FTXs to allow command personnel the opportunity to practice their skills without inconveniencing the troops. This ensures that these skills are well established when the entire unit goes on a field exercise:

> Troops should never be employed solely as training aids for the training of leaders. When leaders are relatively inexperienced an exercise is best "TEWTed" first so that leaders can learn their jobs before the troops are deployed. The same exercise can then be repeated as an FTX, and the leaders, secure in their own roles, are free to provide close supervision to the troops. (CLFCSC 1986)

The aim of a CPX is to practice the command and control functions of whatever unit is being exercised. A CPX can be mounted at any level of command, but it is normally practiced at battalion or brigade level. During the exercise, the various command posts of the different units and sub-units are deployed, meaning that the officers, and the other ranks who work in the command post (signalers and clerks for example), are employed in cells separate from each other, but are in radio contact with each other as well as with "higher control" and "lower control."

The extent to which the cells are realistically deployed varies. Sometimes the cells are set up in different classrooms of a lecture building, with the radios and maps installed as they would be in a proper command post. At other times, the actual command post vehicles are deployed. If the command post vehicles (usually armored vehicles) are used, there will be canvas attached to them (as they would be in the field) and the site is camouflaged. However, this is a feature used simply to add an atmosphere of realism, rather than to replicate a wartime experience. Cells communicate with each other, and with superior and subordinate elements, through the use of normal battlefield means such as radio, telephone links, or messengers. Higher control is responsible for presenting a scenario, and for acting as the superior element or higher headquarters. Subordinate elements in CPXs are not fighting soldiers; rather, they are "lower control"—personnel who move markers on a battle map in response to commands from the exercise participants.

Although exercise planners may decide on a relatively realistic scenario, the actual experience of the CPX does not approximate realism, except with respect to time. The game may go on for twenty-four hours a day in an attempt to simulate the fatigue that would be a factor in war. It is common practice in telephone exercises, and less common in field CPXs, for exercise play to occur only during normal working hours (between 0800 hours and 1700 hours daily), so that the problems of sleep deprivation that are a part of FTXs are avoided (which in itself compromises the authenticity of the exercise), and to save money. However, because it is considered necessary to practice a battle through the entire range of activities of a 24 hour day, "exercise" clocks are set in each cell. While the play is progressing "exercise time" is in effect. When the players break for the night, the exercise clocks are stopped and "real time" is in effect until play resumes the next morning. To enhance the sense of reality, the windows are usually sealed; therefore, participants are not aware of the weather and light conditions outside. It can be extremely disorienting to stand down during the middle of the night in

107

"exercise time" and to step out of the sealed room into the bright light of 5pm "real time." The different types of time parallel the difference between the "exercise" and "no-duff" frames.

Tactical Exercises Without Troops (TEWTs), where the aim is to teach tactics to officers, are even less realistic than CPXs and are, perhaps, better categorized as case studies rather than simulations. TEWTs may be organized at any level of command at which there are a number of officers. It could be organized, for instance, from the company level and up, or a platoon might even hold a TEWT for the section commanders, though this is less common. On TEWTs, officers are presented with a scenario that would include the resources available to the officer (size of unit, number of weapons etc.) as well as the information intelligence supposedly acquired about a hypothetical enemy. The enemy is purely notional and there are no actual troops or equipment, but officers are expected, normally as a group, to develop a plan that would involve putting in place troops, weapons systems, and obstacles such as minefields. The complexity of the plan depends on the level of the organization that the game (and I use this term purposely as it is what officers call the exercise) is being played.

New Direction 4.3

While there is some attempt to make the scenarios reasonably realistic, they are primarily designed to teach particular tactical principles. Thus, these training goals take priority over realism and not much of an attempt is made to make the actual experience of playing the game realistic.

TEWTs are often used on officers' courses, where the participants are expected to play a role at least one level higher than the rank they currently hold. Officers are assessed when they present their plan to the Directing Staff (DS), who also debrief them. TEWTs may be played either on maps, which permits a wide variety of terrain to be used but, in turn, removes the exercise even further from any correspondence with the real world, or they may be played on the actual ground, which enables officers to see the terrain rather than to try to visualize it from the two-dimensional map or three-dimensional miniaturized map board. TEWTs are useful for teaching tactics and they are relatively cheap to run; only the officers and a small support unit (drivers, etc.) are required. Although debates often occur about how realistic particular plans are, nobody suggests, generally, that TEWTs are remotely realistic. The reason is because there are no troops involved; therefore, the plan is never actually put to the test and played out, which makes the effectiveness of any plan ambiguous and constantly debatable. During the debriefing phase of a TEWT, one often hears comments from the DS such as "we can't debate tactics, because we don't know if this will work or not." What officers are being tested on is their command of, and ability to apply, current military doctrine as well as their knowledge of the characteristics of weapons systems (ranges and rates of fire for example), their knowledge of the enemy's doctrine, and their presentation skills.

While there is some attempt to make the scenarios reasonably realistic, they are primarily designed to teach particular tactical principles. Thus, these training goals take priority over realism and not much of an attempt is made to make the actual experience of playing the game realistic. There are no troops, no actual weapons, and often officers are permitted a longer time in which to develop their plans than they would have available to them in a combat situation. Again, the aim is to drive home certain training points rather than to mimic or replicate a combat situation.

The type of exercise that attempts to mimic war is the FTX or Field Training Exercise, of which there are many possible formats depending on, among other factors, the command level of the exercise and the lessons that are meant to be taught. For an FTX, the unit deploys to the field tactically, meaning that the soldiers are playing the game as if they were participating in a war. It is important to note that there are different types or dimensions of reality that a particular type of FTX is designed to emulate.

One of the factors to be considered when planning an exercise is the use of live ammunition, laser simulators, or blank ammunition. During ordinary FTXs, blank ammunition is used, which provides a satisfying noise when the weapon is fired. However, there is no way of evaluating the effectiveness of an attack because, of course, there is no actual damage done. Umpires (who are discussed in more detail below) may assess damage based on the observed movement of soldiers on the battlefield and on the number of rounds fired, but there is no way to measure the accuracy of those rounds. Moreover, there is no sense of danger; the soldiers, of course, know that the rounds are blank and any sense of danger is a result of playacting or the organizational scripting of emotion as described by Zurcher (1985).

One effective, though expensive, way of getting around the problem of evaluating the effectiveness of an attack is the use of various types of laser receptors worn by soldiers, which buzz or give some other sign when a laser beam attached to a weapon hits the receptor. Laser simulators certainly increase umpires' abilities to evaluate the effectiveness of an attack. They also allow soldiers to evaluate their own accuracy with weapons as well as their own use of the ground to avoid being hit. There are, however, problems with lasers apart from their high cost. One of the problems pointed out to me by a number of soldiers during one exercise using lasers is that even light foliage and small trees, which would be destroyed by real machine gun ammunition, can effectively screen the laser beam allowing soldiers to hide during a simulation in places that would provide no safety at all in a wartime situation.

Another problem is that the laser receptors are attached to the webbing of the soldier, not to the soldier himself. On one occasion, I was acting as the number two on a machine gun crew during a simulated attack when the number one tried to fit himself into a small depression in the ground so that he could find a good firing position and not be seen. Finding that his bulky webbing was preventing him from achieving a good position, he removed it and set it to one side within easy reach. Within minutes his webbing beeped, indicating that he had been shot. Confused, he told me that he could not have been shot because he was in a good location, then we both realized that he had not been shot, but that his webbing had been hit, triggering the beeper. With laser receptors, as with blank ammunition, there is still no authentic sense of danger, yet FTXs that use blank rounds, or laser receptors, are realistic in the sense that the activity on the battlefield is free-flowing and based on the assessments by commanders and individual soldiers of the ground, and the enemy's disposition and behavior.

In contrast, "live-fire" exercises are frequently held in which live ammunition is used, including machine guns and tank cannons. The stated reason for the use of live ammunition is that it replicates the noise and danger of the battlefield, forcing soldiers to "take the game seriously." This increase in risk, however, necessitates sacrificing the realistic free-flow of movement on the battlefield because limits must be placed on how close soldiers may fire at others and movement must be strictly controlled in the interests of safety.[3]

In addition to the problem of what sort of ammunition to use, the officer in charge of planning an FTX has many factors to consider in his or her design of the training. The main factor is the training goal which dictates the form the exercise will take. This goal can be constrained by such factors as safety, and the availability of time, space, equipment, and ammunition. The officer must decide which units will be involved, where and when to hold the exercise (the spatial and temporal boundaries), and what elements of the participating units are to be exercised. For instance, is the exercise designed to practice assaults or will logistical and medical systems be practiced as well? If he or she decides on the former, then there is no need "to play casualties" and, therefore, logistical support is part of the real world, not the simulation. If the latter option is chosen, then there must be a system for identifying simulated casualties and for evaluating the effectiveness of their treatment, as well as for distinguishing between actual and simulated casualties and accidents.

The organizer must decide not only the constitution of the friendly force, but also of the enemy. One option is to use a small enemy force, under control of the exercise staff, which informs the enemy force of the movements of the friendly force. This option allows the organizers more control over the achievement of the training goals because the smaller force can be inserted and extracted at will; but choosing this option may somewhat diminish perceived authenticity. Another option is to have evenly matched forces, where neither is privy to information about the other force except the information that their intelligence elements are able to acquire. This option makes it much more difficult for the exercise staff to control the exercise play; but the resulting unpredictability is supposed

---

New Direction 4.4

All these policies are established by the organizer of the exercise, but they are subject to interpretation and ongoing re-interpretation by exercise participants.

---

to have tremendous training value, and the competitive spirit that is engendered is considered valuable.

The third group that must be constituted is the umpire staff. During simulations, umpires are required to establish the outcome of any engagement, using parameters laid down by the exercise commander. Umpire teams travel with every formed unit of the friendly forces and, if the second enemy scenario described above is chosen, teams also accompany the enemy forces. The organizer must decide how these three different groups will be identified. It is usual for enemy forces to wear some sort of identifying marker on their uniforms in order for them to be distinguished from friendly forces. The umpires are meant to be invisible during the course of the exercise. They are there to observe, not to interact during the course of the battle. But, paradoxically, as the combatants are camouflaged, the umpires are in effect made invisible by being highly visible. They do not wear camouflage and may be identified by the use of colored armbands. In addition, their vehicles are also marked in a certain fashion, rather than camouflaged.

All these policies are established by the organizer of the exercise, but they are subject to interpretation and ongoing re-interpretation by exercise participants. Cicourel explains this principle:

> General procedural rules are laid down for members, and members develop and employ their own theories, recipes,

and shortcuts for meeting general requirements acceptable to themselves and tacitly or explicitly to other
members acting as "supervisors" or some form of external control. (Cicourel 1976:1)

With this in mind, I turn now to an analysis of how
soldiers participating in a number of FTXs, ones in which I
also participated, employed their own theories and recipes to
constitute situtations as "tactical" or "no-duff," and to evaluate
the level of realism of the exercises.

Prior to one of these exercises, the Company
Commander told me that he would be conducting a heliborne
exercise and wondered if I would be interested in attending. A
heliborne exercise is one during which troops are transported
by helicopter and I knew that there might be some difficulty
acquiring permission for me to participate, but I was certainly
interested in attending. He said that if I wanted to attend he
would find a way to write me into the exercise because having
an acknowledged observer would compromise authenticity.
Inasmuch as everyone participating would be playing a role,
he felt my presence would be acceptable if I, too, had a simulated role to play. The scenario he designed entailed having a
civilian electronics expert assist in a covert operation to
destroy an "enemy communications installation."[4] Because of
budgetary restraints, all the planning phases of the operation,
including orders, briefings, and debriefings, were conducted
in garrison and the troops only went into the field for the
actual "fighting" of the "battle." In a conventional exercise,
the briefings and debriefings would have taken place in the
field in a defended location under "tactical conditions."
However, because this exercise was heliborne, the actual location of the briefings was irrelevant, and tactical conditions only
came into effect when the troops were loaded on the helicopters.

114

Before the beginning of any exercise, commanders at all levels give formal orders to their subordinates. These orders establish the spatial and temporal framework for the exercise by specifying exercise timings and spatial boundaries. Commanders tell their subordinates which locations of the training area are to be considered tactical, and which are "real." They also inform the participants which members of the organization are to be considered players (both enemy and friendly), which are to be considered non-players, and how these different roles are to be identified. Orders also establish the criteria for defining a situation as tactical or real, as well as the codes used to interpret the status of these criteria. The following is an excerpt from a transcript of a tape-recording I made of the Company Commander's Warning Order, or preliminary order:

> OC: Okay. This warning order then is exercise secret. Situation: enemy forces. The enemy that we will be principally concerned with is the forces garrison in the Calgary area. If you look up on the map here, you will see that there's two main positions across the Sarcee area in Harvey Barracks. There is an enemy-mounted Quick Reaction Force on thirty minutes notice to move right here. That's important to us. And they have a number of prepared battle positions inside the buffer zone...Also, in the area of Curry Barracks there is an enemy infantry company. And they're responsible to man a number of vital points throughout the city that are indicated, including the airport, and the uh ...support key bridges and intersections and that kind of stuff. (Irwin 1996a)

115

Embedded in this warning are explicit instructions for the orders to be understood as part of an exercise, so that when the OC sets the security classification of the orders as "exercise secret," which everyone should understand to mean for exercise purposes only, the orders are to be treated as if they were secret. But beyond that, the instructions are embedded in the very activity of issuing the orders. The orders were being issued in a nice warm building in a conference room. Although the soldiers were dressed in combat clothing, and some of them had red faces from exposure to the cold during rappel practice, no one could mistake this for the "real thing." What is noteworthy is that for much of the process of issuing orders, the simulation/reality dichotomy is not problematic. The interpretation of the situation as a simulation was informed by the knowledge these soldiers shared. For instance, they knew there could be no enemy in the same building where they were sitting, receiving their orders. Any references to the enemy, then, had to be understood as instructions to treat this event as an exercise.

Several times while he was giving orders to platoon commanders, the OC stepped out of the exercise frame and adopted the no-duff frame, which was done in order to delineate the appropriate approach to realism that he wanted the troops to take. In the following segment, he was encouraging realism by reminding soldiers that while in the actuality of the real world they would have access to what would become enemy territory once the exercise proper began, they were not to take advantage of the no-duff situation:

> Good. Okay, then we'll bash on with the updated warning order, just so everyone knows what's going on. First of all, just a couple of other sort of no-duff points have come up…given the fact that the target area is

fairly close to here and obviously you have access to it and so on, um…let's have no more recce [reconnaissance] other than the helicopter recce yesterday, into the Harvey Barracks area. That's not going to happen. In operations you'd have air photos, you'd have maps, and you wouldn't be able to walk into the enemy position, so now that you are going to get an idea of where your actual objective is physically, we don't want guys out there crawling around, sort of, tonight, and so on, and figuring out where their OPs [observation posts] are going to be, what the navigation route is, and so on. Use your map and if there's any surprises in the process, then so be it. (Irwin 1996a)

And later on, at another briefing:

And the last thing: No recce into Harvey Barracks now, gentlemen—honor system okay? I know we all know the area well enough as it is, but let's do our planning off maps and the air photos that are available and so on just like we'd really have to do it. So we don't want to be down there tonight—Honor system. Okay, that concludes the whole shooting match. (Irwin 1996a)

On another occasion, the OC stepped out of the exercise frame in order to remind the platoon commanders that the exercise was, indeed, a simulation and that they were to refrain from causing any real damage to equipment or injuring other soldiers. At the same time, he reminded them of the cues to be used to determine whether vehicles should be considered part of the exercise or not:

All good stuff…Anything else? [pause] okay then, I'll finish off with just a couple of no-duff points. Common

117

sense prevails out there. You know we don't want to be cutting fences in the link fences there. You're going to have to crawl underneath, push up, that sort of thing; or scale fences and that's when you—I know it's a bit of a hassle but I think you understand we just can't be out there crashing up the compound [laughter]...The other thing, the armored vehicles that we're going to destroy, we're going to simulate destruction and [the Pioneer officer] is going to explain that in just a sec. We have charges to detonate and so on, but obviously we're not getting ready to do it in smashing up mode—smashing a periscope and some of that good stuff. I know you wouldn't do that [laughter]... anyway, we just want to be careful of obvious, uh, destruction of facilities...we want to be careful there so we can't actually destroy it, obviously...when you're defending the bridge you're only going to stop in-play personnel and vehicles. Okay? In-play enemy personnel—we know what they're going to look like, we've identified that in-play vehicles, all of them, will all have a large white piece of mine tape that will come off the top of the antenna. So, if you see a jeep with a long white thing dangling behind it, it's in play so, cut-off, let him have it okay? But if it's just a real MP on patrol, they know we're out doing the exercise, so don't be jumping out there and hauling him out [laughter] zap-strappin' him [laughter]. (Irwin 1996b)

It became evident during these series of briefings that there were some elements upon which the OC had insisted for the sake of authenticity and training value, which required some convincing of the NCOs on his part. In particular, in the absence of mortar ammunition, he insisted that troops be required to carry bricks to the objective. And it seems clear

118

from the explanation he gave for this requirement that he suspected that perhaps the NCOs did not share his opinion:

> OC: Mortar ammunition...we're simulating that, eh, with sand in the tubes?
> Sgt. M: Actually, we uh...we couldn't get the tubes, Sir, I already talked to the 2-i-c [second-in-command] about it, we tried to get 'em up from Wainwright. I went through the ammo guy here, but we couldn't get 'em.
> OC: So we're going to carry red bricks instead?
> Sgt. M: Okay.
> OC: Okay, we need something to simulate it. I know, I know the old story, there's got to be a harder way, but we've got to simulate this. You need troops to help you haul ammo and there's some lessons, there's some real good lessons to be learned there, hauling the real weight. I'd like you to look at something there if you can. (Irwin 1996b)

The leadership challenge facing the OC throughout the orders and briefing phases of this exercise was to ensure that his subordinates had the required resources available to them to interpret any situations that arose in a way that would be consistent with his wishes; and yet there was no way for him to predict all the possible situations that might have arisen. He also had to convince them that his image of what constitutes a realistic scenario was reasonable.

The field notes I made during another set of orders revealed the time that the company would be leaving its bivouac for the tactical area. Other "no duff" matters included the Commanding Officer (of the battalion) paying the company a visit to observe its performance, the manner in which meals would be served, and the requirement for casualty cards to be issued as the unit would be "playing casualties" during the exercise. On another occasion, during orders preceding a live fire attack, platoon and section commanders were told by the Company Commander that the safety staff on the firing range was not there to control the tactical activities, but only to intervene if safety was at stake.

Before another major exercise, I recorded the following orders of the company commander: "The moment our wheels cross the start point, we are in the tactical mode until the end of the exercise. Air sentries up, covers off the guns" (Irwin 1992a:21). Air sentries and uncovered guns would then be used by participants as evidence that the situation was a tactical one. Zimmerman has demonstrated that "whatever 'context' is required to organize a particular interaction, it is locally activated and interactionally achieved and sustained" (Zimmerman 1992:36). This is very much the case during war games, as the following comment, overheard in a "tactical" location, demonstrates: "Since we've got a generator, I guess we're not tactical, are we?" (Irwin 1992b:185). Tactical locations are supposed to be quiet, well-hidden, and well-protected. For this soldier, the presence of the noisy generator precluded the location from being defined as a tactical one.

The criteria that the commander uses to establish the tactical nature of an exercise does not, however, define the situation for the entire exercise. These criteria become, instead, resources used by participants to define a situation as tactical or no-duff and, as noted above, defining the situation is an ongoing process. It is not decided "for once and for all." But, as pointed out by Cicourel, "participants also use their *own* categories to depict their perception and interpretation of the social environment. Further, members of a group methodically employ categories for depicting their life circumstances and the grounds for their action" (Cicourel 1976:16).

120

Participants are engaged in a continuous process of deciding whether a situation should be defined as tactical or no-duff. They must use the resources presented by their superiors and their own categories to constitute the situation appropriately. The following excerpt from my field notes describes a situation when no-duff events interrupted the progress of a tactical exercise:

> We continued with platoon attacks—practice for the "real" one this afternoon. Apparently, the reason the one this afternoon is considered real is because of having an enemy from another company. On the fourth attack, however, Master Corporal T threw a smoke grenade and some grass caught fire and very quickly turned into a major burn...had to call for assistance. The second in command came over in his carrier but eventually range control came and took over. Two big fires were going all afternoon so we had to stand down. We're on 15 minutes notice to move to fight the fire, with all the fire fighting equipment in the battalion loaded on the company's carriers...did have time to do the "real" platoon attack, but dismounted. (Irwin 1992b:187-8)

Soldiers, then, become adept at switching from tactical mode to no-duff mode on an ongoing basis. The definition of a given situation as no-duff or tactical is worked up through the interactions and conversations of the participants, and they use a wide range of resources to accomplish this social act. Moreover, the definition of the situation as tactical or no-duff is made available to participants so that they know how to situate their actions as well as to have a context for their behavior. Some of the resources used by members to constitute the situ-

121

ation as tactical include the practice of camouflaging people and vehicles. In making their appearance less visible, they are signaling their status as tactical elements. Conversation is another strategy or resource. Exercise radio traffic can be interrupted with a message preceded by the term "no-duff," to make clear to participants that the message concerns a real, not tactical, situation.

This is not to say that mistakes do not occur. Mistakes do occur quite regularly, and are often reacted to with laughter, teasing, or ridicule. During the orders for the heliborne operation discussed above, I recorded the following interaction:

> OC: You want a photo of the bridge eh? Good idea.
> Lt.: 'cause it's a critical choke point almost.
> OC: Okay, so I need you [looks at the Corporal photographer] to study this map 'cause we won't necessarily...we probably won't be on headset so to save us yelling back and forth, have a good look at the map. And for that you may have to actually lean out and take a shot forward to get a nice angle into the bridge.
> PHO: If needs be, maybe I could go down tomorrow as well, take a truck down, we won't get the same height but...
> OC: How the *fuck* are you going to drive into the enemy territory? [laughter]
> Lt.: Good one, Sir.
> Sgt. A: Cheater.
> OC: The only photos that you'll be printing are ones that you take out of the helicopter.
> PHO: Okay, sir. [laughter]
> OC: Don't be too hard on him. He wasn't at our big scenario brief.
> Sgt. B: Play the game, son [laughter]. (Irwin 1996b)

In this case, the young Corporal/photographer who had not been present at the briefing, which had spelled out the parameters of the simulation, was not operating in the same frame as the others who were involved in the interaction, and his breach was marked with laughter and ridicule.

One of the more important and more powerful resources used to constitute the situation as real or tactical is the status of the participants themselves as tactical or real. Watson has commented on the roles of the anthropological fieldworker and informant:

> They do not just happen to be fieldworker and inform-
> ant, they have to make themselves available as such.
> They have many statuses and, at any particular time,
> even in the field, it is not necessarily the statuses of
> fieldworker and informant that are activated. (1992:21-22)

The same is true of soldiers in the field: they have many statuses, including both real and simulated statuses, and, at any particular time, one or the other or even both may be activated. The situation of the Company Quarter Master Sergeant (CQ) is a case in point. He is responsible for the issuing of rations and for organizing the feeding of the company when it is deployed in the field. There are several methods of feeding troops. Each depends on such factors as the training aims, the tactical situation, and the availability of "IMPs" (Individual Meal Packs), known to the troops as "hard rations."[5] If IMPs are unavailable, the most common method of feeding troops in the field is for the CQ and his staff to transport hot meals from the bivouac kitchen, in large thermos containers called hayboxes, to the troops in the tactical area. The troops may "stand down" for such haybox meals during which case the exercise stops. Everyone takes a break and the

123

situation is defined as real. Alternatively, the meal may be defined as a tactical feed, in which case it is often held at night in the dark, quickly, quietly, and with sentries defending the location.

When the CQ delivers a haybox meal to the field, he moves from the real world of the bivouac kitchen across a boundary into the tactical location. He activates both his real status and his tactical status simultaneously. He demonstrates that he is activating his tactical status by camouflaging his face and his vehicle and by carrying a loaded weapon (with blank ammunition, to be sure; remember this is simulation, not real war). But he is delivering real food, and often has soft drinks and cigarettes available for purchase from the company canteen; hence, he is concurrently activating his real status.

Umpires also have both real and tactical statuses, although their situation is quite different from that of the CQs. In their status as real people, they are charged with deciding the outcome of engagements between the friendly forces and the enemy forces (i.e., the amount of men wounded, the amount of armored vehicles destroyed, the amount of weapons destroyed, etc.), with debriefing participants on their perform-ance, and with keeping the exercise coordinators informed of the progress of the exercise. In their tactical status they are, quite simply, supposed to be non-existent. Ironically, as mentioned above, this is achieved through heightening their visibility.

When umpires activate their tactical status, they are co-present with, but not interacting with, exercise participants. As soon as an exercise participant (in his tactical status) enters into an interaction with an umpire or, indeed, any person acti-vating a real status, the situation is constituted as a real one. It is next to impossible to sustain the definition of the situation as tactical in the face of an interaction with a real person.

There is much power in this construction, and much potential for manipulation, as we will see. Sometimes simple mistakes occur, causing a person exercising a tactical status to mistake someone exercising a real status for a tactical one. This is demonstrated in this excerpt from my field notes:

> Interesting mix of play/reality occurs when someone (e.g., the company commander, the second in command, or the sergeant major) observes an attack. For instance...there was a mounted platoon attack where A mistook the company commander's carrier (39) and the headquarters carrier (3) for the enemy and missed the enemy which were one bound farther up the trace [one tactical move farther up the map]. The company commander had come on the air earlier and said he wasn't playing. (Irwin 1992a:95-96)

In this case, the enemy and the non-combatants were not specially marked, but the lead platoon commander should have recognized the commander's and the headquarters' vehicles by their identifying numbers (39 and 3), and should have remembered that they were not "in the game." But, he did not. He engaged them with fire (blank, of course), and was subject to a public rebuke over the radio by the company commander.

Therefore, statuses are mobilized to help in defining the situation as a tactical one or a real one. Tactical statuses are activated to create a tactical situation, and real statuses are activated to create a real situation. Often, however, statuses are mobilized to achieve different ends from what one might expect, and, at times, the situation itself is defined in a particular way in order to achieve a particular goal.

It is quite common for individuals attempting to achieve tactical ends to activate a real status, forcing their

125

interactive partners to define the situation as real, rather than tactical—as this example from my field notes illustrates:

> Last night—the aim of Sgt. M's patrol was to find the "enemy" (a platoon from another company) command post and destroy it. In effect, this meant marking it with camouflage paint—doesn't wash off—or throwing a can of footpowder at it—"hand grenade"—the white powder would mark it and be hard to wash off...This morning just after brushing his teeth the platoon commander happened to glance over at Sgt. C's carrier (33A) and said "oh fuck." Marked on it in pink chalk was "good night from the pioneers" and on the front "Hey Scotty, Angus was here. Harleys suck long live Hondas." He shows everyone in the platoon "Oh fuck, we'll hear about this." They wash off the chalk as well as possible. Turns out that a couple of pioneers who were buddies of T's showed up and he let them into the hide and even told them the password and radio frequencies...Lots of talk about the problem of the "enemy" being somebody you know. (Irwin 1992a: 139-140)

In this case, the individuals acting in their tactical statuses as the enemy invoked their real statuses as friends of the sentry, who was acting in his tactical status. The imperative for him to produce the situation as a real one was strong. Later, I found out that he had even served them coffee, along with telling them the passwords and radio frequencies in the course of a long friendly visit and conversation about the progress of the exercise. As they left him, they ceased to invoke their statuses as friends and "sabotaged" the section commander's armored personnel carrier. This scenario is not unusual, but is replayed on many occasions. It is one of the disadvantages of a small scale exercise, where all the participants are known to one other, and have mutually known multiple statuses to activate.

Another way real statuses are used to achieve tactical ends is a product of the paradoxical nature of the invisibility/ visibility of the umpires. In this case, individuals acting in their tactical status do not use their own status but, instead, the real status of the umpire to try to predict the course of the exercise, such as in the following incident recorded in my field notes:

> This exercise is really a three-way war—friendly, enemy, umpires. People watch the umpires all the time to try to figure out what's going to happen next. Master Corporal A said last night that if you see lots of umpires around you know something is going to happen there. But that didn't hold true last night. We were expecting a helibome assault and there were all kinds of umpires around. Nothing happened in the end so we finally got some sleep. Also, he said that I don't have to worry about having my respirator handy until I see the umpires carrying theirs because they know the scenario. In fact, from the chats I've had with the umpires, Lts. A, B, and C and Sgt. G, it seems that, at least at their level, they don't know very far ahead what's going to happen either. (Irwin 1992b:145)[6]

In the above case, exercise participants used the umpires' real statuses as resources to attempt to predict the forthcoming tactical situation. We are not concerned here with their motivations, which may indeed involve the real world. They may want to know what is going to happen, so that they can use that information tactically, or they may simply want to predict when they are likely to have the next opportunity to eat

127

> ### New Direction 4.5
>
> The distinctions between reality and the simulated world of the war game are an accomplishment of the participants in the exercise. Through their interactions with each other, they make available to one another their interpretations of what the situation should be.

or sleep. What is significant for this analysis is not the motivation but, rather, what sorts of ends are achieved—real or exercise.

Not only do soldiers use real statuses (by observing their activation or by activating them) to achieve tactical ends, but they also define situations tactically in order to achieve real ends. When military units are in the field, they use a system of accounting for materiel that is much more lenient with respect to lost or damaged items than the one used in garrison. Many items of stock that are accountable in garrison (and hence must be paid for by the soldier if lost) are considered expendable in the field. It is common practice for CQs to save up reports of lost or damaged stores until after a field exercise, when field accounting takes place. In this instance, they are manipulating the tactical situation in order to achieve the real end of protecting the soldiers from their own negligence.

I have been told that another common practice is to use the field or tactical situation in order to pay back superiors for what are considered abuses. I was told "anything can happen in the field" and "anyone can be got." The more authentic the simulation is, the higher the risk of accidents; and some of these accidents are "paybacks" rather than actual accidents. This is another example of how soldiers manipulate tactical situations to achieve real ends. Nevertheless, the one strategy that I never witnessed or heard about was misusing the term "no-duff." The reason for this, I believe, is self-evident. If the use of the term "no-duff" were to become subject to manipulation or practical jokes, its use as a safety measure would be compromised, as would the safety of the soldiers themselves.

The distinctions between reality and the simulated world of the war game are an accomplishment of the participants in the exercise. Through their interactions with each other, they make available to one another their interpretations of what the situation should be. Using a variety of resources, including verbal cues like "no duff" and visual cues like vehicle markings and facial camouflage, they interactively work up a definition of the situation which holds "for now," but which is always subject to revision and reconstitution. Among the most important resources available to them are the statuses to which each participant has access. Different statuses are activated at particular moments, defining the moment as a real one or as an exercise. We have seen how these statuses can be manipulated or interpreted to achieve real or tactical ends.

This paper has been an attempt to employ an ethnomethodological perspective to explore some of the complexities surrounding the problems of realism and reality in military exercises. I hope I have demonstrated that the frames of the no-duff (or real world) and of the make-believe (or exercise world) cannot be decided once and for all by commanders, planners, or participants; rather, these frames are constantly subject to interpretation and negotiation throughout the course of military exercises. Soldiers use these frames to interpret behavior as no-duff or exercise, but they are also adept at manipulating these frames and using them as resources to achieve aims, which may or may not be those expected by commanders and planners. I have demonstrated, as well, that realism is not some objective authenticity that exercise planners aspire to, but a negotiated and contested notion; and that part of the leaders' challenge in a peacetime army is to ensure that their versions of realism and reality are the ones to which their soldiers are oriented.

SUMMARY

Using an ethnomethodological perspective, this chapter explored the complexities surrounding the problems of realism and reality in military exercises. In line with the ethnomethodological tradition, the author offered extensive descriptions and narrative accounts to support and illustrate her analysis. Issues such as the frames of the "no-duff" (or real world) and the "make-believe" (or exercise world) are analyzed, demonstrating that they cannot be decided once and for all by any particular commanders, planners, or participants. Rather, these frames are constantly subject to interpretation and negotiation throughout the course of military exercises. Lastly, the paper showed that realism is not an objective phenomenon. It is a negotiated and contested notion, which is an important part of the leadership challenges of officers in a peacetime army, as they have to ensure that their versions of realism and reality are the ones to which their soldiers are oriented.

KEY TERMS AND CONCEPTS

• Ethnomethodology	• Realism
• Reality	• Interpretation
• Simulation	• Frames
• Military training	

STUDY AND DISCUSSION QUESTIONS

1. How important is realism to training soldiers for war or peacekeeping?

2. How important is prior socialization in accepting others' viewpoints on reality? Is military training brainwashing? Explain.

3. If the military became better at integrating its various realities, is it possible that, in the long-term, this could threaten its hierarchical structure?

4. In spite of its extreme brutality, do you think warfare is socially constructed?

5. How would you explain the concept of the social construction of reality to a practically-oriented military person?

NOTES

1. I conducted participant observation fieldwork with a Canadian Regular Force infantry battalion in 1991-1992 and again in 1995-1996. I acknowledge with gratitude the support of the Social Sciences and Research Council of Canada Doctoral Fellowship 752-94-0219 from 1994 to 1998. I am grateful as well to the participants in the University of Manchester Department of Social Anthropology Post Graduate Seminar for their helpful comments on an earlier version of this paper.

2. Here, and in the reference list, "field recordings" refers to conversations tape recorded with permission of those present during the course of participant observation fieldwork. "Field notes" refers to notes written up during the course of field work. In both cases, identities of those present

have been disguised to ensure anonymity in accordance with the ethical guidelines that I followed.

3. The year before my second period of fieldwork with the battalion, one of the soldiers had been killed during a live-fire attack, and the investigation to determine responsibility for the death was reopened during the course of my fieldwork.

4. In the end, we were unable to obtain permission for me to be transported by helicopter, so my participation in this particular exercise was limited to the planning and debriefing phases of the exercise.

5. These are individually packed meals, easily carried, and easily reheated, although they are often eaten cold. They are not pleasant meals and they are extremely expensive. Thus, they are used only when the exercise scenario dictates "tactical feeding" (when, for instance, the company is practicing patrolling rather than platoon attacks).

6. Interestingly enough, several of the soldiers interpreted the fact that I had been specially issued a respirator by the CQ as evidence that we would be exposed to real gas before the end of the exercise. In fact, the CQ had told me that he did not know himself, but wanted to make sure that I would be safe if, indeed, gas was used.

REFERENCES

Anderson, R. J., J. A. Hughes, and W. W. Sharrock. 1987. "Executive Problem Finding: Some Material and Initial Observations." *Social Psychology Quarterly* 50:143-159.

Caputo, P. 1996. *A Rumor of War*. New York: Henry Holt and Company.

Cicourel, A. 1976. *The Social Organization of Juvenile Justice*. London: Heinemann.

CLFCSC. 1986. *Training (TRG/3)*. Kingston, Ontario: Canadian Land Forces Command and Staff College.

Crookall, D., C. S. Greenblatt, A. Coote, J. Klabbers, and D. Watson. 1987. *Simulation — Gaming in the late 1980s: Proceedings of the International Simulation and Gaming Associations's 17th International Conference.* Oxford: Pergamon.

Crookall, D. and R. L. Oxford. 1990. *Simulation, Gaming, and Language Learning.* New York: Newbury House.

Irwin, A. 1992a. Field notes Vol. II. January - April.

_____. 1992b. Field notes Vol. III. April - October.

_____. 1996a. Field recording by author. Tape recording. Calgary, Alberta, 16 January.

_____. 1996b. Field recording by author. Tape recording. Calgary, Alberta, 17 January.

_____. 1996c. Field recording by author. Tape recording. Wainwright, Alberta, 26 April.

MacPhail, S. 1991. Interview by author. Tape recording. Calgary, Alberta, 24 October.

Malinowski, B. 1984. *Argonauts of the Western Pacific.* Prospect Heights, Illinois: Waveland Press.

Watson, D. R. and W. W. Sharrock. 1990. "Realities in Simulation/Gaming." Pp. 231-238 in *Simulations, Gaming and Language Learning,* edited by D. Crookall and R. L. Oxford. New York: Newbury House.

Watson, G. 1992. "Twenty Nine Lines of Fieldnotes." *Manchester Sociology Occasional Papers* 34:1-35.

Zimmerman, D. H. 1992. "The Interactional Organization of Calls for Emergency Assistance." Pp. 418-469 in *Talk at Work: Interaction in Institutional Settings,* edited by P. Drew and J. Heritage. Cambridge: Cambridge University Press.

Zurcher, L. A. 1985. "The War Game: Organizational Scripting and the Expression of Emotion." *Symbolic Interaction* 8(2):191-206.

C h a p t e r 5

THE SPIRITUAL ARMAMENT OF THE GERMAN OFFICER CORPS

Ulrich vom Hagen
Bundeswehr Institute for Social Research
Strausberg (Berlin), Germany

LEARNING OBJECTIVES

After reading this chapter, you should be able to

- describe military affairs outside the categories of simple cause and effect;
- understand that the military institution is also extremely complex with respect to its social mechanisms of human action;
- explain how religion influences the armed forces as an indirect mechanism;
- understand that military forms such as discipline and austerity are not necessarily military in their origin;
- identify how military culture shapes the military institution.

The existence of a cultural framework is important for the internal integration of elites and professional groups, as far as their cohesion is concerned. This framework arises out of a commonly shared "social space" with, among others, a common religious determination and common religious bonds; the importance of which should not be underestimated. In the German military, commitment to the Protestant church has played a prominent role since the time of the reign of the Prussian King, Friedrich Wilhelm I, in the early eighteenth century. Thus, even today, you find expressions in the German military that have a religious connotation such as "Seele der Armee" (soul of the army) or "geistige Rüstung" (spiritual armament).[1]

Traditionally, the Protestant church has had a significant influence on the German armed forces, especially in the formation of the officer corps. Ideologically, Protestantism dominated, cultivating the basic convictions of the officer corps. The Prussian King was not only the supreme employer of the Prussian Army, but also head of Prussia's Protestant Church. The Prussian King, and later German Emperor, was particularly important since Prussia dominated the Contingent Army[2] of the German Reich (1871–1918) and the kingdoms of Saxony and Württemberg, which were already Protestant. Thus, Bavaria was the only kingdom to have a predominantly Catholic officer corps. The close ties between the Protestant church and the Prussian state created a Protestant state Church in Germany (Plessner 1935:66). And, because of the central role of Protestantism in Germany, belonging to one of the established German Protestant regional churches was crucial to the career prospects of individual officers in the German armies. Protestant socialization not only affected one's chances of becoming an officer, but also increased the ease with which an individual could negotiate the societal subculture of the German military.

135

New Direction 5.1

The Protestant church has had a significant influence on the German armed forces. Ideologically, Protestantism dominated, cultivating the basic convictions of the officer corps.

In this essay, I will analyze to what extent the Protestant ethic continues to exist in the Bundeswehr and how it shapes *military culture*.[3] The analysis will show that even if an officer belongs to one of the two state churches in Germany, this fact does not have any *direct* impact on his[4] prospects of promotion to the military elite. I will then examine the importance and relevance of the Protestant ethic, which even today influences the German armed forces in various ways. I will discuss the dominant military culture, which evolved in context with the Protestant tradition of the German officer corps. The military, here, is understood as a social institution with rules, principles, and values, including (and especially) the *Protestant ethic* and *military ethics*. Therefore, the extent to which the Protestant ethic and military ethics are in accord with one another will be investigated. This will facilitate an understanding of German military culture. It is assumed, here, that the *ascetic Protestant ethic* and the *military ethic of austerity* perform an institutional function in the military that can be termed "spiritual armament," particularly for the German officer corps.

These issues are then placed in a theoretical context, employing Max Weber's sociology-of-religion approach and Pierre Bourdieu's concept of *habitus*. After comparing Weber's central concept of the *Protestant ethic* and my construct of the *military ethic of austerity*, the concept of *state nobility* will be investigated briefly. The application of this concept performs a theoretically integrating function that helps for a broader understanding of *military culture*. Finally, the objective of this essay is to contribute to the theoretical compatibility of the subdiscipline of military sociology, along with the theoretical discourses of general sociology, by discussing these approaches within the framework of Weber's interpretative sociology and with reference to Bourdieu's theory of *social practice*. A social practice approach enables a profound understanding of the general concept of culture and, thereby, of military culture as a specific construct.

The Military Elite of Germany

The term *military elite* is used following the positional approach of elite research, so that only generals and admirals are considered the elite of this professional group.[5] The career of an officer and, particularly, the promotion to the rank of general or admiral is characterized by certain specifics[6] which set the military profession apart from other professions. Being a member of the military elite implies not only a generous wage rate, but also social recognition and influence.

Until the middle of the nineteenth century, the German officer corps was primarily comprised of members of the nobility. With the increased significance of technical branches of service, such as artillery and engineers, officers with technical training were required. In addition, the forming of mass armies meant that the influence of the nobility through participation in the officer corps had decreased. However, the German Reichswehr in the Weimar Republic (1918-1933) slowed down this development to some extent because it was limited to 100,000 men under the Versailles Treaty. As such, the nobility dominated the German military elite until World

War II, with the aristocratic tradition of the officer remaining unbroken.[7] As in a social and value pyramid of Estates, noblemen preferably succeeded to the higher officer ranks with their participation increasing with the height of the ranks (Bald 1982:93). In this context, Bald speaks of the *nobility pyramid* as a structuring element in personnel recruiting that constitutes a selection mechanism. In the Reichswehr, the percentage of noblemen among general grades was 45.5 percent on 1 May 1932 (Jung 1990:119). Following the army enlargement in the mid-1930s, the percentage of aristocratic generals serving in the Wehrmacht army still amounted to 20 percent in 1943 (Schössler 1977:181). Considering that the percentage of nobility among young officers of the German Bundeswehr in the early 1960s was just 2 percent, the aristocracy continues to be overrepresented in the military elite because after nearly the length of a military career in 1985, the participation of the nobility in the military elite was 6 percent (Jung 1990:119).[8] It appears that the Protestant spirit of the nobility in the German military is still alive.

The basis of recruiting underwent a transformation when, in the context of the army enlargements during the Prusso-German wars of unification in the 1860s, the German officer corps opened up to the so-called desirable bourgeois circles.[9] In fact, the young German officers of the year 1967 were the last age group still to be registered as applying the criteria of the *desirable circles,* which had been introduced more than 100 years before (Bald 1982:61). Today, the officer corps of the Bundeswehr is mainly recruited from sons of families from the advancement-oriented lower middle class (Bonneman and Hoffmann-Broll 1999:23) who use the profession of an officer as a means of social mobility.[10]

According to Schössler (1977:181), the military elite in the mid-1970s was still being recruited from the upper middle class of the Federal Republic of Germany. At that time, Schössler predicted this recruiting pattern of the military elite would continue to exist because the field grades came from this social stratum.[11] In fact, the Mannheim elite study of 1981 proves that the rate of participation in the German military elite is described by an extreme overrepresentation of the lower middle class. The Potsdam elite study of 1995, however, demonstrated that the social disproportion of the German military elite has significantly decreased; today, there is even a proportional share of generals and admirals with a working-class background (Schnapp 1997:78ff.).

In terms of the military elite in Germany, however, those officers who have successfully completed the command and general staff officer grade course (Army and Air Force), or the flag staff officer (Navy) grade course, play the most important roles. Although there is no active general staff in the post-war German military, it is nonetheless a prerequisite for career-oriented officers of the Bundeswehr to have successfully completed that particular grade course. Line officers in the Bundeswehr who made it into the military elite are a rare exception. According to Kutz (1991:60), 22 percent of the families of general staff officers who succeeded in the 1983/84 grade course still meet the profile of the so-called desirable circles. On that basis, Kutz concludes that the basic tendency of even this group of officers—who in effect make up the new generation of military elite—is a social democratization. A similar development was observed in the United States of America.[12]

Representative surveys of the whole officer corps of the Bundeswehr in the 1990s continue to show a structural predominance of Protestants over Catholics (45 percent and 33 percent respectively) (Bald 2000:46). Furthermore, the percentage of officers with a religious affiliation—78 percent

139

of which are members of one of the Christian churches—is clearly higher than that of the general German population at 65.1 percent in 1999 (Frerk 2002:40ff.). In terms of religious affiliation, the average in the military elite departs strongly from the average of other sector elites in Germany. It is clear that the percentage of Protestants is higher in the military elite than among others. Nevertheless, Jung (1988:298) states that those holding high ranking-positions in the military regard religious affiliation to be of little importance in their lives.

Out of the 135 officers in the general and flag grades who were interviewed in the Potsdam elite study,[13] 23 percent were Catholics, 60 percent were Protestants, while 17 percent had no religious affiliation (Schnapp 1997:108). The average length of time between joining the Bundeswehr and attaining their current position was 32.5 years (Rebenstorf 1997:174). This means that the high ranking officers interviewed had joined the Bundeswehr in the early 1960s. For the 1960s, however, data regarding the religious affiliation of lieutenants is only available for the year 1966. According to that data, 26.1 percent were Catholic, while 67.2 percent were Protestant (Bald 1982:77). These figures prove that the structural under-representation of the Catholic population in the top military leadership (44 percent of West Germans were registered as belonging to the Catholic Church in 1966), had been handed down. Nonetheless, this does not show that the relative partic-ipation of Protestants in the German military elite is higher than the relative participation of Protestants in the new gener-ation of junior officers in 1966. Although there is evidence of clearly disproportionate participation of Protestants in the German military elite, there seems to have been no structural preferential treatment of Protestant officers in this sample, as far as their chances for advancement to the military elite of the Bundeswehr were concerned. Thus, it is not the case that officers with a Protestant affiliation are overrepresented in the German military elite. Rather, Protestants tend to join the German armed forces more likely than Catholics do, and are therefore overrepresented at all levels of the German officer corps.[14] Officers with a Protestant affiliation have been over-represented compared to Catholic officers for a long time (Bald 2000:46).[15] If social structure alone does not account for the overrepresentation of Protestants in the German officer corps, then it may be that there exists elements that are common to both Lutheran Protestantism and the military. An examination of the possible existence and impact of the Protestant ethic in the German military is therefore relevant.

Ascetic Protestantism and the Military Ethic of Austerity

One of the major features of the Protestant ethic is its empha-sis on *discipline*. Disciplining the personality of the Christian is significant to Protestantism because its doctrines extend to the everyday life of the individual. Thus, the Protestant ethic gives rise to a specific *ethos* that Weber understands as an indi-vidual's or group's set of behaviors, which are linked to specific values. The Protestant ethic involves an accumulation of peculiarities, as well as patterns of behavior that are typi-cally Protestant, and thus manifest themselves together as a specific ethos. According to Weber, the doctrines of *vocation* and *predestination,* as well as the emergence of *free churches,* are of central importance to the Protestant ethic—i.e., an inner-worldly asceticism set within a rational way of life.[16] I will now focus on the significant effect Lutheran Pietism has had on the Prusso-German military.[17] Lutheran Pietism, which influenced the Protestant ethic of the German army, values the principles of steadfastness and the perseverance for one's convictions against others, the ideal of internal and external

141

New Direction 5.2

The loyal performance of professional duties bestowed one with honor because it supported the welfare of one's country. The formation of the Prussian officer corps under the "Soldier King" necessitated the creation of an ethos specific to the pietistic Lutheran moral values of self-sacrifice in one's duty toward God and the state.

---

order in one's life, the ideal of diligence and industriousness in the service of others, the ideal of modesty and frugality in one's style of life, and the ideal of a sense of duty and obedience (Müller-Bahlke et al. 2001:71ff.).

The "Soldier King" Friedrich Wilhelm I in[18] Prussia (1688-1740), thought it necessary to create a spirit of voluntary obedience among his soldiers. Although officially Calvinist, like the rest of the Hohenzollern line, he supported the acceptance of the values of hard labor and self-sacrifice exactly as they stood for the Pietist movement, a movement that developed in the seventeenth century and sought to reform the church, the state, and society. In accordance with the Pietist ethos of vocation, Friedrich Wilhelm I expected his officers to regard their professional duties as the central factor of their lives. To promote this idea, the Prussian king introduced Pietist Lutheran army chaplains who had been graduates from the Theology Faculty of the University of Halle (Marschke 2001:339). The overwhelming majority of the Prussian chaplaincy in the eighteenth century happened to be graduates of the "Halle school." Halle Pietism sought to promote a direct relationship between believers and God and arouse out of a debate internal to German Lutheranism (Bach

142

2001:285). The loyal performance of professional duties bestowed citizens and officers with honor because it supported the welfare of one's country. The formation of the Prussian officer corps under the "Soldier King" necessitated the creation of an ethos specific to the pietistic Lutheran moral values of self-sacrifice in one's duty toward God and the state, as well as in practical, efficient, and straight-forward approaches to tasks (Hübner and Mies 2001:188). The spiritualization of the Pietist work ethos constitutes the motivation behind the conscious obedience that became such a particular feature of the Prusso-German officer corps.[19] The ethos of service to the state is, therefore, a central part of the honor code of soldiers; and fidelity to the head of state is a central characteristic of officership. A current booklet on etiquette in the army's officer corps—issued by the cadet school of the German army in Dresden—emphasizes that the first toast should always go the head of state in an expression of willingness to serve.

Protestantism, in all its facets, emphasized daily work and raised it to a level of moral worth. Whereas an occupation had, in the Christian world, always been regarded as a necessary means to an end, with the reformation, work took on a spiritual dimension. As a result, one's occupation became both the completion of work and the fulfillment of a moral life—work became vocation. The resonance of this is still present the meaning of the word vocation: a calling. Martin Luther regarded one's earthly occupation to be an obligation imposed on the individual, by God, to seek moral activity in the world. The only way of living acceptably to God was solely through the fulfillment of the inner-worldly obligation to work imposed upon the individual. Each honorable occupation was considered to be God's will (Weber 1904/05:71). Luther remained a strong traditionalist. For him, the individual

143

> ### New Direction 5.3
>
> Hardness toward one's self and toward others is regarded as integral to being a soldier. Suffering austerity and, above all, the willingness to suffer austerity, have become values in themselves.

Christian was to remain in the position God had assigned to him or her. In other words, the vocation is a calling that one must follow. In contrast to Calvinism, Lutheranism considers the attempt to leave one's assigned position—even through hard labor—as godless conduct (Weber 1904/05:76ff.). By doing this, Lutheranism advances a conservative social view, and is thus guaranteed support from the privileged social strata.

According to Lutheranism, vocation flows from the certainty of God's guidance and faith in eternal grace. Work is the general occupation of humankind. Practicing a special occupation, such as that of an officer, means fulfilling God's will. Practicing one's vocation can not constitute a means for moral improvement but, rather, as defined by the Lutheran doctrine of election, a mode of sanctification through which God himself has given his grace to humans. At the cost of privations and foregoing enjoyment, one is called on to act in God's world and to transform it according to his ideas. This asceticism renders the occupation—perceived as lived asceticism—intensively charged with ethical meaning.

"Praised be what hardens you!" so goes the military counterpart to Protestant asceticism. The *ethos of austerity* that is so specific to the military accounts for the high degree to which the often meager living conditions of the armed forces are valued. Things that would help make the soldiers' lives more pleasant are considered unsuitable. The ethos of austerity refuses anything that might possibly render soldiers

---

New Direction 5.4

It was the Prussian and Protestant virtue of discipline that had a formative influence on the German military. In Protestant Prussia, discipline formed part of the established canon of its ascetic ethic.

---

effeminate.[20] Hardness toward one's self and toward others is regarded as integral to being a soldier. Suffering austerity and, above all, the willingness to suffer austerity, have become values in themselves. The ethos of austerity, traditionally known as the "spirit of the troops," has an effect on training and the practical application of command and control. Thus, Wiesendahl (1980:110) speaks about the value order of a professional estate that is shaped by the ideal of monk-like ascetics, and which constitutes a male community of self-denial. He argues that being a member of the military profession means to remain apart from civil life and to subordinate one's life and one's lifestyle to the military community.[21]

In the military, the priority given to *discipline* is as high as in Protestantism. For Max Weber, the military is specifically a rational instrument of governmental control, but it is also part of the process of rationalization in terms of common *discipline*, because "army discipline is the mother of discipline in general" (Weber 1921:686; translation by the author). It was the Prussian and Protestant virtue of discipline that had a formative influence on the German military. In Protestant Prussia, discipline formed part of the established canon of its ascetic ethic. The overwhelmingly Protestant nobility[22] played an outstanding role in the military, both in terms of the enforcement of discipline and other Prussian virtues such as patience and perseverance, as well as in terms of the model of performance of one's duty (Hübner and Mies 2001:187).

State Nobility: The German Military Establishment

In a casuistic argument concerning the emergence of estates, which he did not complete, Max Weber began investigating the warrior estate. However, scattered through his works are various remarks concerning the conceptualization of the military as one of the estates. In his considerations of the military, Weber regards the structure of the military as dynamic, evolving out of sociopolitical processes. The structure reflects the bureaucratic type of army that was necessary for forming professional standing armies (Weber 1921:565). According to Weber, this phenomenon is necessarily coupled with the professionalization of the commanding personnel, which called for *exercising one's office as one's vocation* within a bureaucratic framework. It seems to be of special importance that the self-conception of these professional civil servants (in military uniforms) is associated with belonging to a particular estate (Weber 1921:550ff.). By the same token, being a servant to the state implies a superior position toward those who are ruled by the state. The bond of service and loyalty between the civil servant or professional soldier—as servants of the state— and the state, constitutes the central issue.

In particular, Weber pointed to the dependence of professionalization on bureaucratization, and analyzed the modern military as a large bureaucratic-technical organization in which the civilian structures of functional organization increasingly gain in importance. Analogous to Weber's conceptualization of the military as an estate of warriors whose leading members are bureaucrats, I want to conceptualize the military establishment as *state nobility* (la noblesse

146

The ethic of serving goes beyond internal military requirements, and refers, rather, to obligations toward state and society as well as to the claims derived from them both.

d'état). On the one hand, this construct involves the soldierly self-conception of officers, one which is derived largely from the aristocratic *ethic of serving* and, on the other hand, it involves their inclination to the state. The *ethic of serving* goes beyond internal military requirements and refers, rather, to obligations toward state and society as well as to the claims derived from both. Janowitz (1960:6) uses a broad-based concept of *military establishment* to encompass all those who possess power in the military. The construct of state nobility is loosely based on the Janowitz conceptualization of military establishment, yet tries to be more specific concerning the group of officers involved and more precise when considering the qualities of theses officers.

German officers who successfully complete the command and general staff officer/flag staff officer grade course are expected, through their training, to acquire and develop certain qualities and characteristics. These, together, are sociologically conceptualized as state nobility. This construct is useful in this context for it allows an assemblage of the aristocratic idea of the serving warrior, the element of modern bureaucracy in the military profession, and the neo-liberal strife for the top positions in one's organization and society in general. Moreover, the construct of state nobility allows for the integration of the occupational characteristics that are specific to a professional officer, who is both a

147

warrior—following the aristocratic tradition—as well as a modern bureaucrat in a large organization.

Pierre Bourdieu (1989) elaborated the construct of state nobility in terms of the French civilian elite arising out of France's elite universities (grandes écoles). This construct, in the German context, is particularly applicable to the military establishment.[23] The general focus of Bourdieu's work is the social and mental structures of the state nobility that determine the mechanisms of elite selection. More specifically, Bourdieu turns his attention to the role of the *esprit de corps* that serves the formation of the state nobility. The esprit de corps specific to the military (after all, the terms had its origin in this area) fits with Bourdieu's concept particularly well.

In his analysis of social distinctions, Bourdieu concentrates on those codes with which only certain social groups are familiar; what he terms a *habitus*. In this context, the habitus is something like a second nature to the acting individual. Without the notion of the habitus, the social field in question is quite unthinkable. The habitus as a durable, transferable, and characteristic set of dispositions (Bourdieu 1979:25, 98) acts here as a scheme for judging, thinking, and perceiving human activity in everyday life, which Bourdieu calls practical sense (*sens pratique*). Bourdieu explains his construct of habitus in the context of his social practice theory in the following way:

> I am attempting to show that there is a connection between the position which the individual takes within a social sphere and his lifestyle. However, this connection is not a mechanical one, this relationship does not directly imply that somebody who knows where somebody else is standing also knows the latter's taste at the same time. What I call habitus, i.e., a general frame of mind or a disposition toward the world, acts as a link

between the position and standing [of a social actor] within the social sphere and [his or her] specific practices, affectations etc... (Bourdieu 1982:25; translation by the author)

Thus, the habitus is linked with a long history of social structure, which in itself is structured by the past and, therefore, a structure of knowledge that precedes the individual actor. At the same time, the habitus is itself an incorporated structure that structures social practices; it allows the individual actor to understand given situations through a practical sense and to be flexible when dealing with given situations within different social fields. The concept of habitus enables Bourdieu to describe the dialectics of structures that are, on the one hand, objective and incorporated and, on the other hand, subjective and embodied. According to Bourdieu, what pressures the different sides in the "plays"[24] of social practice to make them act in the ways they do, can be reconstructed through their habitus, which both reflects and informs the dispositions of the acting individuals (Bourdieu 1985:69). Therefore, what Bourdieu (1982:25) calls the "general frame of mind," the habitus, serves to illuminate structures of knowledge and the use of "adequate behavior" or "adequacy" in the military. The habitus resembles the posture, attitude, manner, behavior, and conduct of an individual from a certain social strata within the social field of the military.

The *military ethic of austerity* is composed of numerous traditional ideas and images of the soldier, and has its origin in the repertoire of conservative thinking and in the soldierly virtues of obedience, loyalty, discipline, decency, truthfulness, honor, and readiness to make sacrifices: It has had, and still has, a huge influence on the formation of *military habitus*. The inner-organizational subordination to the military

value and social-order of renunciation, self-denial, and sacrifice, can be understood as another aspect of asceticism in the
military (Wiesendahl 1980:110). It may just be this orientation
toward the soldierly virtues of keeping one's composure, a
readiness to make sacrifices, and of unselfishness that helps to
describe the apparent paradox of an objective meaning without
a subjective intention, that the military habitus embodies. The
cultivation and reproduction of these values, principles, and
virtues, occur simply by the extent to which they define social
success in the military. However, there is a close interrelation
between these values, principles and virtues, and the Lutheran-
Protestant ethic. Protestant socialization, and assimilation of
the Protestant ethic, consequently seems to foster the appropriate and desired conduct of the individual soldier in the German
military.

Conclusion

Military habitus and *esprit de corps*[25] form central component
parts of the *state nobility* concept. This concept makes it possible to analyze the character, the self-conception, and the
mechanisms of selection and reproduction of not only the
German military establishment but also of the German officer
corps in general. If we imagine the military as an extremely
complex social field, this approach enables us to better understand the social practices of this social institution.

Considering the importance of Lutheran Protestantism
for the German military, it should be noted that the implications of the German military's being dominated and defined by
the Protestant ethic are not to be understood in terms of cause
and effect (i.e., by furnishing proof of better career possibilities for Protestant officers in the German military). Rather, the
social mechanisms of human acting and social structures are

extremely complex; the relation between cause and effect in social institutions is an indirect one. Therefore, if the *Protestant ethic* and *military ethics* are perceived to have a great deal in common with one another, one should endeavor to develop a sociologically informed understanding of a social institution like the military. A theoretical approach that attempts to go beyond the dichotomy of objectivity and subjectivity helps us understand the individual actor within social structures.

The ascetic Protestant ethic (in particular, the version of Lutheran pietism upon which these considerations have been based) and the *military ethic of austerity,* as it is describe above, can actually be regarded as the "spiritual armament" of the German officer corps. Military sociology will need to follow up on how these military ethics will be maintained throughout the changes in the soldier's job profile toward modern professionalism, and on how a continued marginalization of the two state churches in German society affect the relationship between cross and sword.

The military enjoys the exclusive right to use force for the purpose of regulating the external relations of the state. As a result, it does continue to have a social significance that should not be underestimated. At the same time, however, sensitivity to any use of force has significantly increased in many democratic societies. This has an effect on the self-legitimization of "the managers of professional use of force" (Lasswell 1941) within democratic societies that are, on principle, committed to the norms of non-violence, equality, and freedom. Therefore, the interrelation between the development of societal values and the values shared within the military must be further compared.

SUMMARY

This chapter analyzed the extent to which belonging to the Protestant church continues to be important in the Bundeswehr, and to what degree military culture is shaped by this condition. The analysis first showed that an officer's membership in one of the two German state churches does not have any direct impact on his prospects of promotion to the military elite of the Bundeswehr. The chapter discussed the importance of the Protestant ethic for the German Bundeswehr and the tradition of Prusso-German armies. Above all, the interrelations between the Protestant tradition of the German officer corps and the dominating military culture of the German armed forces are examined. The military, here, is understood as a social institution with explicit rules, and implicit regularities, principles, and values, among which are the Protestant ethic and military ethics. Therefore, the extent to which the Protestant ethic and military ethics are in accord with one another is investigated. Indeed, this is particularly relevant to understanding the German military culture. It is assumed that the ascetic Protestant ethic and the military ethics of austerity perform an institutional function in the military, which can be regarded as "spiritual armament," particularly for the German officer corps. The issue is then placed in a theoretical context, relying upon Max Weber's sociology of religion approach and Pierre Bourdieu's concept of habitus. After comparing Weber's central concept of the Protestant ethic and my construct of the military ethics of austerity, the concept of state nobility was briefly expounded. The application of this concept performs a theoretically integrating function that facilitates a broader understanding of military culture.

KEY TERMS AND CONCEPTS

- Ethics
- Military culture
- Protestantism
- Religion
- Habitus
- Esprit de corps
- Elitism
- Social practice

STUDY AND DISCUSSION QUESTIONS

1. How can we conceptualize military culture?

2. What are the specific values and primary virtues of the military?

3. What makes people choose the military profession?

4. Do you think religion has an influence on the military institution of your country? Explain.

5. How important are ethics for a military institution? Discuss.

NOTES

1. I would like to thank Sarah Clift vom Hagen for her constructive criticism on an earlier version of this text and for helping polish my English.
2. In 1913, the 25 German army corps that existed in peacetime were comprised of nineteen Prussian, three Bavarian, two Saxon, and one Württemberg corps.

153

3. James Burk (1999) offers the most promising concept of military culture so far. He emphasizes that "war fighting still determines the central beliefs, values and complex symbolic formations that define military culture" (Burk 1999:448). For Burk, military culture consists of at least four central elements: discipline, professional ethos, ceremony and etiquette, and cohesion and esprit de corps.
4. When making reference to a soldier I will use the masculine "he" since my data predates 2001, the time when the German military became completely open for women.
5. Morris Janowitz's usage of the term "military elite" in his landmark *The Professional Soldier* is rather vague: he defines it simply as "the highest ranking officers" (Janowitz 1960:6).
6. They include, among others, the willingness to kill and to die for one's country in the context of war.
7. The nobility has never played a prominent role in the German naval officer corps, and so never produced many admirals.
8. The percentage of nobility within the total population of Germany is estimated to be a little less than 0.1 percent.
9. "In 1865, the nobility could only just maintain its majority among the entire officer corps at 51.1 percent—definitely for the last time in Prusso-German military history" (Bald 1982:86; translated by the author).
10. See also Janowitz (1960:4, 81) for a similar description of a situation in the United States in the first half of the twentieth century.
11. After German reunification, young officers from Eastern Germany will have reached the necessary length of service requirements to be eligible for advancement to the military elite only after many years. Former NVA officers who were taken over by the Bundeswehr, generally, have no chance for this.

12. Janowitz (1960:89-92) describes such a development for the American case in the 1950s.

13. In the Potsdam elite study of 1995, 135 out of the 157 German officers in the general and flag grades were willing to participate in interviews. This means 86 percent of all possible interview partners were covered, which is the highest percentage of all the sector elites interviewed (Machatzke 1997:65).

14. That even today the participation rate of Protestants in the German officer corps is higher than Catholics cannot be explained at the statistic aggregate level, i.e., by a higher or lower number of potential applicants coming from regions with a low share of Catholics and/or a high share of Protestants in the population. Contrary to public opinion, e.g., the applicant potential from wealthy Baden-Württemberg (about half the population are Catholic) is clearly above the average in Germany, while the applicant potential from the poorer states, Bremen and Lower Saxony (high share of Protestants), is clearly below the German average (see Heikenroth 2000:34 f). For more than a decade now, 40 percent of the officer candidates come from the mainly atheistic Eastern Germany (while only 20 percent of the total population in Germany live there). The social structure of the German officer corps is changing.

15. Janowitz (1960:97-99) explains the traditional overrepresentation of Protestants in the American military citing the social composition of the American officer corps, which has predominantly a southern, rural, upper middleclass background.

16. Weber employs a descriptive approach, which limits itself to the academic description of ideas of morale and does

not lay claim to the establishment of scientifically normative statements.

17. Therefore, I will not discuss in more detail the specifically
Calvinistic doctrine of predestination and the Free
Churches, which are to be found particularly among
Puritans who, in Germany, were long denied careers as
officers in the military.

18. He could not use the term "of Prussia" because his father
Friedrich I had crowned himself "Rex Brandenburgicus in
Prussia" outside of the territory of the German empire in
Königsberg in 1701.

19. The idea of conscious—and not blind—obedience is still
central to the Bundeswehr's concept of "Innere Führung"
(self leadership and moral guidance).

20. In this respect, Dunivan (1994:533ff.) speaks of the traditional model—in contrast to the evolving model—of the
"combat, masculine-warrior" (CMW) paradigm.

21. The question of whether or not the armed forces of
Western countries really are such *total institutions*, as
Wiesendahl (1980) and many other military sociologists
suggest, remains an open one. However, there is good
reason to conceive of the military as a *total profession*
because the soldier's contacts are predominantly with
others within his profession. In this respect, the military
profession is unlike other professions. Because of the
extremely hierarchical structure of the military organization, the degree of surveillance by superiors within the
military is constant and intensive.

22. After all, the nobility enjoyed supremacy in the German
military at least until the July 20th 1944 conspiracy against
the NS-regime.

23. The *grandes écoles* are particular to the French educational
system, but they could, perhaps, be compared to the

156

universities of the Bundeswehr and the Command and Staff College in the German system (although these only admit military officers). However, as far as their function as a point of entry to top careers in politics, administration, and economy is concerned, these French institutions have no counterpart in Germany.

24. Bourdieu uses the term "game" in order to highlight the active nature of social structures on the one hand and their competitive nature on the other.

25. Congruent with its French meaning, "corps" can be understood as a kind of body with a large number of integrated parts. In that sense *esprit de corps* and *habitus* are closely related since both of them imply the act of incorporating and/or embodying social conditions as a means by which those social conditions are reproduced.

REFERENCES

Bach, Tom. 2001. "Throne and Althar: Berlin and Halle, 1727-1740." Pp. 285-295 in *Gott zur Ehr und zu des Landes Besten* (For God's Honor and the Best of the Country), edited by Thomas Müller-Bahlke. Halle: Verlag der Frankeschen Stiftungen zu Halle (Saale).

Bald, Detlef. 1982. "Der deutsche Offizier. Sozial- und Bildungsgeschichte des deutschen Offizierkorps im 20. Jahrhundert" (The German Officer. Social and Educational History of the German Officercorps in the 20th Century). München: Bernard & Graefe.

_____. 2000. "Zur Reform der Bundeswehr. Militärischen Mentalität versus Innere Führung" (On the Reform of the Bundeswehr. Military Mentality versus Innere Führung). *Wissenschaft & Frieden* 3:45-48.

Bonnemann, Arwed and Ulrike Hofmann-Broll. 1999. "Studentische Orientierungen zwischen akademischer und soldatischer Lebenswelt" (Students' Orientations between Academic and Military Lebenswelt) *HDZ der Universität der Bundeswehr Hamburg*, manuscript.

Bourdieu, Pierre. 1979. *Die feinen Unterschiede. Kritik der gesellschaftlichen Urteilskraft* (Distinction. A Social Critique of the Judgement of Taste). Frankfurt: Suhrkamp.

_____. 1982. *Satz und Gegensatz. Über die Verantwortung des Intellektuellen* (On the Responsibility of the Intellectuals). Frankfurt: Fischer.

_____. 1985. *Sozialer Raum und Klassen. Leçon sur la leçon. Zwei Vorlesungen* (Leçon sur la leçon. Two Lectures). Frankfurt: Suhrkamp.

_____. 1989. *La Noblesse d'État. Grandes Écoles et Esprit des Corps* (The State Nobility: 'Grandes Ecoles' and the Esprit de Corps). Paris: Les Editions de Minuit.

Burk, James. 1999. "Military Culture." Pp. 447-462 in *Encyclopaedia of Violence, Peace, and Conflict*, edited by Lester Kurtz. San Diego.

Bürklin, Wilhelm et al., eds. 1997. *Eliten in Deutschland. Rekrutierung und Integration* (Elites in Germany. Recruiting and Integration). Opladen: Leske and Budrich.

Dunivin, Karen O. 1994. "Military Culture: Change and Continuity." *Armed Forces & Society* 20:531-547.

Frerk, Carsten. 2002. *Finanzen und Vermögen der Kirchen in Deutschland* (Finances and Property of the Churches in Germany). Aschaffenburg: Alibri.

Heikenroth, André. 2000. "Wer will zur Bundeswehr? Eine Potenzialanalyse" (Who wants to go to the Bundeswehr? An Analysis). *SOWI-Working Paper* No. 123, Strausberg.

Hübner, Michael and Anke Mies. 2001. "Prediger und Patrioten. Die Franckeschen Stiftungen und die preußische Militärpolitik" (Preachers and Patriots. The Franke Foundations and the Prussian Military Policy). Pp. 187-227 in *Gott zur Ehr und zu des Landes Besten* (For God's Honor and the Best of the Country), edited by Thomas Müller-Bahlke. Halle: Verlag der Frankeschen Stiftungen zu Halle (Saale).

Janowitz, Morris. 1960. *The Professional Soldier. A Social and Political Portrait*. Glencoe, Ill: Free Press.

Jung, Matthias. 1988. "Generalität–Eine Elite wie jede andere? Anmerkungen zu Rekrutierungs-, Karriere- und Einstellungsmustern in der bundesrepublikanis- chen Militärelite" (The Generals – an Elite like Any Other? Comments on the Patterns of Recruiting, Career and Attitudes of the Federal German Military Elite). Pp. 287-300 in *Militär als Lebenswelt. Streitkräfte im Wandel der Gesellschaft (II)* (The Military as a Lebenswelt. Armed Forces in a Changing Society), edited by Wolfgang Vogt. Opladen: Leske and Budrich.

———. 1990. "Die Bundeswehr-Elite. Eine Bestandaufnahme nach 30 Jahren" (The Elite of the Bundeswehr. A Stock-taking after 30 Years). Pp. 109-123 in *Eliten in der Bundesrepublik Deutschland* (Elites in the Federal Republic of Germany), edited by Landeszentrale für politische Bildung Baden-Württemberg. Stuttgart et al.: Kohlhammer.

Kurtz, Lester, ed. 1999. *Encyclopaedia of Violence, Peace, and Conflict*. San Diego: Academic Press.

Kutz, Martin. 1991. "Karrieren und Kriterien. Herkunft und Leistungsstand von Generalsstabs- und Admiralsstabs- soffizieren" (Careers and Criteria. Social Origin and

Performance Level of Officers of the General- and Admiral-Staff). *Information für die Truppe* 10:56-62.

Landeszentrale für politische Bildung Baden-Württemberg, ed. 1990. *Eliten in der Bundesrepublik Deutschland* (Elites in the Federal Republic of Germany). Stuttgart et al.: Kohhammer.

Lasswell, Harold. 1941: "The Garrison State." *American Journal of Sociology* 4: 455-468.

Machatzke, Jörg. 1997. "Die Potsdamer Elitestudie – Positionsauswahl und Ausschöpfung" (The Potsdam Elite Survey – Choice and Benefit). Pp. 35-68 in *Eliten in Deutschland. Rekrutierung und Integration* (Elites in Germany. Recruiting and Integration), edited by Wilhelm Bürklin et al. Opladen: Leske and Budrich.

Marschke, Ben. 2001. "The Collaboration of Halle Pietism and the Military State. The Development of the Chaplaincy in Prussia through the Middle of the Eighteen Century." Pp. 337-347 in *Gott zur Ehr und zu des Landes Besten* (For God's Honor and the Best of the Country), edited by Thomas Müller-Bahlke. Halle: Verlag der Frankeschen Stiftungen zu Halle (Saale).

Müller-Bahlke, Thomas, ed. 2001. *Gott zur Ehr und zu des Landes Besten* (For God's Honor and the Best of the Country). Halle: Verlag der Frankeschen Stiftungen zu Halle (Saale).

Müller-Bahlke, Thomas, Carmela Keller, and Ralf-Thorsten Speler 2001. "Bildungsweg und Tugendpfad. Halle als bevorzugter Standort preußischer Bildung und Erziehung" (The Path of Education and Virtue. Halle as Preferred Location of Prussian Education and Learning). Pp. 71-104 in *Gott zur Ehr und zu des Landes Besten* (For God's Honor and the Best of the Country), edited by Thomas Müller-Bahlke. Halle: Verlag der Frankeschen Stiftungen zu Halle (Saale).

Plessner, Helmuth. 1935 [1959]. *Die verspätete Nation. Über die Verfügbarkeit bürgerlichen Geistes* (The Delayed Nation. On the Dispositions of Bourgeois Spirit). Stuttgart: Kohlhammer.

Rebenstorf, Hilke. 1997. "Karrieren und Integration – Werdegänge und Common Language" (Careers and Integration – Professional History and Common Language). Pp. 123-156 in *Eliten in Deutschland. Rekrutierung und Integration* (Elites in Germany. Recruiting and Integration), edited by Wilhelm Bürklin et al. Opladen: Leske and Buedrich.

Schnapp, Kai-Uwe. 1997. "Soziodemographische Merkmale der bundesdeutschen Eliten" (Sociodemographic Features of the Federal German Elite; UvH). Pp. 101-122 in *Eliten in Deutschland. Rekrutierung und Integration* (Elites in Germany. Recruiting and Integration), edited by Wilhelm Bürklin et al. Opladen: Leske and Budrich.

Schössler, Dietmar. 1977. "Militärische Elite" (Military Elite). Pp. 181-184 in *Bundeswehr und Gesellschaft. Ein Wörterbuch* (Bundeswehr and Society. A Dictionary), edited by Ralf Zoll, Ekkehard Lippert, and Tjark Rössler. Opladen: VS Verlag für Sozialwissenschaften.

Schulz, Karl-Ernst, ed. 1980. *Streitkräfte im gesellschaftlichen Wandel* (Armed Forces in a Changing Society). Bonn: Osang.

von Scotti, Michael. 2001. "Die Seele der Armee ist verletzt" (The Army's Soul is Hurt). *Loyal* 11:24.

Vogt, Wolfgang, ed. 1988. *Militär als Lebenswelt. Streitkräfte im Wandel der Gesellschaft (II)* (The Military as a Lebenswelt. Armed Forces in a Changing Society). Opladen: Leske and Budrich.

Weber, Max. 1905 [1920]. *Die protestantische Ethik und der Geist des Kapitalismus* (The Protestant Ethic and the Spirit of Modern Capitalism). Pp. 17-206 in *Gesammelte Aufsätze zur Religionssoziologie I* (Collected Essays in the Sociology of Religion). Tübingen: Mohr.

_____. 1920. *Gesammelte Aufsätze zur Religionssoziologie I* (Collected Essays in the Sociology of Religion). Tübingen: Mohr.

_____. 1921. *Wirtschaft und Gesellschaft. Grundriß der verstehenden Soziologie* (Economy and Society. An Outline of Interpretative Sociology). Tübingen: Mohr.

Wiesendahl, Elmar. 1980. "Demokratischer Wertewandel und militärische Subkultur" (Democratic Change of Values and Military Subculture). Pp. 95-123 in *Streitkräfte im gesellschaftlichen Wandel* (Armed Forces in a Changing Society Change), edited by Karl-Ernst Schultz. Bonn: Osang.

Zoll, Ralf, Ekkehard Lippert and Tjark Rössler, eds. 1977. *Bundeswehr und Gesellschaft. Ein Wörterbuch* (Bundeswehr and Society. A Dictionary). Opladen: VS Verlag für Sozialwissenschaften.

C h a p t e r

6

NAVAL PROFESSION, CHIVALROUS CADETS, AND MILITARY UNIONS: THE FIGURATIONAL APPROACH TO MILITARY SOCIOLOGY

René Moelker
Royal Netherlands Military Academy
Breda, The Netherlands

LEARNING OBJECTIVES

After reading this chapter, you should be able to

- develop an understanding of the figurational approach based on the work of Norbert Elias;
- understand how conflicts between groups can be analyzed through the figurational approach;
- understand the genesis of new institutions and the formation of habitus, particularly in a military context;
- appreciate how distant historical events can still have a substantial impact on military institutional processes;
- appreciate the complexity of the social construction of military identity.

163

Figurations and Their Uses

It is remarkable that the work of a key sociologist like Norbert Elias, who wrote so much on violence and civilizing processes (Elias 1939, 1969), has only scarcely been used in military sociology. The "Studies in the Genesis of the Naval Profession" (Elias 1950), while so evidently devoted to military sociology, are not mentioned in recent reviews and studies on the military profession (Caforio 1994; 1998). More remarkable is the omission of *The Civilizing Process* (Elias 1939) as the most important work about the correlation between the use of the military as a tool of state formation and changes in culture or, if one prefers, the psychological makeup of personality structure. Over time, violence becomes channeled and the warriors are tamed as instruments of state and, parallel to this development, the personality structure is civilized, inhibited, and emotions are increasingly controlled by the individual.

Elias's work has initiated a large series of studies that are mostly labeled "figurational studies." Figurational scholars usually object to being categorized, but they do share a special approach to the study of social behavior. Strangely, there are many figurational studies[1] that are related to the topics of war, state formation, violence in and between societies etc., but there are only a few figurational studies in the field of "military sociology." For a long time, scholars in military sociology neglected a relevant paradigm that could have been a strong heuristic tool for understanding the military.

What, then, are figurations and why are they relevant to the study of the military? By figuration, Elias (1978:130) means "the changing pattern created by the players as a whole—not only by their intellects but by their whole selves, the totality of their dealings in their relationships with each other. It can be seen that this figuration forms a flexible latticework of tensions. The interdependence of the players, which is a prerequisite of their forming a figuration, may be an interdependence of allies or of opponents." Robert van Krieken (1998:214) points out that as figurations are meshes of interdependence, they limit autonomous action. Nevertheless, despite this limitation, figurations do consist of independent human beings. The relationship between individuals can be studied most effectively by analyzing shifts in asymmetrical power balances. Figurational studies are valuable because the paradigm focuses on relationships and interactions. System analysts, like Talcott Parsons, are rejected as strongly as is the psychological reductionism of George Homans. They are rejected because both the system and the individual emerge from the interactions between individuals. The study of changing social structures and processes—what Elias called sociogenesis—is linked to the analysis of psychogenesis, or the changes in personality structures or habitus (the socially learned "second nature" that individuals acquire in the process of social learning). It is the study of the network of interactions that distinguishes figurational studies from system approaches and psychological individual perspectives. That is why Elias's earliest work mentions the terms "Verflechtungsfigur" or "Menschenflechtwerk" (interweaving of humans). In modern translations of *The Civilizing Process* "Menschenflechtwerk" is translated as "figuration."

There are many possible figurations but the most illuminating example by Elias is the "royal mechanism" (Elias 1939) that drives state formation and the civilizing process. The example is especially adequate as it illustrates the shifts in power between the parties involved in this figuration. In a three-party figuration, the King tries to balance the nobility and the bourgeoisie. He will favor whatever group is in the

165

lesser position. Before the sixteenth and seventeenth century, the nobility was, in most cases, the dominant party and had to be counterbalanced by the King, who would give rights and advantages to non-noble groupings. From the seventeenth century onwards, the urban bourgeoisie in western European countries has been on the rise and therefore the King favors the nobility. By balancing the two groups the King secures his own position,[2] but the unanticipated consequence of the "royal mechanism" is that social institutions like the military or parliament evolve and change as a result of the rivalries, antagonism, and power shifts in the network of relationships. One consequence is that the military evolves into a profession, first noticeable in the naval profession (Elias 1950; Moelker 2003a, 2003b). A second consequence essential to state formation was that both the monopolies of violence and taxation came to rest with the King or the state.

From the above example, more distinguishing characteristics of figurational studies can be extrapolated. Figurations are best studied by analyzing the historical processes that are responsible for their development. In the study of these processes, the focus is on the interactions between the parties in the figuration. As a result, many figurational studies lean heavily on historical data and analysis. Furthermore, the result of the tensions in the figuration is unanticipated and difficult to predict. Civilization processes are therefore characterized by optimism and by temporary setbacks. Change is in the direction of growing civilization, but there are many reversals and counter processes of decivilization (as was demonstrated by Zwaan 2001; see also Wouters 1976). In comparison with Parsons, Foucault, Ahrendt, and Baumann, Norbert Elias is the most optimistic scholar (Smith 2001). Elias's work is not unilinear, and so Smith (2001) points to the possible uses of the figurational approach in postmodern theory.

The relevance of the figurational approach for military sociology may already be clear from the above. On the one hand, there is a strong correlation between the soldier and the state. Tilly (1992) expresses this correlation eloquently, saying "the state made war, and war made the state." On the other hand, the military is the cause and consequence of the civilizing process and the figurations that include the military as one of the parties are well worth analyzing from this perspective. Demonstrating the relevance of the figurational approach for military sociology is the main issue of this chapter, but it is a goal that can best be achieved by looking at examples. First, some methodological notes will be made to clarify the uniqueness of the approach. After answering the question of why figurational studies have not gained recognition in military sociology in section two, the chapter will continue by looking at three different examples. The first example elaborated upon is derived from a partly unpublished work by Elias himself on the naval profession. The second example will investigate the cultural aspects of personality formation and habitus by examining the mores, culture, and etiquette of the Royal Netherlands Military Academy (RNLMA) Cadets' Corps. The third example concerns the special figuration of which the military unions are a part. In the concluding section, the possibilities for future uses of figurational studies in military sociology are discussed.

Some Notes on Methodology

If a branch of science is to be accepted as an independent discipline, it is required that it has a methodology of its own. Sociology fulfills this requirement because, according to Emile Durkheim (1947), it has a unique methodology where "social facts" are explained by "social facts." By this definition, figurational studies belong to sociology, but, at the same time, they are interdisciplinary in character. Figurational studies have much in common with history and political science. But there are more disciplines that enable symbiotic relations with figurational studies.

Figurational studies do have methodological peculiarities that make them different from other approaches to the study of society. In the Norbert Elias Archive in Marbach am Neckar, Germany, the author of this chapter found notes by Elias explaining the method he used for the major part of his work. One note bears the title *Die Eliassche Methode* and contains the key phrase "Makrostrukturen durch die Untersuchung von Mikrostructuren sichtbar zu machen" (to reveal macro structures by researching micro structures) (Norbert Elias Archive 518, hereafter cited as NE). Another note is also illuminating. It states "the history of a profession is part of the social and economic history of its country" (NE archive 517). This note was related to Elias's "Studies in the Genesis of the Naval Profession," but it was not only the origin of the naval profession in which Elias was interested. The studies are, in fact, studies into England's culture,[3] national and international politics, social structure, and economy. By studying the roots of a part of English culture—i.e., the genesis of a profession—Elias tries to gain an insight to the specific civilizing processes that made Britain an empire.

Furthermore, Elias claims his method and theory to be superior to the Marxist dialectic method. The Marxist method studies societal tensions by contrasting thesis and antithesis. The tension is overcome by a synthesis. In its turn, the synthesis might, at one point later in time, become the new thesis that provokes a new antithesis. Elias agrees with the conflict sociology in the work of Marx. In particular, the concept of an "axis of tensions," which is developed by Elias in the "Genesis

168

of the Naval Profession" (1950), is an example of this dialectical approach. From tensions between nobility and bourgeoisie in the seventeenth century, to the eighteenth and nineteenth century, "the main axis of tensions shifted more definitely to the commercial and industrial section of the population, dividing it into two camps, the working classes and the middle classes" (Elias 1950:301). Taken together with the remark quoted above that the history of a profession is part of the social and economic history of a country, Elias—in these studies—is very close to a Marxist perspective. In his Parisian lecture in 1983, Elias himself articulated a resemblance to Marx, but he also stated the Marxist schema to be too rough: "The Marxist model...is surely not wrong, but it is rough!...What is missing in the Marxist division of classes is the fact that the king and the nobles form a kind of focus of power in its own particular way, that is not equal to the nobility" (NE archive MISC-D X = Paris 3:13; translated by author).

Elias criticizes Marx's two-party dialectics and advocates a three-party kind of dialectics that is embedded in the royal mechanism. In figurational studies, a sophisticated version of Marxist conflict sociology is introduced.

The particular methodology used in figurational studies differs from main stream sociology. Because of these differences, military sociology can profit from this new direction for research for it is sure to generate new knowledge.

Why Has the Figurations Approach Not Been Used Much in Military Sociology?

When the epistemology and methodology of figurational studies can generate new findings, why then has the approach scarcely been used? The answer to this question may be found in military sociology itself but also in the life history of Norbert

Elias. Military sociology began to flourish after World War II. Many renowned scholars of those days started in military sociology. They were also the heydays of functionalism. Functionalism lost its dominance in the 1970s, though it remained relevant in military sociology because it was a fitting perspective for many problems of the military organization. It was a non-threatening, not-too-critical theoretical stance and a good starting point for applied research.

The life history of Norbert Elias also explains why figurational studies have received little attention in military sociology. The lack of attention is visible when one tracks the reception of the "Studies in the Genesis of the Naval Profession" (1950). This gemstone of military sociology was never published as intended; only part one was issued, though three parts were planned.

The "Studies in the Genesis of the Naval Profession" were written during a difficult time in Elias's personal life. A Jewish refugee in the United Kingdom since 1935, Elias obtained a Senior Research Fellowship at the London School of Economics in 1940, shortly after the publication of *The Civilizing Process* (1939). Work for the LSE was interrupted by internment in 1940 (Mennell 1989). During this same

---

New Direction 6.1

Functionalism lost its dominance in the 1970s, though it remained a relevant perspective for dealing with the problems of the military organization. It was a non-threatening, not-too-critical theoretical stance and a good starting point for applied research.

---

period, he lost his mother as a result of the brutalities of the Nazi regime (Korte 1997).

After the war, Elias made a living teaching extra-mural classes and giving psycho-therapeutic sessions. He also went into psychoanalysis himself. When asked why, he said it was because he wrote so slowly, although he also wrote to Cas Wouters that the analysis helped him get beyond "an ineradicable guilt feeling that I was unable to get my mother out of the concentration camp before she died in a gas chamber" (Wouters 1993:10; Heerma van Voss and Van Stolk 1989; Krieken 1998).

Elias acquired a permanent position in the academic world (Leicester) in 1954 at the age of 57. In short, Elias experienced hard times. In terms of recognition, these years were also difficult. *The Civilizing Process* was received positively by a limited group of reviewers (especially in the Netherlands), but the work was hardly known in the United Kingdom. It was translated into English about thirty years later. Recognition did come until late in his life, in the 1970s after he had retired.

During this difficult period, Elias worked on, among other things, the naval profession project. In 1950, a first part of the work was published in the *British Journal of Sociology* (BJS). Goudsblom (1987:86) rightly observed that if the public had known the work of Elias they would have recognized the general sociological importance of the article. Undeniably, it was a study based on the theoretical foundation laid down in *The Civilizing Process*. The impact the article made, however, was negligible. Most readers probably thought of the article as a "historical contribution of limited importance" (Goudsblom 1987:86) One of the reasons why the other studies were not published must have been that the first one did not provoke any response. Goudsblom (1987) tracked

---

New Direction 6.2

"Interestingly, in the origins of the naval profession, as represented by the British Navy, there was greater reliance on middle and even lower-class personnel in the officer corps, because men were needed to perform the arduous and skilled tasks of managing a vessel and its crew" (Janowitz 1960:23).

---

references to the article by subsequent sociologists. In footnote 18 he states "the only references to the article on the genesis of the naval profession I know are found in Lammers (1969) and Teitler (1972; 1974; 1977)." These references belong to the field of military sociology.

In military sociology, Elias's work has been noticed by some scholars like Janowitz. A small but interesting reference to Elias is made in Morris Janowitz's classic *The Professional Soldier* (1960:23).

As mentioned earlier, more references are found in studies by Lammers (1969) and Teitler (1972, 1974). For purposes of comparison with Elias's work, the latter is the most interesting. Teitler's thesis (1974) was translated and published in 1977 by the most important institution in military sociology, The Inter-University Seminar on Armed Forces and Society. Significantly, the book was called *The Genesis of the Professional Officers' Corps.*

Teitler studied sociology at the University of Amsterdam. Jacques van Doorn (1956, 1965; Van Doorn and Janowitz 1968), during Morris Janowitz's time one of the most renowned military sociologists, was Teitler's promoter. Van Doorn collaborated with Janowitz and Lammers on many occasions and must have been familiar with Elias's most prominent Dutch advocate, Johan Goudsblom. As the work of

Elias first became popular in Amsterdam, these biographical facts concerning Teitler explain why he was aware of works like *The Civilizing Process*, *The Court Society* and the 1950 *BJS* article. Teitler did not know Elias's unpublished work, but the similarities between the two authors are striking.

As Elias began to receive recognition in the 1970s, a translation of the study "Drake and Doughty" (1977), which had formed part of the unpublished second article for the *BJS*, was published in a Dutch literary magazine called *De Gids*. Though the story told in this translation is wonderful, it made no sense publishing it out of context. The powerful meaning of the story vanishes, for it depends on the totality of the argumentation. In fact, this was also the weak point for the first study published in *BJS*, but the effect of isolation proved to be more detrimental to this second piece published in Dutch. When read in context, the story stands out as an illustration strengthening the central argument—one of the jewels in the crown, sparkling and shining brightly. As a stand alone article it is merely an anecdotal story about a conflict between two long dead privateers.

The impact of the *BJS* article was evident partly, and indirectly, through his colleagues and students at Leicester. Elias's ideas in the article "Gentlemen and Tarpaulins" influenced the authors of a chapter entitled "The Professions" in *Human Societies, an Introduction to Sociology* (Hurd 1973:124). One of the students from the Leicester period, Dandeker, who also published on the naval officer's profession in the *BJS* (1978), introduced Eliasian ideas into military sociology.

In 1998, Goudsblom and Mennell published a small part of the *BJS* article in *The Norbert Elias Reader*, a reader that is intended as a "biographical selection." Recently, two translations of the *BJS* article have been published in Portugese (Elias 2001) and in French (2003). The latter publi-

173

cation concerns an issue of *Les Champs de Mars*, a French journal in military sociology.

Example 1: The Genesis of the Naval Profession

Exactly what figurational studies may signify for military sociology can only be demonstrated with examples. The first example to be discussed is derived from Elias's "Studies in the Genesis of the Naval Profession," which was recovered from the Norbert Elias Archive in Marbach am Neckar in Germany by Moelker (2003b). As mentioned above, only the first of the three studies was published. If all of Elias's original research had been published, perhaps he would have been considered a seminal figure in military sociology. However, due to personal circumstances and because recognition came late in his life, the other two studies were never published in English. As mentioned, one part concerning the rivalry between Drake and Doughty was published in Dutch (Elias 1977).

The unpublished articles form a coherent whole. The subject of inquiry, briefly, deals with the social origins of key institutions in British society, the Navy and its officers' corps. In general, the work is built on the strife between the nobility and the bourgeoisie. The studies are a continuation of Elias's earlier research in civilizing processes. The rivalry between these two groups forms the dynamic factor causing change. The rivalries and conflicts contribute to the institutionalization of a new occupation, the naval officer. Comparisons with Spain and France demonstrate that the rivalry was essential both for England acquiring a competitive edge and for its dominance of the world's seas. These rivalries and conflicts were subdued in Spain and in France with detrimental results on nautical skills and military competence. The latter quality, following Elias, stems from the values and standards of nobil-

174

ity (courage, discipline, fighting spirit, collaboration, and hierarchical command structures). Nautical skills originate from seamen or "tarpaulin commanders" who have learned the tricks of the trade as young apprentices at sea. Only the rivalry between the two socially divergent groups could result in a fusion of military and nautical skills or, in other words, in the genesis of the naval officer. While often the subject of dispute, the need for officers to acquire nautical skills became more and more evident. But the noblemen resented being forced to do what they regarded as the lowly work of the seamen, whose manual labor, an inherent part of a mariner's job, was deemed dishonorable for gentlemen. Therefore, Elias formulated the following leading question: "How could a gentleman become a tarpaulin without losing caste, without lowering his social status?" (NE archive 505).

The first study in "The Genesis of the Naval Profession" (Elias 1950) is on the social origins of tarpaulins and gentlemen, the seamen from bourgeois descent, and the noble members of court society. Military commanders/officers of noble descent did not want to lower themselves by doing the manual labor that came with learning the tricks of the sea trade. The officers regarded themselves as gentlemen, whose main task was commanding men and leading them into battle, getting them to board hostile ships and leading them in man-to-man combat. Whereas seamen commanders would eat and sleep with the sailors—only protected from the weather by a piece of canvas washed over with tar (hence the nickname "tarpaulin" or "tar")—the gentlemen officers would eat their meals in private or with their peers. The men on board cultivated the social distinction of the sailors "before the mast" and the officers "behind the mast." A seaman captain "might, as Sir William Booth did, sleep for years on deck with nothing over him but a tarpaulin that his seamen be the better contented" (Elias 1950:301).

In the late sixteenth century, ships proved to be useful platforms for guns. This enabled ships to fight at a distance. Nautical skills became more important in sea battle. Military commanders needed to acquire more knowledge of sailing in order to lead in battle. This shift in required skills made it possible for both seamen commanders and gentlemen commanders to rise in the military hierarchy. Members from both groups could be commissioned as admirals.

In the second study, the argument concerning conflicting relations is formulated more sharply: conflicts between nobles and commoners are seen as causing changes in the profession. In this study, the conflicts are the social tissue, the figuration, from which a new institution develops (Elias 1977; NE archive 507; NE archive 508).

First, Elias discusses an exemplary conflict between Drake and Doughty and then proceeds with a comparison of naval warfare under Henry VIII and Charles I. During the sixteenth and seventeenth centuries—with the exception of the period of the Commonwealth when only professional seamen were appointed as commanders—many conflicts occurred between the two socially distinct groups of nobles and commoners. Elias focuses on the matter of recruitment: "from which of the two groups of officers (seamen or gentlemen) should be recruited?" (NE archive 508). The answer to this question depends on political and societal power balances in the broader society. Elias explains that "under Henry VIII, and to some extent also under Elizabeth, the seamen gained a fairly strong position. Under the early Stuarts, the gentlemen were in the ascendant. They disappeared from the Navy with a few exceptions under the Commonwealth...under Charles II and James II the gentlemen again gained the ascendancy over the seamen...as in terms of influence and power, they were the favorites of the court" (NE archive 508:20).

176

The logic that determined which group was in a favorable position was described by Elias in *The Civilizing Process* (1939) as the royal mechanism; the group that is on the rise is counterbalanced by the commissioning policy of the King. Through this system of balance, the King manages to ensure his own position as the sovereign. In Henry VIII's time, the old nobility was already on the decline but was still the most powerful group. To counterbalance the influence of the old nobility, the King frequently appointed men of inferior status as commanders. During the reign of Charles I, the balance of forces in the country had changed and the urban bourgeoisie was definitely on the rise: "The King persisted in appointing courtiers, in spite of their professional shortcomings, as lieutenants, captains and flag officers in preference to professional seamen not only because he himself was by upbringing a courtier, but because he knew that in the country's internal struggle they were on his side while the seamen...had close links with the groups which, as he saw it, denied him his right as King" (NE archive 508:25).

In the third study, Elias formulates an answer to the question "How could a gentleman become a tarpaulin without losing caste, without lowering his social status?" The answer was to create a position for the training of young recruits not before the mast, not behind the mast, but amidships. Young people from both groups could be trained there. Working with their hands would, in this manner, not be below the station of a young gentleman. Hence, at the beginning of the eighteenth century, the institution of the "midshipman" evolved.

This training system gave the English a competitive advantage. It was possible for people from both groups to acquire nautical skills, become seamen, and, at the same time, learn to behave as gentlemen.

177

Elias not only provides insights into the institutional-ization of a profession, but also describes the political and societal processes of change in England leading to maritime supremacy. He went on to compare these processes with conti-nental developments in Spain and France. According to Elias, when the political structure employs this "royal mechanism," a healthy antagonism between nobility and commoners is enabled and, as a result, processes of change (leading to new institutional arrangements such as the fusion of noblemen and seamen into the profession of naval officers) are put in motion. Bringing conflicts out into the open is the first condition for change. A second condition for social change is fulfilled when the social structure allows men from lower stations to climb the societal ladder and, in turn, the social structure permits a certain degree of openness.

Spain and France faced the same problem as England. Their officers lacked nautical skills and their seamen were not trained to be military leaders. However, in Spain and France the societal structure was not open and conflicts between commoners and nobility were suppressed:

> The greater superiority and exclusiveness of the mili-tary class was reflected in the barrier between gentlemen officers and craftsmen officers on board the ships...Generally speaking one could say these barri-ers were higher and more rigid in France than in England and higher in Spain than in France. (NE archive 505:15)

The French Navy proved to be inferior to the English naval forces. Bureaucracy was one of the reasons for the "infe-riority" of the French naval forces because it caused the French officers to be overcautious. Whenever an action went

178

wrong, officers had to give a full account of events for which they were held fully responsible. This caused them to avoid risk-taking and to resort to fighting using guns only. The French preferred not to fight using the old boarding techniques and kept their distance, forcing the English to do the same. The English preferred to rely on their nautical skill for they were far more skilful sailors than the French. Another, no less important factor in the decline of the French Navy and its more or less constant inferiority to the naval force of England was the social distance between sailors and commanding nobles, which was reinforced by Louis XIV's constitution for his naval forces. This constitution assured supreme control for the nobles.

Example 2: Chivalrous Cadets
or the Habitus of the Cadets Corps

The second example examines a figuration that results in the formation of a habitus or a set of values like chivalry, courtesy, politeness, courage, and honor. The figuration comprises all the parties that make up the network of interactions that influence cadets' standards of behavior at the Royal Netherlands Military Academy. Not all cadets will know "how to behave." One reason for this may be their changed social origins, but there are also the changes in society whereby the traditional rules of conduct no longer provide guidelines. In the days that officers were solely recruited from higher circles of society, everyone knew how to behave. After all, the existing etiquette had been developed by society's elite—the nobility. In many ways, chivalrous norms and values have persevered at the academy.

Outward Appearance

Obviously, a training institute has many rules and regulations regarding dress. The most interesting ones, however, are those that relate to the off-duty hours of the cadets. After all, they will reveal the way in which the rules of conduct have an effect on an individual's life.

In their spare time, many cadets are casually dressed, but in 1993-94 serious discussions were held on whether it should be allowed to go into town "collarless" (t-shirt). The official guidelines of the Corps, as laid down in the *Blue Book* (Royal Netherlands Military Academy (RNLMA) 1993), were very explicit, indeed. Men were not allowed to wear earrings and they had to have a decent hairstyle. The armed forces as a whole have freedom of hairstyle, but the Cadets' Corps had different rules. Sideburns were not allowed to grow past the middle of the ear and a beard was forbidden. Clothing had to be decent. Jeans were allowed, but not with repairs and/or damaged or bleached. Ladies in military dress were expected to wear long hair held together by means of a ribbon or clip in neutral colors. With regard to trousers, the same rules applied as for the men. Decent blouses or turtleneck sweaters were recommended, but when a sweater is worn, a collared blouse has to be worn underneath. Needless to say, the length of a skirt was also regulated.

In 2004, these rules still apply. There are some minor differences, but they do not change the essence of the regulations. Thus, in 2004, a beard or moustache was allowed if the direct commander and the Chef du Protocol approved.

Associating with "Fairy" or "Gnome"

In the past, rules with regard to "social intercourse" were very strict. In recent times the rules have been loosened but many of them still apply. On Cadets' Corps parties, of which the Assaut—the Cadets' Annual Ball—is the high point, there are many rules to be observed. The 1993-1994 *Blue Book*, for instance, forbids excessive intimacies. What is to be qualified as such is not specified, however. But the behavior can never get too far out of hand because the cadet is responsible for the behavior of his "fairy" or "gnome." "Fairies" and "gnomes" are the invited guests of the cadets on activities like the Assaut. When evening dress is required (as is the case with the Assaut), the *Blue Book* specifies that the "fairy" has to wear an evening gown "down to several centimetres above the ankle." Some regulations are of a more practical nature, such as "when your 'fairy' is wearing an evening gown, take a taxi instead of a bike or motorcycle." Other rules concern polite manners, such as "never exclude a 'fairy' from conversations with your colleagues," "talk about something else from time to time," and "do not force yourself upon someone else's 'fairy'." Courteous behavior is expressed in such regulations as "assist a 'fairy' when she wants to sit down," and "walk to the left of your 'fairy' and in the street, walk on the street side" (RNLMA 1993).

Table Manners

The Cadets' Corps regards familiarizing aspirant corps members with table manners as one of its tasks. In order to teach them, a very clear instructional video entitled "Table Manners" has recently been made (RNLMA 2003).

The video first explains general civilian etiquette. Table seating, tableware, the arrangement of the many sorts of cutlery, the position and function of the serviette, and all other matters that are of importance at a dinner are discussed. Thus, it is better to wish each other a pleasant meal rather than a "tasteful meal," as this, in fact, expresses some doubt as to the tastefulness of the meal. Under no condition is food to be brought to the mouth with the knife. Handling a fork is quite an art, for instance, in dealing with those awkward peas. What is quite funny on the tape is the use of almost "vulgar language" to explain that eating in a common manner is not allowed. The voice-over in the video says "We do not plant the fork upright in a piece of meat in order to cut slices" (RNLMA 2003). Indeed, the video presents a number of etiquette "instructions" that must be followed:

> Take moderate helpings (do not be greedy), eat without making noises, with your mouth closed, and drink without slurping. Do not hang over the table. Do not bend forward with every bite. Sit up straight, legs next to each other, not crossed. The protective attitude of placing an arm around the plate is rejected as a custom that stems from times of extreme poverty or situations of extreme food rivalry (think of prisons). This sort of behavior clearly is not civilized. (RNLMA 2003)

With regard to specific values and norms typical for the Cadets' Corps, many are well-established. For example when serving out the food, the dishes are to the left. Preferably, the lion emblem is kept clean. Should it become stained, it has to be wiped clean. During a cold meal, a slice of bread is eaten by starting at the right-hand bottom and working counter-clockwise. Second year cadets are allowed to place hands and wrists on the table. Third-year students may rest their elbows on the table between courses. To indicate one has finished, the cutlery is laid down on the plate round side up to show the lion emblem. The knife lies above the fork.

182

Punitive Measures

In order to guard values and norms, the Senate established a Disciplinary Council (originally, in 1957, an honorary Council), and an Appeal Council. The Disciplinary Council is an organ that assesses the behavior of Corps members in case there are complaints from other Corps members.

Corps meetings contributed to a compliance with values and norms. Thus, in 1958, cadets were "held accountable for their behaviour, for instance, being in a public place embracing a 'fairy'" (Klinkert 1998). In the 1970s, there were still punishments for "taking off one's jacket in a public place" (Klinkert 1998). With regard to values of chivalry, the attitude toward the emerging phenomenon of the "female cadet" is of importance. The Corps meeting debated on "the extent to which a female cadet should be accepted as such. In other words, should a female cadet be treated like a male cadet, or as a woman first and foremost?" The meeting decided "a female cadet remains a woman, whom we also have to respect as such, when approaching her as a cadet" (Klinkert 1998).

Severe punishments, including the expulsion from Corps activities, were demanded for a number of fourth-year Air Force cadets in 1996 who had really gone too far. They showed up at the Academy in wrong civilian dress (no collar, shirts hanging out of their trousers), they urinated against the wall of the dining hall and the Cadets' bar, and they stole the piano from the Spijker (the Cadets' bar) with the intention of throwing it down the stairs (Klinkert 1998).

Explanation

Chivalrous values are, in a way, functional for officers. Courtesy and etiquette enabled one to move in diplomatic

> ## New Direction 6.3
>
> As habitus consists of internalized values and norms,
> it allows one to recognize opportunities and grasp
> them at the moment they present themselves. It allows
> one to move in a certain way within a specific group of
> people, to communicate with them, and to function in a
> manner accepted by that group.

circles at Court. Courage and discipline were essential when
ships or men had to be held in line during a firefight. Together
with technical expertise and scientific knowledge these values
and norms form the cultural capital for the officer.

The Netherlands has, for a long time, retained recruitment from the nobility and upper classes. In 1872, 22 percent
of the generals and colonels in the Army were of noble
descent. In 1912, this was 12 percent and, in 1950, 0 percent.
Around 1950, 22 percent of the cadets came from "military"
families. In other countries, a similar development can be
discerned, with a decreasing proportion of nobility (Van
Doorn 1974; Abrahamsson 1972; Moelker and Soeters 1998;
Moelker 2003a). A recent survey by Groen and Klinkert (2003a,
2003b) gives somewhat different data and percentages, partly

**Table 1. Social Status Fathers RNLMA Cadets
1828-2003 in Army and in the Colonial Army[4]**

Year/ Social layer	Layer 1	Layer 2	Layer 3	Layer 4	Layer 5	Layer 6
1828-1830	49	41	9	1	0	0
1836-1895	33	50	11	4	2	0
1896-1934	19	44	22	12	3	0
1935-1940	9	38	28	22	3	0
1948-1974	16	30	27	21	4	2
1975-2003	8	32	30	24	5	1

Source: Groen and Klinkert (2003b:72).

because other methods were used and partly because a different class division was used. However, the trend is comparable.

The changes in the composition of the officer corps have consequences for the values and norms of this corps. Cadets from lower strata of society are not familiar with the norms, values, and behavioral codes of the military elite that derived its standards from nobility. Bourdieu's habitus theory (Bourdieu and Passeron 1977) explains the changes by distinguishing economic, social, and cultural capital. Economic capital can be measured by property and income, and social capital by the social contacts a person possesses. His knowledge, good manners, and good taste make up his cultural capital.

Taste is a way to distinguish oneself—a tool for distinction—from others (Bourdieu 1984). It also betrays one's status. In general, the taste of the social elite enjoys a higher reputation than others. This is even true concerning a sense of humor (Kuipers 2001) Those in higher circles can distinguish themselves through their taste and, because taste is part of their cultural capital, these circles can' reproduce themselves by means of this distinction (hence, the title of Bourdieu's classic from 1977, *La Reproduction*). After all, the chances of acquiring the different capitals are not equal for everyone. The division of chances is dependent on the habitus, the internalized values and norms of the group to which one belongs. Their habitus enables people to react adequately to new situations by means of their expectations. Representatives of higher social circles expect their children to choose an education or profession that offers them a high prospect of economic success. Cultural capital and the habitus acquired in one's milieu facilitate one's career. Because the talent to assess risks and grasp opportunities is reserved to a higher social layer, certain manifestations of cultural capital are beyond the reach of individuals belonging to the lower social layers.

As habitus consists of internalized values and norms, it allows one to recognize opportunities and grasp them at the moment they present themselves. It allows one to move in a certain way within a specific group of people, to communicate with them, and to function in a manner accepted by that group.

Etiquette enables people to interact because it is part of the habitus. They do not have to ask themselves each time "how to behave," but they automatically follow the rules of conduct—if they have internalized them well enough. The theory is clearly evinced by the conclusion that rules of conduct are indispensable in contact with other people; they are a precondition for interaction. Rules of conduct "bring people of diverse backgrounds together and allow them to interact without threat of the situation collapsing into a struggle of competing self-interests...the chances of developing a more civilized society are increased" (Finkelstein 1989:139; Elias 1939).

Etiquette, courtesy, and other values of chivalry are especially important within groups that still show great inequality. Etiquette allows people to interact, irrespective of their social status, and in view of the diverse backgrounds of the present-day cadets; this fact underpins the importance of rules of conduct. Etiquette makes the interaction between people of unequal rank safe and predictable. In his latest book, entitled *Respect in a World of Inequality*, Richard Sennett (2003) maintains that the way in which people can show respect is dependent on the way in which they can develop impersonal manners. These manners manifest themselves in ritual role play (the commanding officer also acts out a role) and accepted rules of conduct. People of "high" and "low" positions can chat in a relaxed manner and make jokes because there are rules that govern polite conversation. Even when one is reprimanded, it is part of a ritual, which makes it a safe situation for all parties concerned.

186

It is important to avoid the cult of personality. This glamorization of the individualistic personality was already the butt of criticism in Sennett's famous *The Fall of the Public Man* (1977). In his latest book, he takes his criticism even further. In his view, it is impolite and offensive—disrespectful—to harp on one's personal merits. The cult of personality only leads to people placing themselves above others, which is something completely different from a person being a functional superior. In the latter case, he only plays a role and emotions, personal feelings, and narcissistic tendencies are kept outside the work atmosphere.

The strict rules of conduct seem to limit self-expression (Wouters 1976; Zeegers 1988), and they seem to become a burden. An author like Sennett, on the other hand, argues that social intercourse is facilitated when certain institutions—rules of conduct—are observed. In his view, it is precisely those rules that allow individual self-expression.

Values of Chivalry without Chivalry

Values of chivalry still have their place in the life of a cadet and, consequently, also in officer socialization. At the same time, the chivalry itself has eroded. The origins of etiquette and the values of chivalry are to be found historically in the nobility and the system of knighthood. Because of the democratization of the recruitment, cadets are increasingly drawn from all layers of society and the natural foundation for the values of chivalry has disappeared. Earlier prefaces to the guides for etiquette identify the changing social composition of the Cadets' Corps as one of the legitimizations for the socialization in manners and rules of conduct.

There are several reasons why the values of chivalry still exist, while the social composition of the cadet corps has

187

changed. The first is that etiquette and values of chivalry are functional for the work of the officer. Courage, honor, and discipline are values that are essential on the battlefield or in air combat. Courtesy and etiquette were once essential requirements because officers often found themselves in diplomatic or court circles. The relevance of these values and norms, however, has not decreased. Today, peace operations require diplomatic skills from the officer-communicator/officer-diplomat (Soeters 1998). Norbert Elias was one of the first to theorize that military academies are suitable institutions to bring about a fusion between civilian knowledge and military-chivalrous values and norms.

The second reason can be derived from Richard Sennett's work. The manners/rules of conduct of the etiquette system give a certain firmness and safety within an environment that is strongly characterized by inequality in rank and status. Not only is there a great inequality between cadre and cadets, but also among the cadets themselves, especially in the relations between senior and junior cadets. Etiquette remains important because there will always be inequality at a military academy. Rules of conduct allow people of unequal rank to communicate with each other in a civilized way.

A third reason is the urge every group feels to distinguish itself. In 1965, Van Hessen maintained that military academies, apart from providing professional knowledge, also fulfilled the function of elite formation. "Elite" in his view meant a group of people who demand a number of privileges for themselves on the basis of very specific knowledge, power of position, values, and standards. When officers were still mainly recruited from the nobility, it was obvious that the values and norms of the officers were also those of the noble elite. Let us leave the question about whether the RNLMA still has the function of elite formation. For the present, this question is debatable. It is, however, possible to speak of what Pierre Bourdieu calls the need to distinguish oneself. Socialization, in a very specific habitus and with regards to cultural capital, results in a professional grouping of officers that reproduces its esprit de corps. In doing this, it distinguishes itself from other professionals, not necessarily as a group that feels superior to others (which would be elite formation), but different (and unique) and therefore distinct from others.

Example 3: Military Unions

The third example concerns military unions. The focus is again on the tensions between groups and on the societal changes that will cause power balances to shift.

Military unions are not allowed in all countries. From our data we know that unions for military personnel do exist in Denmark, Sweden, Norway, Finland, Germany, Switzerland, Austria, Belgium, and the Netherlands (Caforio 2003), and, more recently, also in Spain and Ireland (Van den Bosch 2003; Schouten 2003). Unionization is prohibited in England, the United States, Canada, France, Portugal, Turkey, and Greece. Caforio summarizes many authors who put forward hypotheses explaining the national differences in attitudes toward unionization. One explanation points at the continental political culture where serving in the army is integral part of citizenship and where the collective interests are being negotiated by unions. Alternately, in the United Kingdom the armed forces have a "special relationship with the civil power whereby the rights and privileges of the dominant social group are automatically guaranteed to members of the military; in this relationship there is no need to seek unionization to provide the political, social and economic rights of members

189

New Direction 6.4

The government is in a position to keep the balance by favoring one of the other two parties. In a changing world, a shift can be seen from a traditional alliance between government and military management to a new coalition that is more often favorable to the members of the military.

---

of the organization for these will be always protected by the power elite with which the military is closely associated" (Harries-Jenkins 1977:68). Other explanations accounting for national differences in attitudes examine differences in conscription. Again, another hypothesis states that unionized Armed Forces are not efficient in combat. Another frequent explanation indicates the change in authority structure, where the Armed Forces are becoming more occupational and increasingly conform to enterprises in the civil society. Even though all of these hypotheses have their merits, there are always nations that disprove the general rule.

Figurational studies take a different approach by analyzing the tensions between at least three parties: government, military management (i.e., higher ranking officers, the military establishment), and members of the military (soldiers, Non Commissioned Officers (NCOs), and subaltern officers). Figurational studies investigate the societal developments that change the power balances between these parties. In this figuration of three parties, Elias's royal mechanism seems to apply. The government is in a position to keep the balance by favoring one of the other two parties. In a changing world, a shift can be seen from a traditional alliance between government and military management to a new coalition that is more often favorable to the members of the military. The forerunners were northern European countries, but because of many recent, simultaneous changes, shifts in power balances can be seen in Ireland and Spain where unionism is on the rise.

In the Netherlands, unionism goes back to the late nineteenth century. In 1897, a union for sailors was founded. Unions for NCOs were established in 1898 (Heckers 1998:44). There was an association for Naval Officers as early as 1883. In 1909, three army officers founded an association for officers. Most of these organizations were associations, not unions. Officer associations and religiously inspired associations refrained from political statements and clearly opposed any association with socialist parties in the Netherlands. They were officially satisfied to promote war sciences, religion, and the well-being of their members. NCO organizations promoted the interest of their members in the early decades of the twentieth century by starting housing corporations, savings and insurance institutions, and the like. Whenever they engaged in semi-political work the unions were suppressed, their chairpersons imprisoned, and so on. Though the associations of the military made some progress regarding war widows' pensions in the early years of the twentieth century, the mutiny on HMS "Seven Provinces" in 1933 gave the government a pretext for serious "union busting." After this mutiny, the military management and government easily subdued the wishes and demands of the military associations. Union work was made impossible until after World War II. Military management and government were in a dominant position also because of the fragmentation of the military associations. Each religious faction and each rank had its own association and the associations often disagreed with each other. Although the structural position of the associations remained fragmented until the

1990s, after World War II they played an important role in organized consultative structures discussing salaries, and living and working conditions. In 1977, over 90,000 military personnel were members of one of the associations (the total force numbered 130,000 in those times) but the question whether or not the organizations were associations or unions was debated by the members themselves. Sometimes their answer was "yes" and sometimes "no," depending on the fear of losing negotiating power. In the 1990s, many of the associations merged, corporals and officers associations joined forces and became one union. Nowadays, there are approximately five remaining unions, all affiliated with civilian federative national unions. Membership levels exceed 80 percent, whereas in the larger society membership is declining and is well below 25 percent.

A milestone was the establishment of the VVDM (*Vereniging Voor Dienstplichtige Militairen* or Association for Conscripted Soldiers), a union (though officially an association) of conscript soldiers in 1966. Society was changing a lot during the sixties with increasing emphasis on participation in decision making, democracy, socialist movements, hippie culture, and a great desire for change. In many respects, the government was sympathetic to the societal changes and wanted to break the military establishment just as much as the conscript soldiers wanted to do the same. Defence Secretary Vredeling, a former union man himself, chose the side of the conscripts on many issues, decided positively on the right to wear long hair, abolished the obligation of saluting one's superior, and relaxed many of the suffocating regulations (Kruijf and Lardenoye 1991:71-81). In the early days of the VVDM, subaltern officers were often in coalition with the conscripts union. They helped them formulate action objectives and, by doing so, ameliorated living and working conditions for themselves and their men. The struggle for a salary equal to the professional level was won in phases over a period of about 25 years.

Playing with power balances was an art that was mastered by the military managerial elite. They struck back when the VVDM was inevitably becoming more political. The VVDM used unorthodox methods for reaching their goals such as protest marches in uniform, work-to-rule actions, using the media, and so on. In time, they became associated with socialism, the peace movement, conscientious objector groups, and even anarchistic anti-Armed Forces groups (Kruijf and Lardenoye 1991:115-139). The Military Management began to promote a rivaling conscript union and was successful in this attempt. They made recruitment efforts extremely difficult. A devastating blow to the VVDM concerned their involvement in leaking information on nuclear weapons to the newspapers. This fact was used in an anti-VVDM campaign. Membership dropped from approximately 20,000 to 5,000 and lower.

The conscript union had been successful to a high degree. Not only did the union improve the life of its members, but, most importantly, it also taught the associations of other categories of personnel how to function as a union again. Because of constant repression in the early days of military associations, the organizations had forgotten how to wheel and deal, how to negotiate, and how to reach objectives by the instrument of political action. The present unions still benefit from conscript unionism long after the suspension of conscription (1996).

The royal mechanism that is at work in the process toward participation and representation of the military in the Netherlands is also encouraging change in other countries. As Schouten (2003) demonstrated for Spain, and Van den Bosch

193

(2003) for Ireland, two structural preconditions of society enable the working of the royal mechanism. The first is that military management has to open up to influences outside the elite. The second is that conflicts should not be subdued. Moderate levels of conflict create change. These two preconditions are essential for developing unionism.

In Spain, the nobility traditionally was in charge of the army. The Franco regime depended heavily on this elite and allowed high ranking army officials to also play an important role in politics and civilian enterprises. When Franco died, the dictatorship ended and Spain developed democratic institutions. Power shifted and civilian groups got the vote. The armed forces could no longer be a corner stone of the system and their position weakened in favor of the government. One of the changes in 1987 and 1989 concerned the laws on the Escala Especial: the rules regarding the internal promotion of officers. These groups of officers were threatened by the changes and the reduced opportunities for internal promotion by having officers serve longer in the same rank.

Some of the officers wanted to unite, but unions or "associations with demands" were not allowed in Spain. Having no other option, the officers' wives formed an association until 1995, when the men took over and established an association themselves. The military top management opposed this development, as they already felt threatened by the measures taken by the government. A union would threaten their position even more but, by this time, the government did nothing to stop the uniting officers. The officers were strengthened by support from European union-organization Euromil and because Spain was a member of larger entities like the European Union. The power balances in the figuration military managerial elite, the government, and military unions had shifted in favor of the latter. The government was in need of an alliance with military associations and needed to conform to European consultative structures. This is why it was possible for the balance of power to shift.

In Ireland, a coalition of government and military management tried to prevent soldiers from uniting in the 1990s. However, all parties concerned were dependent on each other. Van den Bosch states "they were each other's enemies and allies" (2003:38). The societal changes that were responsible for a shift in power were connected to the violence in Northern Ireland, the goal of maintaining a good relationship with the United Kingdom, and participation in UN missions. The Irish State could not afford to lose the monopoly of violence, and in order to hold on to central authority it had to give in to the demands of the soldiers. Soldiers on UN missions were ambassadors of Ireland promoting the interests of the state. One of the goals the government tried to achieve by participating in peacekeeping missions was to obtain investments or grants to boost the economy. Now, 90 percent of the Irish soldiers are members. Officers, who originally tried to prevent unionization, are setting up organizations of their own.

Figurational approaches to the phenomenon of military unions can help us understand why they may or may not gain influence and be accepted as negotiating partners. Changes in societal strengths, which promote the openness of societies and which allow for moderate forms of conflict, form the preconditions for changes in power balances. The royal mechanism is at work when a shift in the power balance occurs.

Conclusion: Possibilities for
Future Uses of the Figurational Approach

Figurational approaches to military sociology are very promising. They offer alternative theoretical perspectives to the

> ### New Direction 6.5
>
> Just as Elias wrote about the taming of the warriors, it is likewise useful to study the possibilities for the taming of the warlords in so-called "failed states."

discipline and overcome the functionalist hegemony that is characteristic of this type of sociology. They do so by emphasizing processes and by analyzing the interdependencies between people and groups of people. In this respect, figurational studies enable the study of tensions between groups, postulating the theme that change normally comes from conflict. The royal mechanism is a heuristic tool that provides powerful theoretical leverage. It is conflict sociology, which has overcome the strangulating bias of Marxist structuralism. At the same time, figurational approaches are suitable for studying cultural processes and cultural patterns of interactions.

Though the applicability of figurational approaches is unlimited and the topics may vary infinitely, a few suggestions for further study can be made.

A classic topic in figurational studies concerns state-formation and violence (Zwaan 2001). State structures are connected to civilization and the failure of state formation processes can easily lead to decivilization. Zwaan gives several examples of this kind of research.

Just as Elias wrote about the taming of the warriors, it is likewise useful to study the possibilities for the taming of the warlords in so-called "failed states." Louis XIV used the court at Versailles to tame the French warriors, but what would it take for the United Nations to domesticate warlords in, for instance, Afghanistan?

Formation of a global identity and a common peace-keeping culture, including the way in which this global identity can be blended with the need for localized forms of identity, seems a useful project as well. With increasing inter-dependencies leading to worldwide peacekeeping and peace-enforcing attempts, the need for collaboration between soldiers of different nations grows and so does the need for a global identity directed at world peace.

New missions such as peacekeeping and peace-enforcing ask for a different kind of military. What is needed is a soldier with a strong capacity for self-control and inhibition of violence and thus we are faced with the paradox of the warrior-peacekeeper. We ask soldiers to keep the peace and, at the same time, we ask them to fight wars. The paradox is at its most extreme in those cases where an operation starts as a peacekeeping mission, but escalates into a peace-enforcing scenario. In such a situation, it is difficult for the solders to switch from the one extreme to the other. A related question, whether pacified soldiers from countries who normally only deploy soldiers for peacekeeping missions are able to fight wars, is also relevant from this perspective.

Many other suggestions for future research utilizing figurational approaches are possible, such as studying the uncivilized behavior of peacekeepers from civilized nations, nation building in post-war Iraq, and/or international collabo-ration. Figurational approaches will undoubtedly enrich the study of the military. The examples provided here of the naval profession, chivalrous cadets, and military unions are merely the beginning of a wide array of possible studies.

René Moelker

SUMMARY

Figurational approaches offer fresh theoretical perspectives for military sociology. They overcome the functionalist hegemony that is characteristic of the field. They do so by emphasizing processes and by analyzing the interdependencies between people and groups of people, i.e., figurations. In this respect, figurational studies allow for the study of tensions between groups, postulating the theme that change normally comes from conflict within the figuration. The royal mechanism is an ideal-typical way to portray the tensions in a figuration with three or more groups that resembles Marx's historical-dialectics. But, instead of two parties, as in the Marxist concept, the balancing act with three parties allows one of the parties to be the one who is "sitting pretty" (the tertius gaudens). The result of the tensions is comparable to Marxist dialectics: new institutions (the synthesis) develop from the tensions. The royal mechanism is a heuristic device that provides powerful theoretical leverage. The figurational approach overcomes the strangulating bias of Marxist structuralism. At the same time, figurational approaches are suitable for studying cultural processes and cultural patterns of interactions.

The royal mechanism is used by Elias himself in his studies in the genesis of the naval profession, where the King keeps the balance between the officers of noble descent (the gentlemen) and the nautically skilled seamen-commanders, the tarpaulins, originating from commoners. The naval profession develops out of the rivalries between the gentlemen and the tarpaulins. A fusion of the two groups is made possible by bringing the two groups together amidships, hence the name and origin of the educational institution the "midshipman." In turn, this synthesis creates new figurations and new tensions.

198

This development also contributes to the formation of norms and values, or habitus (Elias points at the parallel processes of sociogenesis and psychogenesis). As the percentage of nobles declines and the civilian component of the cadets' corps at military academies grows larger, there is an increasing need for learning how to behave, learning etiquette, and learning how to become a future member of the officer corps, because the cadets of common descent have not learned these things in their upbringing. Etiquette enhances diplomatic skills (knowing how to behave in every situation) and is therefore functional, even in present times, when the officer is deployed as peacekeeper. Etiquette provides safety in an environment where inequality is an organizational characteristic. Etiquette provides a means of distinction. It defines the groups to which people belong and contrasts them to other kinds of people who behave according to different standards.

The royal mechanism can also be applied to the genesis of military unions. In a three-party figuration of government, military establishment, and members of the military organization, shifts in societal strengths and intra-organizational balances of power create windows of opportunity for the establishment of consultative structures in which military unions play a role.

KEY TERMS AND CONCEPTS

• Figurational approach	• Royal mechanism
• Habitus	• Marxism
• Structuralism	• Etiquette

RENÉ MOELKER

STUDY AND DISCUSSION QUESTIONS

1. What makes the figurational approach different from mainstream functionalism?

2. Why did Elias consider his method and more specifically the "royal mechanism" superior to the Marxist dialectic method? Do you agree or disagree with the point Elias is making about Marxism?

3. How did the military profession evolve in your country? Are there similarities or differences with the genesis of the naval profession in England? Are there other professions that evolved along the same logic as Elias describes in his studies into the genesis of the naval profession?

4. Figurations influence the formation of cultural habits, norms, values, and standards of behavior that are described in etiquette books. What other sets of standards of behavior in or outside the military can you think of and how are they influenced by the figurations they are part of?

5. If military unions are allowed in your country, think of a figuration and of groups/parties using the royal mechanism in a way that could explain the genesis of military unions.

NOTES

1. As there are many studies outside the field of military sociology, it is impossible to give an overview. The interested reader can find such an overview at the site of the Elias Foundation (www.norberteliasfoundation.nl/index_FS.htm).

200

2. Here, Elias borrows from George Simmel the concept of "tertius gaudens." The third party, the king, occupies the best position for he manages to divide and rule the other parties involved.

3. These objectives of the study show a remarkable parallel with the studies that Elias published together with Dunning on sports (fox hunting, boxing, and soccer) and leisure time (Elias and Dunning 1966). In the studies of sports, the object is also the psychogenesis and sociogenesis of English culture.

4. Based on the occupational classification by Van Tulder (1962:22), Layer 1: Mainly free and academic professions, executive officers of large companies, secondary school teachers, very senior civil servants; Layer 2: Mainly higher employees, executive officers of small companies, senior civil servants, large farmers and market gardeners, intermediate technicians; Layer 3: Mainly large to intermediate old and new trades people, intermediate civil servants, intermediate farmers and market gardeners, intermediate employees; Layer 4: Mainly small old and new trades people, skilled laborers, small farmers and gardeners, office clerks, lower employees, lower civil servants; Layer 5: Mainly practiced laborers, lower civil servants; Layer 6: Mainly unpracticed laborers.

REFERENCES

Abrahamsson, B. 1972. *Military Professionalization and Political Power*. London: Sage Publications.

Bourdieu, P. 1984. *Distinction: A Social Critique of the Judgment of Taste*. London: Routledge.

Bourdieu, P. and J. C. Passeron. 1977. *Reproduction in Education, Society and Culture*. Beverly Hills/London: Sage Publications.

Caforio, G., ed. 1994. "The Military Profession in Europe." *Current Sociology* (Special Issue) 42(3).

_____. 1998. *The Sociology of the Military*. Cheltenham: An Elgar Reference Collection.

_____. 2003. "Unionization of the Military." Pp. 311-319 in *Handbook of Sociology of the Military,* edited by G. Caforio. New York: Kluwer/Plenum.

Dandeker, C. 1978. "From Patronage to Bureaucratic Control: The Case of the Naval Officer in English Society 1780-1850." *British Journal of Sociology* 29(3):300-320.

Durkheim, E. 1947. *La règles de la méthode sociologique* (The Rules of Sociological Method). Paris: Plon.

Elias, N. 1939. *Ueber den Prozess der Zivilisation* (The Civilizing Process). Basel: Haus zum Falken.

_____. 1950. "Studies in the Genesis of the Naval Profession." *British Journal of Sociology* 1(4):291-309.

_____. 1969. *Die höfische Gesellschaft* (The Court Society). Neuwied: Luchterhand.

_____. 1977. "Drake en Doughty. De ontwikkeling van een conflict" [Translation by Nelleke Fuchs-van Maaren of the unpublished "Drake and Doughty: A Paradigmatic Case Study"]. *De Gids* 140(5-6):223-237.

_____. 1978. *What is Sociology?* London: Hutchinson.

_____. 2001. "Estudos sobre a gênese da profissão naval: cavalheiros e tarpaulins" (Studies in the Genesis of the Naval Profession: Gentlemen and Tarpaulins). *Mana* 7(1):89-116.

_____. 2003. "Etudes sur les origines de la profession de marin" (Studies in the Genesis of the Naval Profession). *Les Champs de Mars* 13.

Elias, N. and Dunning, E. 1966. "Dynamics of Sport Groups with Special Reference to Football." *British Journal of Sociology* 17:388-402.

Finkelstein, J. 1989. *Dining Out. A Sociology of Modern Manners.* Cambridge: Polity Press.

Groen, P and W. Klinkert. 2003a. *Studeren in uniform. 175 jaar Koninklijke Militaire Academie 1828-2003* (Students in Uniform. 175 years Royal Netherlands Military Academy 1828-2003). Den Haag: Sdu.

_____. 2003b. "Dutch Dilemmas." Pp. 57-80 in *NL Arms 2003 Officer Education: The road to Athens*, edited by H. Kirkels, W. Klinkert, and R. Moelker. Breda: Royal Netherlands Military Academy.

Goudsblom, J. 1987. *De sociologie van Norbert Elias,* Amsterdam: Meulenhoff [The Sociology of Norbert Elias].

Goudsblom, J. and Mennell, S.J. (eds) 1998. *The Norbert Elias Reader: A Biographical Selection,* Oxford: Blackwell.

Harries-Jenkins, G. 1977. "Trade Unions in Armed Forces." Pp. 54-73 in *Military Unions: U.S. Trends and Issues,* edited Taylor et al. Beverly Hills: Sage.

Heckers, J. 1998. *Noch noodig, noch gewenscht. Honderd jaar vakbond voor militairen* (Not Needed, Nor Wanted. Hundred Years Union for Soldiers). Delft: Eburon/AFMP.

Heerma van Voss, A. J. and A. Van Stolk, eds. 1989. *De geschiedenis van Norbert Elias* (The History of Norbert Elias). Amsterdam: Meulenhoff.

Hurd, G. 1973. *Human Societies: An Introduction to Sociology.* London: Routledge and Kegan Paul.

Janowitz, M. 1960. *The Professional Soldier: A Social and Political Portrait.* New York: Free Press.

Klinkert, W. 1998. *100 Jaar Cadettencorps* (100 Years Cadet's Corps). Tilburg: Tilburg University Press.

Korte, H. 1997. *Über Norbert Elias. Das Werden eines Menschenwissenschaftlers* (On Norbert Elias. The Genesis of a Scientist in the Study of Men). Opladen: Leske und Budrich.

Kruijf, F. de and F. Lardenoye. 1991. *Over lef gesproken! 25 jaar VVDM* (Talk about Guts! 25 Years of a Soldiers Union). Breda: De Geus.

Kuipers, G. 2001. *Goede humor, slechte smaak. Nederlanders over moppen* (Good Humor, Bad Taste. Dutch People on Telling Jokes). Amsterdam: Boom.

Lammers, C. J. 1969. "Strikes and Mutinies: A Comparative Study of Organizational Conflicts between Rulers and Ruled." *Administrative Science Quarterly* 14:558-572.

Mennell, S. 1989. *Norbert Elias. Civilization and the Human Self-Image.* Oxford: Blackwell.

Moelker, R. 2003a. "Méér dan een beroep" (More than a Profession). In *Krijgsmacht en Samenleving, klassieke en eigentijdse inzichten* (Armed Forces and Society, Classic and Current Views), edited by R. Moelker and J. Soeters. Amsterdam: Boom.

_____. 2003b. "Elias, Maritime Supremacy and the Naval Profession On Elias' unpublished Studies in the Genesis of the Naval Profession." *British Journal of Sociology* 54(3):373-390.

_____. 2003c. "The Last Knights." Pp. 81-100 in *ARMS 2003 Officer Education. The road to Athens*, edited by H. Kirkels, W. Klinkert, and R. Moelker. Breda: Royal Netherlands Military Academy.

Moelker, R. and J. Soeters. 1998. "Democratization of Recruitment. On the Social Origins of Cadets." Pp. 121-135 in *The European Cadet: Professional Socialisation in Military Academies,* edited by G. Caforio. Baden-Baden: Nomos Verlagsgesellschaft.

Norbert Elias Archive. Inventory of part 1, Marbach Am Neckar, Germany.

_____. 503. Text of outline of "The Genesis of the Naval Profession."

_____. 505. Manuscript with note with heading "Copies of Development in France and Spain and Beginnings in England," pp.13-62, incomplete, carbon copy.

_____. 507. Manuscript of "Studies in the Genesis of the Naval Profession." 2. "The Formative Conflict," pp.1-13, unfinished.

_____. 508. Manuscript with note with heading "Growth Henry VIII t. Charles I," pp.14-25. 1955.

_____. 510. Manuscript of "The Genesis of the Naval Profession. Gentlemen into Seamen," pp.1-22, incomplete, carbon copy with handwritten corrections.

_____. 513. Manuscript with note with heading "Development of Midshipman with French Comparison," pp.7-17, version with mark A, incomplete.

_____. 517. File concerning "Studies in the Genesis of the Naval Profession," with numbered pages belonging to several manuscripts.

_____. 518. File concerning manuscripts of "Studies in the Genesis of the Naval Profession," with notes, unnumbered pages and newspaper clippings.

_____. MISC-D X = Paris 3: Transcription de l'éxposé présenté par Norbert Elias au Colloque Historique Franco-allemand, en date du 17 mars 1983 (Transcript of a presentation at the Historical French-German Colloquium 17-3-1983).

Royal Netherlands Military Academy. 1993. *Blue Book.* Breda, The Netherlands: RNMA.

_____. 2003. "Table Manners" (Videocassette). Breda, The Netherlands: RNMA.

Schouten, J. E. 2003. *Gewapende mannen, geweldloze strijd ... Opkomst en vestiging van een belangenorganisatie voor Spaanse militairen* (Armed Men, Fight Without Violence...Rise and Establishment of an Interest Group for Spanish Soldiers). Master's Thesis, Department of Anthropology, Free University Amsterdam, The Netherlands.

Sennett, R. 1977. *The Fall of The Public Man. On the Social Psychology of Capitalism.* New York: Alfred A. Knopf.

_____. 2003. *Respect in a World of Inequality.* New York: W.W. Norton & Company.

Smith, D. 2001. *Norbert Elias & Modern Social Theory.* London: Sage Publications.

Soeters, J. 1998. "Valeurs militaires, valeurs civiles: vers le soldat-communicateur" (Military and Civic Values, Towards the Soldier Communicator). *Journal of Political and Military Sociology* 26(2).

Teitler, G. 1972. *Toepassing van geweld* (The Use of Violence). Meppel: Boom.

_____. 1974. *De wording van het professionele officiersko-rps. Een sociologisch-historische analyse* (The Genesis of the Professional Officers' Corps. A Sociological Historical Analysis). Rotterdam: Universitaire Pers Rotterdam.

_____. 1977. *The Genesis of the Professional Officers' Corps.* London: Sage Publications.

Tilly, C. 1992. *Coercion, Capital, and European States, AD 990-1990.* Cambridge: Basil Blackwell.

Van den Bosch, F. E. 2003. *The Establishment of the Irish Association for Soldiers.* Master's thesis, Free University, Department of Anthropology, Amsterdam, The Netherlands.

Van Doorn, J. A. A. 1956. *Sociologie van de organisatie* (The Sociology of the Organization). Leiden: Stenfert Kroese.

———. 1965. "The Officer Corps: A Fusion of Profession and Organization." *Archives Européennes de Sociologie* VI(2):262-282.

———. 1971. "Militaire en industriële organisatie" (Military and Industrial Organization). Pp. 207-231 in *Organisatie en Maatschappij*. Leiden/Antwerpen: Stenfert Kroese.

———. 1974. *The Soldier and Social Change*. Beverly Hills/London: Sage Publications.

Van Doorn, J. A. A. and M. Janowitz. 1968. *Armed Forces and Society. Sociological Essays*. The Hague: Mouton.

Van Hessen, J. S. 1965. "Elitevorming door apartheid – Een historisch-sociologische analyse" (Elite Formation through Apartheid – An Historical-Sociological Analysis). In *Beroepsvorming in internaatsverband* (Vocational Training in Boarding Schools), edited by J. A. A. van Doorn. Rotterdam: UPR.

Van Hoof, J. A. P. 1977. "Belangengroepen in de krijgsmacht" (Interest Groups in the Armed Forces). Pp. 323-335 in *Welzijn en krijgsmacht* (Welfare and Armed Forces), edited by H. J. H. Brentjens and C. F. Turpijn. Deventer: Van Loghum Slaterus.

Van Krieken, R. 1998. *Norbert Elias: Key Sociologist*. London: Routledge.

Van Tulder, J. J. M. 1962. *De beroepsmobiliteit in Nederland van 1919 tot 1954. Een sociaal-statistische studie* (Occupational Mobility in the Netherlands from 1919 to 1954). Leiden: Stenfert Kroese.

Wouters, C. 1976. "Is het civilisatieproces van richting veranderd?" (Has the Civilization Process Changed Course?) *Amsterdams Sociologisch Tijdschrift* 3:336-360.

_____. 1985. "Formalisering van informalisering. Veranderingen in omgangsvormen, vooral tussen de sexen in Nederland: 1030-1985" (Formalization of Informalization. Changes in Manners, in Particular Between the Sexes in the Netherlands 1030-1985). *Sociologisch Tijdschrift* 12:133-162.

_____. 1990. *Van minnen en sterven* (Of Loving and Dying). Amsterdam: Bert Bakker.

_____. 1993. "Ja, ja, ik was nog niet zoo 'n beroerde kerel, die zoo 'n vriend had' (Nescio)" (Yes, I wasn't Such a Bad Guy, Having a Friend Like That). In *Over Elias,* edited by H. Israëls, M. Komen, and A. De Swaan. Amsterdam: Het Spinhuis.

Zeegers, W. 1988. *Andere Tijden, Andere Mensen. De sociale representatie van identiteit* (Other Times, Other People. The Social Representation of Identity). Amsterdam: Bert Bakker.

Zwaan, T. 2001. *Civilisering en decivilisering. Studies over staatsvorming en geweld, nationalisme en vervolging* (Civilizing and Decivilizing. Studies into Nation Formation and Violence). Amsterdam: Boom.

C h a p t e r

ARMED FORCES, NATION, AND MILITARY OFFICERS: FRANCE AT THE CROSSROAD?

Claude Weber

Centre de Recherche des Ecoles Militaires de Saint-Cyr
Coëtquidan
France

LEARNING OBJECTIVES

After reading this chapter, you should be able to

- understand that military institutional life cannot be equated directly with specific actions of its members;
- understand how collective perceptions and social representations are not necessarily the same thing;
- appreciate that civil-military relations can take of variety of forms and can be conceived of in multiple ways;
- appreciate how important physical presence is for the military institution in generating positive collective representations of itself;
- appreciate some of the challenges related to the movement from a draft system toward an all-volunteer force.

The subject matter of this chapter concerns the recurring questions and concerns related to the future of the relationship between the nation and the armed forces in France. Indeed, military sociologists must strive to understand the social dynamics of civil-military relations. The social constructs linking a society and its armed forces greatly influence how the military is funded, how its forces are structured, the types of roles it will be assigned, etc. Hence, it is important to look beyond legislation, official discourses, and policies about the armed forces to understand the social dynamics between armed forces and society. An important dimension in uncovering how social constructs emerge is the genesis of social representations, i.e., the long-term mechanisms that allow people to develop perspectives about a given topic.

In France, if one listens to some vocal military officers, it appears that the armed forces are no more part of the French society and that its future is a grim one, and soon they will be forgotten. This opinion is particularly prevalent in the Army (land forces). Such concerns seem to have grown since 1996, when the French armed forces were professionalized (i.e., that France officially abandoned the draft system to move toward an all-volunteer force). However, for the vast majority of people—civilians, soldiers from other services, or other personnel categories—the issue surrounding the nation-armed forces relationship do not mean much. Yet, this theme pervades Army officers' discourse quite significantly, and its persistence warrants further investigation. While considering a number of indicators, this chapter seeks to uncover the basis for such concerns and show that the nation-armed forces relationship in France is a healthy one, and that the armed forces are more touch with new social realties than they have ever been.

First, it is important to understand what is meant by the "nation-armed forces relationship." In the eyes of many people in France, having 300,000 young French men passing through the military institution annually creates the only actual, or at least significant, link between the civilian world and the military one. Hence, for many, there is a unique and positive bond that is created through the draft system between the population and the armed forces. Military personnel systematically stress the values instilled in conscripts (punctuality, hygiene, discipline, and respect). Such a bond is also construed as being highly beneficial to the French Republic at large by providing, among other things, the following benefits: it is a tool for the integration and training of young people; it creates a level playing field by eliminating illiteracy among the conscripts; it allows for the elaboration of useful medical statistical databanks; and it provides a better representation of society within the armed forces as conscripts are drawn from all regions and social classes.

Having said this, it is clear that the nation-armed forces relationship is actually complex and difficult to assess. Furthermore, the expression itself raises a number of issues. First, it does not adequately encapsulate the experience of the concerned military officers. If one questions those who express fear about a rupture between the military and society, it is apparent that the bond they refer to are the ones established, and cultivated, by members of the military institution with individuals, social groups, and organizations outside the military; it is not about the relationship with the "nation" or the "state" itself. Their perspective is, therefore, a very concrete one, but also one that is not comprehensive or institutional in nature, as the linkages with specific individuals, social groups, and organizations are, by definition, idiosyncratic. At best, one could refer to worries about the relationship between the military institution and civil society. It would be more adequate to present those worries as being about civil-military relations or even social-military relations.

The second issue that the expression "nation-armed forces relationship" raises concerns the notion of relationship. The use of the singular term "relationship" seems inappropriate for conveying the reality we are studying. Military officers who are concerned about the status of the relationship seem to have a monolithic understanding of the concept of a bond. It is either good or bad, present or absent. It is not clear if, for instance, they construe civil-military relations as simply a direct phenomenological experience of the military "thing," implying that since the abolition of the draft fewer than ever are experiencing the military "thing." In other words, can we reduce what is likely to be generated by face-to-face interactions with the military to some kind of grand social bond? It appears that many of those worried military officers have a rather simplistic view of what constitutes a national bonding experience.

To be fair to those military officers, however, the abolition of the draft system also caused concerns among civilian authorities who were worried about losing some of the personal advantages they were getting from the draft system.[1] It is not surprising, therefore, that the theme of the "nation-armed forces relationship" became quite prominent within the chain of command. More importantly, however, worries about the future of the relationship were also related to concerns about the loss of some specific benefits to specific individuals. Again, an understanding of the very notion of relationship, or national bond, is not something that should be taken for granted. Obviously, there are different approaches, and conclusions, about how professionalization interacts with the relationship between the armed forces and society.

It is clear that, depending on how we consider the phenomena it may or may not refer to, there are a variety of ways to conceive of professionalization and the relation between

212

the armed forces and society. Our standpoint is (1) direct inter-action is only one among many possible forms of the relationship; (2) this relationship can be positive, neutral, or negative; and (3) a relation can be assessed according to various standards, its presence or its absence, its regularity, and its intensity.

The Origin of the Issue

The issue of the relationship between the armed forces and the nation, although it involves specific and concrete applications, such as the improvement of literacy, is fundamentally about examining the military institution as a whole. Yet, like any collective representation, or social construct, it draws upon multiple roots, but not all are necessarily in line with how reality is lived and perceived. One of the older, and now outdated, perceptions of the military institution in France is linked to the idea of conscripts as the "sons of the nation." In other words, every young man is construed as a "grown-up child," who will support and defend the well-being of his parent (i.e., the Republic) and the rest of his "family" (i.e., French society). This view clearly implies that over half of the French popula-

---

New Direction 7.1

Unless one believes in the supremacy of a man-centered universe or in a patriarchal order, it appears difficult to support the idea that conscription can be used to build a truly encompassing bond between the military world and the civilian one.

213

tion of the age groups concerned (i.e., young women) is rather a liability. Unless one believes in the supremacy of a man-centered universe or in a patriarchal order, it appears difficult to support the idea that conscription can be used to build a truly encompassing bond between the military world and the civilian one.

Another misleading view about conscription has to do with the compulsory nature of these encounters. Military officials are not always fully aware of the diversity of conscripts' reactions to conscription. Those reactions, built over the 10 or 12 months spent in the armed forces, range from indifference to utter rejection. Hence, those who regret the direct physical connection with the military tend to forget that for many young people, the military experience was not always completely positive. The military service itself may, indeed, be a significant contributor of negative views toward the armed forces (especially the Army).

Although the image of the armed forces remains, overall, positive, it is clear that the Army has a somewhat lower popularity score than the Navy or the Air Force (Ministère de la Défense – SGA/DICOD/C2SD 2002).

New Direction 7.2

The discrepancy between the theoretical benefits of the draft system (a certainty to which people in the Army tend to cling) and the reality experienced by the draftees was sometimes significant. The numerous lampoons relating to the experience of some of the draftees bear witness to this discrepancy.

The lower support for the Army may be because the majority of conscripts (60 percent) were sent to Army battalions; whereas the Navy and the Air Force, on the other hand, were more selective in choosing their conscripts. The Army had to handle the bulk of conscripts, which seems to also partly account for the fact that questions and concerns recorded about the future of the nation-armed forces relationship emanated mostly from Army officers and NCOs.

In some of its collective representations, however, the military service is still perceived as a rather pleasant experience, especially once one is discharged from military obligations. The sharing, for example, of so called Army "war stories" (even if they only involve training in the field) is a usual scenario where former draftees tends to value their experience in the Army. Still, military obligations indisputably generate a certain number of negative representations, as well as certain stereotypes about the armed forces in general, and the Army in particular. In those cases, the relationship created is not always positive for the institution, and the officers and NCOs who are rightly concerned about the loss of the direct relationship are not always aware of this. The discrepancy between the theoretical benefits of the draft system (a certainty to which people in the Army tend to cling) and the reality experienced by the draftees was sometimes significant. The numerous lampoons relating to the experience of some of the draftees bear witness to this discrepancy.

The Emergence and/or Consolidation of the Military-Society Relationship

Civil-military relations are actually constructed and conveyed through many other means. Those other means tend to show that since the army has become an all-volunteer force, it appears

215

New Direction 7.3

France is the only country to have set up a one-day drill call up, which shows the significance that policy makers and army personnel attached to the relationship between the French civilians and the armed forces.

---

more able to create stronger, more numerous, and enduring links between civilians and soldiers. This argument is now presented with a number of examples and indicators.

The JAPD[2]

In the wake of the suppression of the military service, the French Ministry of National Defense created the JAPD (a one-day drill call up) to be used as a sort of mandatory information session about the armed forces for all young adults. France is the only country to have set up such a scheme, which points out the significance that policy makers and army personnel attached to the relationship between the French civilians and the armed forces. We can quite logically make the assumption that reducing military duty for young people into one single day within a military structure is an effective way to bring down the number of negative opinions. Conversely, it is doubtful that this limited encounter would establish strong and enduring links. Nevertheless, the truth is that these interactions do exist. On the other hand, that the JAPD concerns young men as well as young women is an indication of a more equitable, more desirable evolution.

216

Communication

The second indicator under study partly derives from concerns related to recruiting, and the associated development of public communication capacities within the French Ministry of Defense. It is clear that the professionalization of the armed forces has tremendously boosted the importance of any activities having to do with communication within the Ministry of Defense and its various services and branches (Weber 2002).

The development of public communication was made possible by setting up adequate human resources (recruiting officers, under contract to the army, specialized in the field of public communication), as well as technical resources (procurement of equipment and technologies). The increase in resources was also accompanied by a restructuring of the administration of recruitment and new partnerships sharing responsibilities in the various fields of public communication within the Ministry of Defense (creation of the Delegation to Defense Communication and Information (DICOD) and a redistribution of tasks). This resulted in the systematic improvement of public communication in an institution that no longer deserves its nickname—"The Dumb Institution." Newspapers, advertising campaigns, encounters with Defense representatives, and collaborations on the production of documentaries and movies, are just a few examples of practices that foster transparency and an opening up of the Ministry of Defense. The fear of being perceived as part of an "inward-looking" community has forced military personnel to learn how to become effective communicators. From our standpoint, constant exchanges with journalists and experts in communication studies, particularly where the training of military communicators is concerned, constitutes a major evolution in the relationships between military and civilian environments.

Communication has now come to the forefront, whereas, in the past, public communication tasks were seen as insignificant (the tasks were "shelved" according to the set expression).

The Link with University and Research

When considering the objectives of openness and transparency, the multiplication of exchanges between the military and the scientific community should be highlighted. Whatever the subject or field of study (sociology, economy, ethnology, law), researchers are taking an increasing interest in the military. The field of military sociology has, for example, quite recently garnered significant attention at the first congress of the FAS (French Association for Sociology, February 2004). Thus, academics are interacting with military personnel, examining their lives, and analyzing military structures, issues, etc. In short, they create links that not only contribute to the acquisition of knowledge concerning an environment too long ignored by the scientific community—as well as by the public—but they are also bringing the civilian world and the military world together. The ministry plays an important role in this process and fosters such positive agendas as increasing the number of scholarships given to researchers working on defense maters, the organization of symposia and conferences, publications, etc.

Recruiting from New Types of Profiles

As soon as the announcement of the reform was made in 1986, the question of the renewal of military strength became central (Weber 2001:49-72). The ensuing requirement of increasing personnel prompted the services to give an even greater place to women, who can today be assigned any tasks apart from

218

assignments on submarines or combat units. Women account for about 10 percent of the army. The representation of women in the armed forces is improving (i.e., the female ratio) and the ratio of so-called "visible" minorities is improving substantially.

In order to deal with the problem of maintaining adequate personnel levels, the armed forces have implemented new recruiting techniques, offering candidates the opportunity of a short-term career if they wish. First, professional experience is provided, providing candidates with the opportunity to acquire training and their first job placement. Considered a method of re-training, these new options enable the armed forces to perform a more thorough selection of candidates and, consequently, create more opportunities to keep the best recruits who are likely to opt, eventually, for a military career. These new recruiting policies further enhance the exchanges between the military and civilian environments. Furthermore, the renewed flow of personnel and skills can improve the relationships between militaries and civilians; the bonds forged often reach far beyond the experience shared during a work-contract period. Even if they do not remain in the military, the training gives many young people their first "break" and, as a result, they have a much more positive view of their military experience.

The Importance of Training

As the largest employer of entry level personnel in France (400 different jobs available in the Army, 35 specialties for the Navy, 50 for the Air Force), the armed forces are increasingly perceived as a national leader in personnel training expertise. The Navy, for example, enjoys a tremendous reputation and an outstanding re-employment rate for its re-trained personnel. Quite a number of specializations have an equivalent in the civilian environment and, as a result, these data show a strengthening of exchanges between military and civilian society.

Here is another illustrative example: Recent reforms concerning the instruction and training of Army officers in Saint-Cyr Military Academy are significant because cadets enjoy greater autonomy and responsibility, and get increasingly involved in their own education. They attend a three-month training course abroad and receive more consistent academic teaching. This curriculum brings them closer to the experience of students in civilian universities, while preserving the specificity of their military education. Let us hope the "rapprochement" will enable these future officers and military leaders to optimize the relations they will eventually establish with their civilian counterparts.

Daily Life in Units

Notably, one can examine activities in the daily life of military personnel, which foster the multiplication and the improvement of exchanges between civilians and the armed forces. Externalization, or contracting out to civilian firms a number of tasks that were once devolved to the military (e.g., catering, cleaning), is a first such example. This new distribution of tasks, sometimes viewed as the intrusion of the civilian world, amounts to the loss of some military prerogatives, while still remaining an obvious source of local exchanges in places where regiments are based.

An important trend is the increasing employment of non-military personnel (an estimated ratio of 15 percent of civilians—all services considered), either on a contractual or permanent basis, within the Defense administration. This trend gradually puts an end to the isolation of soldiers in their barracks, as they interact with civilian co-workers on a daily basis. Parallel to the greater use of civilians, one can also observe the greater use of reservists to support the daily operations of regular units. Both of these human resources policies represent significant methods for maintaining relations between the military and the civilian society.

Even if huge efforts have been made to upgrade housing quarters within units (specifically for the Army volunteers), institutional authorities are increasingly keen on having the soldiers live within the city instead of being isolated by living either in the barracks or a neighborhood inhabited exclusively by military personnel, as was done in the past. This factor, regarded as the outcome of the coming together of civilians and soldiers, may best illustrate the increasing relationship between the nation and the armed forces.

Similarly, military ceremonies (parades and so on) systematically take place within cities. The taking over of military buildings in town centers for exhibitions, symposia, or various events organized by people in uniform, are in keeping with the same logic of a greater presence among the civilian population.

Quality Relations?

Having established the growing relationship between civilians and the military, it is important to also consider the various

---

New Direction 7.4

It seems difficult to believe that this one-day encounter will establish strong and enduring relationships, but we have already pointed out that a few months of life-sharing was no guarantee of success in this field either.

221

dimensions of relationships (direct or indirect interaction, assessment of its presence or absence, regularity, and intensity), to determine the *quality* of the relationship. Whether we proceed from an institutional perspective or, on the contrary, a civilian one, assessments and judgments will obviously vary. The last section of this chapter will enable us to draw conclusions about the quality of the relations established and nurtured between people in uniform and civilians, between the military and society.

The one-day drill call-up indisputably creates a direct link, an encounter, between the representatives of the Army, Air Force, and Navy (as well as the Gendarmerie) on the one hand, and, on the other, all the French people in the age categories concerned. Those in uniform mostly viewed this contact as positive, even if many in the armed forces think the system could be improved (i.e., too short, too costly, etc.). The Army can, indeed, promote a better understanding of itself through drills and awareness days (discussions about the need and the "raison d'être" of defense, the role of the armed forces, etc.), or even appeal to possible candidates about prospective military careers.

As far as young people's outlooks are concerned, opinions are mixed. Some think this day is a waste of time; mere cramming that does not enable one to obtain an adequate knowledge of military or defense matters. Others, on the contrary, find some interest in them. Quite obviously, this relationship has some positive elements for young men and women. In the case of the negative opinion, we may very well think that such an unpleasant one-day experience will have less impact, than several months of military service. It seems difficult to believe that this one-day encounter will establish strong and enduring relationships, but we have already pointed out that a few months of life-sharing was no guarantee of success in this field either.

The JAPD cannot be understood as a regular relationship (one day in all) or as intensive. Yet, the final assessment of the links established by the JAPD seems to be rather positive, on the whole, or at least not damaging to the military in terms of images and opinions.

There is a mutual benefit for both the public and the institution in setting up such direct interactions. The public, regardless of individual motivations, can acquire a better knowledge of military operations, and the military can enhance its positive image, as well as its recruiting capacities. Thus, from a corporate communications perspective, such "Armed Forces Day" events constitute frequent public relations exercises, which are, at times, omnipresent and intense, but dependent on the local context and the diversity of support available.

The relationships between the university and research are of various sorts. They are primarily direct if we consider the case of researchers in contact with military personnel; whereas they are indirect if, for example, we are referring to readers or potential audiences of research work, books, or conferences. It is important to underline, however, that often military personnel consider academic publications and conferences about military affairs as being "out-of-touch" with reality, and that people in uniform are ill-understood or unduly nettled. Yet, those activities are maintained and supported by the senior leadership of the armed forces because, in spite of those academic investigations and limitations, they offer many windows onto this poorly understood institution. This certainly constitutes substantial proof of the military institution's "open-mindedness." These relations are now more or less considered regular, and tend to intensify as noted above.

In considering new recruiting techniques, training, employment of civilians, and the reserve, we are dealing with direct or indirect relationships. The relationship is direct if we consider the interactions between individuals signing a contract (soldiers, civilians, or reservists), during instruction with their new employer, their colleagues, or their instructors. It is indirect if we take into account the exchanges generated by individuals wearing the uniform, or civilians from the Defense, as well as their families and friends within civil society. The influence on friends and relatives of individuals involved in these interactions can, however, be positive, negative, or neutral.

At first sight, with all of these actors being volunteers, the positive dimensions seem logical and, therefore, likely to be passed on to others. Such relationships will remain positive for the enlisted personnel and their friends and relatives if the respective expectations of both groups are fulfilled. If the experience in the Army is rewarding and enriching, military and/or civilian personnel will convey a propitious and positive image of the military. As a result, it is in the interest of the latter to look after its employees (promotions, free training, and regular retraining). These relationships are deemed positive, whatever the standpoint adopted. In addition, we can argue that for the Ministry of Defense, the setting up of short-term contracts, which implies a constant renewal of human resources, creates regular and consistent relationships with society. The same goes for the reserve: Relationships are bound to evolve, and the institution will have to make sure that people in the reserve remain satisfied.

Externalization first fosters direct relations between military personnel and employees of firms called "service-providers." Such exchanges can naturally extend to the close relatives and friends of the various people involved. These links can generally be seen as positive for outside firms because their personnel are offered work by the army. It is also positive for the army because they are free to change partners

---

New Direction 7.5

While reform initiatives have not always run smoothly, they nonetheless indicate growing relations between soldiers and civilians.

---

and explore other relationships. Such interactions are frequent, regular and widespread within the institution.

Another aspect of external relationships is military ceremonies. They foster direct interactions (personnel in uniform coming into contact with the public), as well as indirect ones (i.e., when the public who witnessed the ceremonies share their experience with others who did not attended them). These public manifestations are quite obviously positive, and this is a source of pride for the institution as well as for the civilians, who enjoy these types of parades. From an emotional perspective, these relationships are rather regular and intense.

This inventory highlights how most of the relationships mentioned offer both a direct and an indirect dimension, insofar as they reach beyond the involvement of those directly participating in the interaction. This includes the parents whose children experience the JAPD, readers of texts concerning field studies on the military, friends and relatives of civilian personnel, soldiers, or people in the reserve, and so on.

These initial direct relationships are extended through other relationship configurations and can, in the same way, be considered more or less intense and regular, and, therefore, can have positive, negative, or neutral aspects. The analysis based on the criteria considered also enables us to underline how generalized and comprehensive the relations among all personnel categories are. We can note, for example, that they are not geographically circumscribed.

Therefore, the choice of these few indicators seems to validate our assumption: Military-society relations are multiplying as well as strengthening, while offering optimistic prospects. Though reform initiatives have not always run smoothly and can often cause resistance, disinterest, or even concern over the possible "dislocation" of military specificity in the future (specificity being something many soldiers value), they nonetheless point out the increasing relations between soldiers and civilians. However, there are still some lingering questions for the military institution, such as how can it be better recognized, and how can it be better appreciated? In this field, the factor of time plays a crucial part. We must keep in mind how, in the past, decades of the draft system created, rather than repaired, differences between the military and the civilian world.

Conclusion

This chapter has been concerned with the existence, or absence, of a rift between the military and civilian society. French citizens have a history of a striking lack of interest in defense matters, except in times of crisis (engagement of troops, events, etc.). From this perspective, the professionalization does not seem to have made things worse. On the contrary, the debates generated by this unprecedented revolution in the French armed forces have only contributed to the positive evolution of opinions and representations concerning this institution, together with the men and women who comprise the institution. There is now a greater recognition of the French armed forces as being a more relevant and better-equipped organization, an organization that is more knowledgeable about modern technologies and social realities.

The concerns about the relationships between the nation and the armed forces are acute only among a specific fringe of the military population and, more precisely, within the Army, as our survey shows (particularly affected are officers and NCOs who were a few years into their career and who experienced the former system). Uncertainties are less prevalent among the younger generation of officers and NCOs whose attitudes seem to be in keeping with the logic we have tried to define throughout this article: the existence of a French Army whose relationships with civilian society are more diverse and positive.

SUMMARY

This chapter explored why some military officers in France are worried about a possible rupture of the nation-armed forces relationship. Those worries were generated after the abolition of the draft system in France, which was seen as the end of the actual relationship of so many citizens with the military institution. The nature of those worries is also explored as they are based on a very limited conception of the nation-armed forces relationship. The chapter then examined how new linkages have been created since France changed to an all-volunteer force. Those new linkages are found to be more positive, durable, and innovative than the ones that were allegedly created through the draft system. Overall, the social representation of the French armed forces appears to have been positively changed through the process of transformation toward an all-volunteer force. Therefore, the nation-armed forces relationship can be construed as stronger than ever in France.

KEY TERMS AND CONCEPTS

- Social bonds and relationships
- Civil society
- Social-military relations
- Draft system
- All-volunteer force
- Social representations Recruiting

STUDY AND DISCUSSION QUESTIONS

1. Do you think that abolishing the draft system can cause a "separation" between the military institution and its parent society? Why?

2. Is there really a risk of rupture between the armed forces and society in Western democracies? Where are those worries originating from?

3. How important is the physical presence of the military among the population in the constitution of civil-military relations?

4. Is it possible to effectively analyze the social representations of the military institution, while having the armed forces relatively secluded from the general population?

5. In the United States, there are some people who would like to re-introduce the draft system. Do you think that the re-introduction of the draft system might change the social representations of the armed forces in the United States?

NOTES

1. The Military Service gave some leverage to French politicians and, thus, they were very attached to the draft system (for instance, they could use their power to find a good place in the army for some of their constituents).
2. Journée d'Appel à la Préparation de la Défense.

REFERENCES

Ministère de la Défense, SGA/DICOD/C2SD. 2002. 10 ans de sondages - Les Français et la Défense - Analyses et Références (10 years of surveys - The French Public and Defense - Analysis and References). France: Ministry of Defense.

Weber, Claude. 2002. *La filière communication au sein de la défense: typologie, recrutement, formation et carrière* (The Communication Stream within National Defence: Categories, Recruiting, Training, and Career). France: Les Documents du C2SD.

Weber, Claude. 2001. "'L'armée de terre en 'campagnes': ses stratégies audiovisuelles de recrutement" (The Army in 'Operation': Its Audio-Visual Recruitment Strategies). *Les Champs de Mars, Cahiers du Centre d'études en sciences sociales de la défense. La documentation française, first semestre* 2001:49-72.

C h a p t e r 8

RITUALIZATION OF EMOTIONS IN MILITARY ORGANIZATION

Ljubica Jelusic
University of Ljubljana
Ljubljana, Slovenia

LEARNING OBJECTIVES

After reading this chapter, you should be able to

- appreciate the importance of management of emotions in military organizations;
- describe the difference between entropic and supportive emotions, and their respective importance in a military context;
- identify the critical role of institutional emotions in military organizations;
- explain the role that ritualization of emotions plays in military organizations;
- understand the impact of the postmodern condition on the management of emotions in military organizations.

New Direction 8.2

The military, as a social institution, cannot prohibit emotions. It regulates them in a prescribed way, which gives the impression that the behavior of the military is fully rational (misinterpreted as intellectual).

still remains open, considering that we do not know the answer to Durkheim's classical problem of "what binds the society together."

Emotional Culture

Emotions suffuse all social acts, underline them, and influence them in fundamental ways by establishing interactions and encounters (Perinbanayagam 1989:73). Emotions, in every culture, are expressed through special languages that include tone of voice and gestures, which are, more or less, controlled expressions of the face, hands, and body. Every member of the society must learn these languages, as they show the role, identity, and situation of the individual. Emotions, therefore, are presented in ritualized form, which helps to control, manage, and acceptably express them. People must exercise how to express these emotions, how to manage them, and how to balance them. In the process of a public presentation of emotions, there are specific patterns of meaning expressed in symbols, by which people communicate, maintain, and develop their knowledge of emotions. Gordon defines these patterns as *emotional culture*, transformed by language, rituals, procedures, art, and other symbolic forms (Gordon 1989:115).

Gordon has distinguished between *institutional* and *impulsive* meanings of emotion as two different orientations

233

within emotional culture (Gordon 1989:117), or two alternative sets of symbols, styles, habits, and skills pertaining to emotions. The military regulates the methods and types of emotional expression, which helps to establish the typical *institutional emotional culture. Impulsive emotional culture* refers to a spontaneous, uninhibited expression of emotions, unregulated by institutions, which may also happen in the military but would be a symbol of an undisciplined or a disintegrated military. The individual reaches the ideal of institutional emotional culture when he/she controls their feelings, their expressions, and their values. Impulsive emotions are spontaneous, not controlled or regulated by the institution, and are free of conventions and prescribed external expressions (Gordon 1989:117).

Entropic and Supportive Emotions in Military Organizations

Entropic emotions in the military are those that, traditionally, have been considered inappropriate for combat causing soldiers to be unprepared for warfare including lower rationality, a tendency to flight, disappearance from battles, psychiatric casualties, panics, or even military disintegration. We use the word "entropic" in order to express the consequences of the soldier's reaction that constitute the disintegration of individuals or units in armed conflicts and wars. Entropic emotions are fear, timidity, disgust, anxiousness, and boredom.

Fear, anxiousness, and timidity often derive from an awareness of the possibility of losing life and of the possibility of having to kill the enemy. Human beings are equipped with physiological mechanisms that guard against stress. These natural instincts help the individual recognize dangerous situations and react by fighting, posturing, submission, or

234

flight (Grossman 1996:7). In addition to the physiological reactions, there are cognitive reactions, when a human being evaluates the circumstances and chooses the most appropriate reaction. The ability to rationalize behavior decreases under the influence of stress. The psychological stress and emotional chaos may lead the soldier into physiological illnesses, such as heart troubles, blindness, paralysis, or deafness. As soldiers head into battle, they typically experience the emotion of anxiety. It appears in the form of nightmares, dreams that anticipate the experience of battle. Soldiers experience fear on a variety of levels. They fear death, they fear failure, they have fears concerning moral dilemmas; they are even fearful of showing others (their comrades) their fears.

Soldiers, who are close to the battlefield, or who are on the battlefield without fighting—typical for positional wars— experience the emotion of boredom. Contemporary military activities in peace support operations cause similar cases of emotional boredom in peacekeepers. These soldiers have to observe the dividing line between the opposing sides and often experience a lack of engagement in meaningful activities (Bartone, Adler, and Vaitkus 1998:589). Behavior in coping with boredom is sometimes very similar to a psychological disorder, because the soldier, in nervous exhaustion, often turns to alcohol, tobacco, and/or drugs to overcome this feeling.

The emotion of disgust is usually connected with the experience of a dead comrade or the killing of an enemy at short distances. It sometimes leads to psychological disorders.

The *supportive emotions* are, contrary to the entropic ones, important for creating bonds among soldiers. These emotions help to establish horizontal cohesion (between the comrades in units), vertical cohesion (between the soldiers and the leaders), organizational cohesion (the soldier's consciousness of belonging to the military), and cultural cohesion (the soldier's feeling of belonging to the civil environment and culture, civilization, homeland, or state). Supportive emotions are the basis of military cohesion and the readiness to fight. In peace support operations, where soldiers are not supposed to fight but, rather, are expected to mediate, supportive emotions may help to overcome the boredom, stress from inactivity, and the de-motivation caused by alienation from the mission's mandate and aims. The supportive emotions in the military are courage, eagerness, loyalty, appurtenance, and sometimes also anger and hate. The supportive emotions are not always culturally acceptable; however, they serve as stimulation in military activities.

Historically, in military science and the science of war fighting, the relation between the emotions and techniques of fighting was not always an important topic. More attention was focused on topics such as the economic influence on fighting (Toffler and Toffler 1993) or the impact of technologies on fighting tactics (O'Connell 1989). In addition, emotions have been neglected in fight planning. Gabriel (1987) has argued that military psychiatrists and military medical persons were not taken seriously when they tried to convince the commanders about the risks of psychological disorders. Psychological collapse is a reaction to long-lasting exposure to entropic emotions, deriving from the fear of death, injuries, and war; but, in the history of warfare, psychological collapse was treated as simply the cowardice and weakness of the individual soldier. Although the psychological effects of fighting[1] were known for a long time, the military psychiatric service, which would help in such situations, was only introduced in the U.S. war in Vietnam.

Grossman's discussion on the psychological costs of learning to kill in war and society is one of the very rare surveys on the anatomy of humans killing within their own species. He elaborated upon the concept of emotional distance through killing (Grossman 1996:156-170). The physical distance in war depends on technology, but there is also an emotional distance that increases or decreases the resistance toward killing. Grossman included the concepts of cultural distance, moral distance, social distance, and mechanical distance and their role in war and the act of killing. These various types of distance allow a killer to avoid and deny the reality of killing another human being (Grossman 1996:158).[2] The correlation between distance from the enemy and the proclivity to fire is obvious. The reactions and resistance to killing are less intense at a maximal physical distance from target, while bayoneting, stabbing, or killing with bare hands at "body distance" becomes almost unthinkable (Grossman 1996:97-98).

The most critical moments on the battlefields happen when combatants perceive other combatants as individuals, individuals they may even identify with, and refuse to kill. The so-called "no firers" indicate soldiers who resist firing at the enemy. Some of these soldiers engage in mock firing or do not even fire in the enemy's direction.[3] There are some examples of soldiers not firing because of strong psychological feelings. Gabriel has published the data collected among American

---

New Direction 8.3

Psychological collapse is a reaction to long-lasting exposure to entropic emotions, deriving from the fear of death, injuries, and war; but, in the history of warfare, psychological collapse was treated as simply the cowardice and weakness of the individual soldier.

---

soldiers in the Second World War, and it was discovered that only 15 percent of the soldiers actually fired at the enemy while being attacked. In elite units, which consisted of veterans, the percentage was higher (about 25 percent). According to Gabriel's data, 75 percent of the soldiers in World War II experienced intense fear, which prevented them from firing or defending (Gabriel 1987:70).

The emotional costs paid by soldiers participating in war are higher than the numbers of dead and wounded soldiers. Many demobilized veterans suffer from psychological stress disorder and post-traumatic stress syndrome (PTSS). PTSS was first recognized in the U.S. military after the end of the Vietnam War. For this reason, it was dubbed "Vietnam syndrome." Indeed, every war, or even battle, produces its own syndromes.[4]

The attitude of the combatant toward killing is, therefore, the consequence of a combination of a number factors: physical distance from the target; emotional distance, which is shaped by the recognition of the enemy as an individual human being; cultural distance between the combatants as an expression of similarity/difference of socialization, civilization, or values; and moral distance, which implies a consideration of the legitimacy of fighting objectives. Usually, each opposing side claims the other one as guilty, its leaders as criminals, and soldiers as misled terrorists, bandits, or guerrillas. These simplistic distinctions help build the basic ideology of enemies; the one tool that mobilizes soldiers and civilians against the target population.

The Ritualization of Emotions in Military Organizations

In order to establish institutional emotional culture in the military, the management of emotions must take place. Managing emotions means creating enduring relationships. An emotion is composed of different components. Gordon mentions five components: prototypical triggering situation, subjective feeling, expressive gestures, regulative norms, and the long-term course of consistent action toward the emotion's object (Gordon 1989:126). The military, while managing emotions, tries to redefine the situation of emotions, change the expressive gestures, impose regulative norms, and, sometimes, create consistent action. These attempts might be so powerful that the individual soldier reinterprets the emotion and no longer reflects on himself/herself or on his or her subjective feelings, but, rather, reflects on collective and institutionalized emotions internalized through trained emotional work.

The managing of emotions is, within the military framework, understood as the ritualization of emotions, where the quality, intensity, and duration of feelings, and also the expressive gestures, are normatively prescribed.

Rituals are highly standardized activities, occurring in special buildings or places in special time. The activities are repetitive. They serve as a way of canalizing emotions, and organizing social groups. Rituals are, therefore, symbolic behavior that is socially standardized and repetitive (Kertzer 1988:9).

The military organization, aware of the great risks of entropic emotions, ritualizes the methods of expression of these emotions in order to prevent the soldiers and units from psychological disorder. The individual member of the military, aware (or trained to be aware) of the importance of appropriate social relationship for his/her survival in risk situations, strives to express the socially valued feelings in an appropriate way. If soldiers do not achieve the institutional standards for emotional expression, they accept the responsibility for spoiling the social relationships in a unit.

239

> ### *New Direction 8.4*
>
> The ritualization of emotions may be regulated by military internal laws and prescriptions, or through learned codes of behavior institutionalized in informal ways. It is usually an ingredient of the general military culture that has been passed down from generation to generation of military professionals and privates.

The institutional rituals are helpful "rule reminders" (Gordon 1989:128) for the intensity, direction, and duration of emotional expression. The institutional rituals are not intended to hide emotions, as might be wrongly interpreted. They help to restrict the impulsive emotions—though they occur in immediate situations—to self-controlled or collective-controlled demonstration.

The demonstration of emotions through institutional rituals may be very touching. It helps create the framework to canalize the overloaded emotions, to relax, or to clean the moral burdens stemming from the fighting. Successful military work relies on the supportive emotions that increase the cohesion of the unit, establish the ideals, promote the heroes, and establish collective identity. The ritualization of emotions may be regulated by military internal laws and prescriptions, or through learned codes of behavior institutionalized in informal ways. It is usually an ingredient of the general military culture that has been passed down from generation to generation of military professionals and privates. It is a part of the professional code of conduct, which obliges the officers to generate the knowledge of the rituals in the incoming cohorts of the soldiers. The methods and the intensity of emotional expression depend on the circumstances in which the military

240

exists (peacetime or wartime), on the type of military social organization (institutional or occupational), and on military tradition.

Every military organization is aware of the possibility that entropic emotions may decrease soldiers' readiness to fight, and that exaggeration of the supportive emotions (like exaggeration of courage) may lead to mistakes and losses. In order to escape such developments, military organizations establish drills of emotional expression and/or activities concerned with the regulation of emotions. Indeed, emotions are among the most important tools for effective military results. In the terminology of the sociology of emotions, emotions in the military serve as the "emotional work" (Hochschild 1979, 1983; Šadl 1997:226), in which soldiers learn to regulate their emotions and adapt them to their occupational role.

The emotional work is of special value for military commanders. Military commanders do not experience a "market" relationship with soldiers (as do patrons and customers in the civil world of production). Nevertheless, they must regulate their emotions; they often have to pretend when using certain specific emotions; they often have to make a display of their emotions to be an effective leader; and they often use their own emotions to solicit supportive emotions from the soldier or to regulate the expression of entropic emotions in the unit. A well-trained unit is able to regulate the negative emotions, to change them in the spirit of expected tasks. For example, they are able to change sadness and grief over a dead comrade into anger against the enemy.

The military leader knows that he/she must prevent subordinates from expressing stressful emotions in public, in a military collective, in a unit, or among staff. The stressful emotions are doubt, fear, anxiety, tension, confusion, uncertainty, and depression (Šadl 1997:321). Doubt, confusion, and uncertainty are produced by a tentative situation on the battle-field, when there is a lack of communication, when comrades are not trustworthy, and when leaders are weak. The expression of these emotions is regulated and balanced through adequate military training, in which soldiers and commanders gain military skills, expertise, and professionalism.

If emotions are the basis for interaction between individuals, then they must be expressed in a way that enables the interaction of mutual understanding. The military strives to institute very clear interaction because of the possibility of mistakes in preparing for armed clashes. The regulative and expressive dimension of emotional ritualization or the "symbolization of emotions," is very important in the military. The gestures and expressions of emotions must be exact in order to help soldiers recognize them very quickly. Often, emotions are expressed in words, which because of the rationalization of time, is less acceptable for the military. The military most often uses gestures, symbols, rituals, and procedures. Excessive forms of emotional expression are not well accepted in the military, because they might destroy the cohesion of the unit, the collective identity, and the will to fight.

The military organization cannot abandon entropic emotions, even though these emotions might destroy the military's existence or the survival of its parts. By practicing and ritualizing the expression of entropic emotions, as well as exaggerated supportive emotions, the military helps soldiers react rationally, or in congruence with learned procedures, in psychologically trying circumstances. The learned behavior, which almost reaches the level of instinct, helps hide real emotions from the enemy.

The institutionally ritualized emotions may also cover real emotions. Šadl warns that the management of emotions, or even the exclusion of emotions in the institutional emotional culture, may not automatically produce "emotional robots" (Šadl 1997:242). The members of institutional emotional culture may pretend to follow the rules of emotional expression but, in reality, their subjective feelings are very different. This statement is perfectly valid for the military organization. In military activities, there are many unknown variables. The soldiers need education, training, and exercises in circumstances very near to reality in order for them to develop the necessary skills for survival (Shay 1994). Additionally, training that is exceptionally real, helps soldiers recognize the emotions that may develop among the unit in extreme circumstances.

Military Rituals

Generally, military organizations value and prefer collective expressions of emotion. There are different rituals for collective expressions of emotion: ceremonies, celebrations, parades, the singing of military songs, oaths, and farewells to dead comrades. The celebrations, especially parades, serve as rituals that increase eagerness, enthusiasm, inspiration, loyalty, and belonging. The rituals are full of symbols, such as military and country flags, ideological flags, and the unit's ensign. The soldiers are supposed to salute the flag in a special ritual, which is the way to greet and acknowledge the collective identity. The ritual of an oath entails the collective readiness to sacrifice. The songs and marches, sung by all soldiers, are usually drawn their military history; they help establish the feeling of permanence as a collective.

The farewell dedicated to dead comrades is one of the most touching military rituals. Most often, it is comprised of regimented procedures, which include a collective arrival to

243

the graveyard, lining-up, a collective volley fire, a special way of marching, a last farewell and tribute involving the waving of the unit's flag, singing or playing a chosen song, and a collective and controlled departure from the graveyard. With the exception of specific cultures that prescribe the expression of grief according to traditional and, perhaps, institutionalized forms (such as the traditional Balkan societies of Serbia and Montenegro where women are supposed to express grief in a special way of crying called *naricanje*), farewell rituals in civil society are generally not as regimented or controlled and are more impulsive, informal, and individualistic then the collective experience of military mourning rituals. The military must cry in collective and rationalized ways: all shouts, screams, cries, and farewells to dead comrades are expressed in one controlled volley fire. The burial of dead comrades is only one part of the military attitude toward death. After finished battles, militaries always try to collect dead bodies; sometimes there are organized services to collect corpses for hygienic reasons and as an expression of emotional support. All soldiers, prior to entering a war, must have the feeling that the military will bring him or her back to their family—to home—to be buried, with all military honors, and that the sacrifice that he or she is about to make will not be forgotten.[5]

An important part of military culture is piety toward dead comrades, even toward dead enemies. Militaries, during ceasefires, negotiate first for the exchange of corpses, injured combatants, and prisoners of war. Military graveyards[6] are an expression of military culture and are some of the most visited monuments of human history. Often they are arranged in a special way, with many simple tombstones lined up resembling a military formation. The similarity of the monuments is a symbol of equality in military organizations; military members are equal before death and in death.

The military celebrations, with parades and exhibitions of weapons, are devoted to forming a collective identity among military members and also between military and civil society. The military lives in two separate worlds: military praxis and the world of perception. In praxis, the military has to deter and defeat enemies, help in disaster relief, and contribute to stability and order. In the world of perception, the practical activities of the military are less visible, but people can still feel safe. The feeling of safety is a result of the *presence* of the military, not of its activities. The public has little direct contact with the military. This is unfortunate because it is on the basis of civilian-military contact that the military contribution to societal welfare can best be analyzed and evaluated. The number of people in Europe having direct experience with the military is rapidly decreasing, particularly in the past decade when the abolition of conscription took place all over the continent. The "decline of the mass armies" (Haltiner 1998) resulted in fewer conscripts passing the compulsory military service and, consequently, lower levels of military knowledge in civil society. In order to overcome this gap, the military must open the collective ceremonies to the public, showing the level of its readiness and also the representative pattern of social values among the soldiers.

The rituals enhancing the emotions of belonging are part of the professional culture and are formative for military cohesion. Military cohesion is an objective that assists soldiers in the execution of military activities. In units where soldiers know each other very well, and their emotional ties are very strong, unit cohesion prevents entropic emotions such as fear, uncertainty, and panic.

The rituals that develop the emotion of courage are connected with the emotions of belonging and unit cohesion. A brave soldier is ideal, and is needed to serve as an ideal type

245

for other soldiers. Heroes are awarded in rituals. This, in turn, encourages other soldiers to find their own courage and heroism.

Postmodern Military and the End of Collective Emotions

In the military sociology of the past decade, the paradigm of the postmodern military (Moskos, Williams, and Segal 2000) has gained a lot of attention and surveys. The researchers of the military also warn that the postmodern military cannot be confused with the post-cold war military organization (Booth, Kestnbaum, and Segal 2001). The *postmodern* military is a social structure distinguished from earlier military models by five organizational characteristics: (1) mutual interrelation of the military and civil sphere, (2) lower differences between the combat and logistic services, (3) change of mission from war-like to less intensive humanitarian and/or constabulary tasks, (4) tasks are executed in a multinational and less unilateral environment, under international oversight, (5) and the inter-nationalization of the armed forces (Moskos et al. 2000:2). These characteristics stem from the adaptability of the military to various value changes in the civil society and the global uncertainty of institutions in the future (Dandeker 1999).

In a *traditional* military organization, the institutional emotional culture prevails because it is developed on the basis of the collective identity and collective goals. In modern indi-vidualized society, and also *modern* military society, the collective goals are less prioritized. The readiness of the indi-vidual to adapt to group expectations is lower. The military organization, if it expects a thorough subordination of the indi-vidual, may end up with a lack of recruits. It is challenged by the contradiction between its collective identity and social individualization. There is also a significant change in the missions the political elite are posing to the military. The new

246

New Direction 8.5

A postmodern soldier must develop an institutional emotional culture that would help him/her to survive in the military group as well as in the relations toward the civilian population. The soldier would still need a great deal of solidarity with comrades, but also understanding and empathy with, and toward, civilians.

---

missions, such as humanitarian activities, peace support operations, and crisis response operations, would require a different organizational format for the military, as well as more specialized units to engage in these missions. The will to fight, incorporated into the collective identity, must give priority to the will to mediate, negotiate, understand, listen, and cooperate. The individualization of activities pleads for a variety of changes on the emotional level of military readiness. A postmodern soldier—the soldier of new missions—must develop an institutional emotional culture that would help him/her to survive in the military group as well as in the relations toward the civilian population. He/she would still need a great deal of solidarity with comrades, but also understanding and empathy with, and toward, civilians. In the traditional military, the collective identity was a dividing line between the military and civil society. In the postmodern military, the collective identity means forced and unauthentic emotions, which create a deeper gap in the emotional world of the individual soldier between his/her own impulsive emotional culture and the expected organizational collective culture of the military. However, the lowered importance of military collective culture, in the postmodern military, does not necessarily mean the exclusion of collective emotions; perhaps, it signifies a readiness to recognize more impulsive patterns of emotional culture.

Conclusion

The military organization is challenged by the traditional dichotomy of intellect and emotions. In order to escape the negative consequences of the intense emotions produced by the expectation of taking the lives of human beings, the military has developed rituals to manage these emotions. The result is an institutional emotional culture in which the entropic and supportive emotions are used to increase the readiness and effectiveness of the military. Impulsive emotions are, to a great extent, negated and the military collective is trained to canalize the expression of emotions that are easy to control. The postmodern military is placing less importance on the military collective and unit cohesion is subjected to the changed patterns of motivation.

SUMMARY

The expression and management of emotions is very important for the functioning of military organizations. There are two main groups of emotions that are significant to interaction in the military: entropic and supportive. Entropic emotions, often, are caused by the possibility of losing one's life in war and/or by the possibility of killing other human beings. If not managed properly, these emotions would lead to psychological stress and post-traumatic stress disorder. The supportive emotions are developed to create and improve unit cohesion, readiness for training, and the will to fight. A military organization must ritualize the expression of entropic and supportive emotions in order to lower the disorder, panic, and psychological causalities. In terms of the sociology of emotions, there are institutional and impulsive emotions in all organizations, as well as in the military. The institutional emotions are the most desired in the military, but in some specific situations the impulsive emotions are acceptable too, for example in heroic acts, which serve afterward as a group ideal. Modern military organizations are facing the loss of traditional and institutional characteristics, as well as the entrance of post-modern values, because of the individualization of behavior and freedom—a more impulsive expression of emotions. The rituals governing the expression these emotions are consequently more lax, modest, and even absurd.

This paper elaborated upon military emotions on the basis of paradigms from the sociology of emotions. It explained the entropic and supportive emotions in the military and continue with the phenomenon of the ritualization of emotional expression, which may be organized as institutional interaction or impulsive. The paper also interpreted current paradigms on the postmodern military, considering the process of change from collective emotions to more individual ones. A few of these military rituals were explained as examples of an elaborated theoretical approach.

KEY TERMS AND CONCEPTS

• Entropic emotions	• Psychological stress
• Supportive emotions	• Institutional emotions
• Management of emotions	• Ritualization
	• Postmodern military

STUDY AND DISCUSSION QUESTIONS

1. Discuss the importance of the sociology of emotions for the military.

2. Explain the emotional dimension of military life in cognitive and institutional terms.

3. Considering emotional culture, how are institutional and impulsive manifestations of emotion different?

4. Discuss the importance of managing emotions through ritualization within the military.

5. Does the postmodern military mean the end of collective emotions?

NOTES

1. The Yugoslav partisan troops in Second World War have experienced the so-called "storm illness," as the illness of those who had been fighting in storms (mostly to break the encirclement around the units).

2. Grossman supported his ideas using the examples from the Vietnam War. Nowadays, it is possible to observe similar problems occurring between U.S. soldiers and the local populations in Iraq. Soldiers strive to avoid the burden of killing by undermining the human characteristics of the "other side." Cultural distance means soldiers think of the enemy as someone distinctly different from themselves. It is based on ethnic and racial differences. Moral distance means an unshakeable conviction in one's own moral superiority. Social distance implies the socially stratified

250

perception of opposing sides. Mechanical distance refers to the effects of screens, thermal sights, sniper sights, through which the killer observes the victims as unreal, dehumanized (Grossman 1996:160).

3. The veterans from the Slovenian Ten-day war for Liberation in 1991 reported that sometimes they did not shoot into the direction of the soldiers of the opposing Yugoslav Peoples Army (YPA), but they postured or fired into the air. They were afraid that among YPA servicemen there might still be some Slovenian conscripts, or innocent conscripts in general, sent to the battlefield by orders of the pro-Serb nationalists against their will.

4. The war in Croatia (1991-1995) has produced several syndromes, mostly stemming from the longer battles of besieged cities (Vukovar, Dubrovnik).

5. The burial of the combatant might be, in extraordinary circumstances, executed on the battlefield, but after military operations have ended, the comrades come back, search for buried buddies, and re-bury them at home or at the military graveyards. The Albanian writer Ismail Kadare, in his novel *The General of the Dead Army*, harrowingly describes the military re-burial of Italian soldiers killed in Albania during the Second World War by Albanian partisans.

6. Part of the care for dead soldiers is a care for military graveyards. It is prescribed in military codes and in manuals designed to encourage and motivate the soldiers. The Manual of Austro-Hungarian Military *Mitt Gott für Keiser, König und Vaterland! Ein Patriotisches Soldatenbuch* by Carl Lutsch (1898) devoted two chapters to military death: one about honoring the military sacrifices, and the other dealing with the military graves.

251

REFERENCES

Bartone, Paul T., Amy B. Adler, and Mark A. Vaitkus. 1998. "Dimensions of Psychological Stress in Peacekeeping Operations." *Military Medicine* 163(9):587-593.

Booth, Bradford, Meyer Kestnbaum, and David R. Segal. 2001. "Are Post-Cold War Militaries Postmodern?" *Armed Forces and Society* 27(3):319-342.

Collins, Randall. 1990. "Stratification, Emotional Energy, and the Transient Emotions." Pp. 27-57 in *Research Agendas in the Sociology of Emotions,* edited by Theodore D. Kemper. New York: State University of New York Press.

Dandeker, Christopher. 1999. *Facing Uncertainty. Flexible Forces for the Twenty-First Century*. Karlstad: Swedish National Defence College.

Franks, David D. and McCarthy, E. Doyle, eds. 1989. *The Sociology of Emotions: Original Essays and Research Papers*. Greenwich: JAI Press.

Gabriel, Richard. 1987. *Nema više heroja. Ludilo i psihiatrija u ratu* (No More Heroes. Madness and Psychiatry in War). Zagreb: Alfa.

Gordon, Steven L. 1989. "Institutional and Impulsive Orientations in Selectively Appropriating Emotions to Self." Pp. 115-135 in *The Sociology of Emotions: Original Essays and Research Papers,* edited by David D. Franks and E. Doyle McCarthy. Greenwich: JAI Press.

Grossman, Dave. 1996. *On Killing. The Psychological Cost of Learning to Kill in War and Society*. Boston: Little, Brown & Co.

Hochschild, Arlie R. 1979. "Emotion Work, Feeling Rules, and Social Structure." *American Journal of Sociology* 85:551-575.

_____. 1983. *The Managed Heart: ·Commercialization of Human Feeling*. Berkeley: University of California Press.

Haltiner, Karl W. 1998. "The Definite End of the Mass Army in Western Europe?" *Armed Forces and Society* 25(1):7-36.

Kemper, Theodore D., ed. 1990. *Research Agendas in the Sociology of Emotions*. New York: State University of New York.

Kaldor, Mary. 1999. *New and Old Wars. Organized Violence in a Global Era*. Cambridge: Polity Press.

Kertzer, David I. 1988. *Ritual, Politics, and Power*. New Haven: Yale University Press.

Little, Roger W. 1964. "Buddy Relations and Combat Performance." In *The New Military,* edited by Morris Janowitz. New York: W. W. Norton & Co.

Lutsch, Carl. 1898. *Mit Gott, für Kaiser, König und Vaterland! Ein patriotisches Soldatenbuch* (With God, for Kaiser, King, and Homeland! A Patriotic Soldier's Book). Czernowitz: Bukowinaer Vereinsdruckerei.

McCarthy, E. Doyle. 1989. "Emotions are Social Things: An Essay in the Sociology of Emotions." Pp. 51-72 in *The Sociology of Emotions: Original Essays and Research Papers,* edited by David D. Franks and E. Doyle McCarthy. Greenwich: JAI Press.

Moskos, Charles C. 1988. "Institutional and Occupational Trends in Armed Forces." Pp. 15-26 in *The Military More than Just a Job?,* edited by Charles C. Moskos and Frank R. Wood. Westpark Drive: Pergamon-Brassey's.

Moskos, Charles C., John Allen Williams, and David R. Segal, eds. 2000. *The Postmodern Military*. New York: Oxford University Press.

Moskos, Charles C. and Frank R. Wood, eds. 1988. *The Military More than Just a Job?* Westpark Drive: Pergamon-Brassey's.

O'Connell, Robert L. 1989. *Of Arms and Men. A History of War, Weapons, and Aggression.* New York: Oxford University Press.

Perinbanayagam, R. S. 1989. "Signifying Emotions." Pp. 73-92 in *The Sociology of Emotions: Original Essays and Research Papers,* edited by David D. Franks and E. Doyle McCarthy. Greenwich: JAI Press.

Shay, Jonathan. 1994. *Achilles in Vietnam. Combat Trauma and the Undoing of Character.* New York: Atheneum.

Šadl, Zdenka. 1997. *Custva kot predmet sociološke analize* (Emotions as Subject of Sociological Analysis). Ljubljana: Fakulteta za druzbene vede.

Toffler, Alvin and Heidi Toffler. 1993. *The War and Anti-War. Survival at the Dawn of 21st century.* New York: Little, Brown & Co.

Zunec, Ozren, Siniša Tatalovic and Tarik Kulenovic. 2000. "The Post-Conflict Restructuring of Armed Forces: War Veterans in Croatia." In *Defence Restructuring and Conversion: Sociocultural Aspects,* edited by Ljubica Jelusic and John Selby. Brussels: Office for Official Publications of the European Communities.

Chapter

9

DIVERGENCES IN TRADITIONAL AND NEW COMMUNICATION MEDIA USE AMONG ARMY FAMILIES

Morten G. Ender
United States Military Academy
West Point, New York, United States

LEARNING OBJECTIVES

After reading this chapter, you should be able to

- understand the social history of communication media use in U.S. households;
- describe the key dimensions of social presence theory;
- identify the intersection of military sociology and communication studies;
- apply social presence theory to military communication contexts;
- distinguish between types of interpersonal communication activities.

255

C ommunication media have achieved critical mass in American families in general, and in military families specifically. VCRs have deeply penetrated family life. Telephones and mail have relatively universal access to most Americans and are convenient. Telephones have significantly affected sociability in family and community life (Fischer 1992). Computer-mediated communications facilitate telecommuting from the home and have initiated the redefinition of work and family domains (Kraut 1989; Reymers 1998; Sanchez 1987; Schepp 1990). One in three U.S. households has a personal computer, one in seven has a modem attached, and there does not appear to be any abatement as the purchasing of CD-ROM devices and other multi-media peripherals has become increasingly popular (Miller 1995). Information technologies are clearly vying for the time of family members (Silverstone 1993).

In terms of technology, some foresee a three-fold paradigmatic convergence of media—communication (telephone), information (computer), and entertainment (television) to include a subsumption of publishing, retailing, and financial services (Adler 1995). Moreover, while this convergence of media continues, it does not equate to homogeneity (Schement 1995). Indeed, Schement (1995) suggests that the homogenous domestic media audience environment of yesteryear is breaking down into fragmented and segmented media markets. Rather than homogeneity, convergence is fostering diffusion, with varied media markets among nations, communities, groups, households, and within a household.

Social science research examining communication media at the work-family intersection remains sparse at best (Wellman 1997). Increasingly, researchers are striving to understand the human dimensions of computer-mediated communication in family and community life (Wartella and

256

New Direction 9.1

Rather than homogeneity, convergence is fostering diffusion, with varied media markets among nations, communities, groups, households, and within a household.

Jennings 2001; Wellman et al. 1996). The burgeoning communication media revolution provides a new context for studying the assumptions of the sociology of the military family and considering the implications of those findings for other work and family situations. War, and military situations other than war involving the deployment of soldiers, such as peacekeeping duties, offer the social scientist an historical, cross-sectional view of the transference of information under extreme conditions, where social order maintenance and reestablishment are more pronounced (Collins 1989). War situations can be devised in simulations, but human subjects will likely respond unnaturally in such laboratory settings. Service members and their families, in times of actual, real-world military deployments, provide the naturalistic environment.

In the present study,[1] we examine the perceived effectiveness of, and personal experiences with, traditional and new communication media use among U.S. army families for communicating between home and war-front during a future (anticipated) military intervention and their actual experiences. Many of the soldiers in this study participated in *Operation Uphold Democracy* in 1994—the U.S. interventionist nation-building effort in Haiti. This provided an opportunity to survey different modes of soldier and family communication activity through different devices. The next section provides the theoretical foundation for the study.

257

Theoretical Framework

Social Presence Theory

Communication media provide alternatives to, or extensions of, human senses (McLuhan 1964). Studies of traditional modes of communication, such as face-to-face interaction and letters, provide the conceptual basis for studies of newer, more interactive modes of communication, such as video, tele- phones, FAX machines, and computer-mediated communications, among others.

The Communications Research Group published a monograph titled *The Social Psychology of Telecommunications* (Short, Williams, and Christie 1976) and can be considered the pioneers of the theory of social presence. Oriented toward the extension of human senses, or "personal-ness," social presence is defined as "the degree of salience of the other person in the interaction" (p.65) or immediacy facilitated by communica- tion. Social presence is a quality of the medium itself and communication media may vary in their degree of social pres- ence. For example, face-to-face communications are high in social presence offering the most stimuli for conveying infor- mation in an interaction. In contrast, voice or letter mail provides fewer stimuli in the conveying of information. Social presence distinguishes between and among modes of commu-

---

New Direction 9.2

Social presence is a quality of the medium itself and communication media may vary in their degree of social presence.

---

nication and the kinds of activities that are accomplished via different information technologies.

The early research methods of social presence theory involved laboratory tests of how participants in a communication exchange would respond to semantic differential scales such as "unsociable-sociable," "insensitive-sensitive," "cold-warm," and "impersonal-personal" relative to the medium being used. In this sense, researchers hypothesized that written text, including letters and email, would score low in social presence relative to more verbal (and nonverbal) oriented interaction, including telephone and face-to-face conversation.

Williams and Rice (1983) adopted, expanded, and confirmed previous research using the theory of the social presence of communication media. Their mean ratings of five modes of communication from highest to lowest social presence included face-to-face, television, multi-speaker audio, telephone-audio, and business letter. The key features of the differentiation of social presence are' "stimulus-conveying" restrictions of some communication media compared to others and their ability to simulate face-to-face communication. For example, some communication media, such as the written word, only convey verbal communication and significantly limited non-verbal communication.

Three additional qualities of media are important to understanding social presence: interactivity, privacy, and context (Fulk, Schmitz, and Steinfield 1990; Williams and Rice 1983). Interactivity refers to the technological nature and the degree of real-time (two-way) interaction versus lag-time (one-way) interaction provided by a communication medium. Privacy (versus public) issues refer to the degree that others are perceived to have access to an information exchange. In terms of social presence, the greater the privacy the higher the social presence. Finally, context refers to one's subjective view

---

New Direction 9.3

Social presence theory, specifically, and communications studies, in general, offer new vistas of analysis for military sociologists. Ironically, the relationship between communication studies and military sociology are linked.

---

of a communication medium and its degree of social presence. All three qualities vary in social presence in a work organization context.

Rice (1993) has been one of the most productive social presence researchers. He developed a Media Appropriate Scale (MAS) to measure social presence in organizational contexts. The scale expands the semantic differential procedure and laboratory experiments of earlier research to a five-point Likert scale ranging from appropriate to inappropriate. The eleven activities analyzed were (1) exchanging information; (2) problem solving and making decisions; (3) exchanging opinions; (4) generating ideas; (5) persuasion; (6) getting the other on one's side of the argument; (7) resolving disagreements or conflicts; (8) maintaining friendly relationships; (9) staying in touch; (10) bargaining; and (11) getting to know someone.

"Exchanging confidential information" and "exchanging timely information" complemented the list of activities based on empirical research of email use (Rice 1993). The comparative method was used to explain traditional and new media and assesses the reliability and dimensionality of the scale across six different organizational sites (Rice 1993). These latter studies confirmed the earlier research by the Communications Research Group on social presence by showing that "personal-ness" is defined by the quality of a communication medium.

Social presence theory, specifically, and communications studies, in general, offer new vistas of analysis for military sociologists. Ironically, the relationship between communication studies and military sociology are linked—both emerged out of war—specifically through *The American Soldier* series during and after World War II (see Siebold 2001). While military sociology built on volumes one and two of the four volumes (*Adjustment during Army Life* and *The American Soldier: Combat and Its Aftermath*), volume three, titled *Experiments on Mass Communication,* served as a foundation for communication studies. The two fields, however, developed separately. In the past ten years, though, the studies of war and communications have again crossed disciplinary boundaries (see Roach 1993). At the macro level, some researchers have theorized about a new military-information society (Levidow and Robins 1989).

Other links between communications studies and military sociology are available at the mezzo level of analysis. Social presence theory has been examined almost exclusively in white-collar work organization contexts (Morris and Ogan 1996). Thus, the degree and quality of social presence offered by a medium begins to provide an explanation for understanding interpersonal communication in military work (Ydén 2005). Further, because soldiers are required to be physically and socially separate from family members during military deployment, we would expect both groups to use different available communication media to communicate different activities to overcome the separation. The social history of soldier-family communication has shown this to be the case (Ender 1996; Ender and Segal 1996; Schumm et al. 2004). The next two sections link military families and communication more directly.

Military Families

Problems associated with the physical and social separation of a soldier from his family surfaced during World War II (Campbell 1984). Social research addressing the military family soon followed the research on soldiers. Hill's (1949) now classic study of World War II families was the first to measure the effects of military separation on families. Military family researchers focused on family separation from the soldier as a major demand of the war-time environment; others focused on issues of soldier isolation from his significant others as a major demand.

A military-family research tradition emerged in the 1970s following the recognition of extreme conditions of soldier isolation and family separation (see Hunter and Nice 1978; for a review, see Hunter 1982). The impetus for that research was the experiences of soldiers held as prisoners of war (POWs) and missing in action (MIA) during the Vietnam War and the impact on their families (McCubbin et al. 1974).

By the 1980s, a solid set of concepts outlining the defining features of military organization and family was developed (Hunter 1982).[2] Mady W. Segal (1986) adopted Coser's (1974) concept of "greedy institutions" as a theoretical perspective for conceptualizing the military and the family. Features of the military institution provided a set of demands that, taken collectively, set the military family apart from civilian families. Demands imposed by the military, which are characteristic of a "greedy institution" (demands found individually in many organizations, but not found collectively in other organizations) include (1) risk of injury or death; (2) geographic mobility; (3) separations; (4) residence in foreign countries; (5) masculine-dominated culture; (6) long working hours and shift work; and (7) normative constraints. These demands reflect an institution whose constant objective is to maintain a state of military readiness. Collectively, these demands affect the family.

Similarly, the family places demands on its members including expecting an emotional commitment to the family by all members, identifying with the unit, affections, and the fulfillment of role obligations. These demands exist within a context of social change including a move toward various family configurations and changing gender roles. These changes have influenced the military family.

The U.S. military responds to the changing needs of their people at the intersection of the military and the family. Grassroots movements among family members, advocates, and applied social science researchers have influenced military policies (Stanley, Segal, and Laughton 1990). Recognition of the family's importance relative to military effectiveness has become a major concern of the military and the relationship between family well-being and soldier functioning is a positive one (Stanley, Segal, and Laughton 1990). However, significant policy changes have generally lagged behind the human experience. In other words, the military has traditionally been rather reactive to family concerns. The military, based on social science research, should be increasingly proactive in its anticipation of social changes. Such a position will help crystallize the complementary relationship between the military and the family that scholars have prescribed (Stanley et al. 1990). More recently, military family research has been placed within a more abstract theoretical framework of work and family called the "spillover hypothesis" (Segal 1989). A major assumption of the hypothesis is that the separation of the "worlds of work and family" is a myth; aspects of one domain overflow into the social domain of the other (Kanter 1977). Essentially, the spillover hypothesis is viewed as a more contemporary and dynamic view, linking work and family domains. In contrast, the segmented model of work and family is based on the notion of instrumental versus socioemotional needs, the latter associated with stereotypical characteristics of women and the former with men. Likewise, the compensatory model views the two domains as separate, but one tends to fulfill social psychological needs for the individual that are not fulfilled by the other. The spill-over model provides a more integrative, dynamic, and encompassing perspective and applies to multiple levels of analysis including the institutional, organizational, interpersonal, and individual (Segal 1989).

Military Families and Communication Media

There are new ways of thinking about the military family (Bell et al. 1996; Schumm et al. 1999; Schumm et al. 2004). New, available, and expedited communication media provide an impetus to question many of the assumptions of military family research and to develop, implement, and enforce new policies that would address the needs and interests of soldiers and families and have some application for "civilian" work and family contexts. A new direction for military sociology is the link to communication studies at the organizational and interpersonal levels—the sociology of the military in the information age should include the examination of the uses and implications of communication media during wartime (see Ender 1996; Ender and Segal 1996, 1998).

Soldier-family communication during war has a dynamic history. During warfare, soldiers seek the means to exchange information with the home-front (Ender 1996; Ender and Segal 1996). Traditionally, physical and social isolation of soldiers from other military units, family, and the larger society has been a defining feature of a military forward deployment (Williams and Smith 1949).

Scattered among the research literature are a few studies that include an examination of the role of communication media in the lives of the spouses of forward-deployed soldiers. Cohen and Dotan (1976) provided a groundbreaking study that directly linked family, war and peace, stress, and communication activities. In particular, they found increases in the use of interpersonal and mass communication by spouses separated during war compared to the patterns of use during peacetime separations. Similarly, during both the Persian Gulf War and the humanitarian effort in Somalia, results from survey data provided evidence that the uses of information technology (including one and two-way communication media) helped U.S. spouses cope with their soldiers' forward deployment (Bell, Teitelbaum, and Schumm 1996). During the Gulf crisis, 75 percent of soldiers' spouses reported sending eight or more letters per month. Further, a cornucopia of mail addressed to "Any Soldier—Persian Gulf" sat on pallets at airports in Saudi Arabia long after the war (Powell 1995; Schwarzkopf 1992; U.S. Post Office Department 1991). Telephone calls and videotape exchanges also increased: 82 percent of the spouses interviewed had made at least two telephone calls per month and 38 percent mailed one or more videotapes per month (Bell et al. 1996).

During Operation Restore Hope (ORH) in Somalia, spouses and other family members on the U.S. home-front relied on email to obtain information from their significant others (Ender 1997). Despite the lack of telephones during the early phases of ORH, and approximately 10,000 email messages, the number of snail mail letters from spouses approximated those sent during Operations Desert Shield and Desert Storm (Bell 1991).

Recent historical research has described the importance of letter mail during World War II when family letter writing was strongly encouraged and radio slogans stated "they're doing the fighting, you do the writing" (Litoff and Smith 1991:126). A new V-mail (Victory Mail)[3] system accommodated the increased bulk of letters (Litoff and Smith 1990, 1991). However, letter writers felt it was too impersonal, "as though they had received only a post-card" (Litoff and Smith 1991:123). The major limitation of the medium was a lack of privacy.

In sum, a new direction of military family research includes the direct examination of communication media during military deployments from the perspective of soldiers, units, families, and the larger society. Specifically, this interdisciplinary perspective offers new ways of thinking about the family. This study examines past and future uses of traditional and new communication media in military families. The goal of the study is to investigate the possible future or anticipated uses of communication media and communication activities. The study aspires to empirically assess some of the old and the new mediated communication in a family context. The findings may assist the military and families to thwart social problems that might upset the fine balance between the military and the family before the devices for communication have become a regular part of social interaction. The uniqueness of the military family as an institution with specified demands found individually in American society, but not collectively, and their communication experiences should begin to fill the research gap between families and new communication media. The next step is to identify the modes different families use to communicate, under what situations, and to what degree. Finally, the research should seek to assess the degree of convergence and divergence of media in a military context.

266

The present study confronts the lacunae of research on new communication media in this area and explores the use of it in a work and family context.

Here are some of the major research questions: how and why do soldiers and family members use communication media during a forward-deployed military context and what are the social, psychological, and organizational implications, if any, of using communication media?

Methodology

The Department of the Army (DA) sponsored a study that eventually included open-ended and closed surveys with soldiers and spouses of soldiers from the 10th Mountain Division, Fort Drum, New York. A social science research team, including the present author, sponsored by the Army's, Chief of Staff Office, visited Fort Drum, New York, during February 1995. The primary research objective was a study of Operational Personnel Tempo (OPT). OPT refers to multiple forward deployments by the same soldiers and their units in a short time period. For example, the 10th Mountain Division had deployed previously on three missions in three years: Dade County, Florida following the devastation of Hurricane Andrew; humanitarian relief effort in Somalia; and democracy restoration in Haiti.[4]

Two surveys were administered. We divided the sample frame of 1000 (500 for each survey) soldiers to accommodate each study. The survey for the present consists of 113 closed-ended and four open-ended question items focusing on dimensions of communication during the deployment and questions about uses in future deployments.[5] The other survey focused on OPT questions and attitudes toward the military. Results of the latter study, including the traditional issues of soldier cohesion, morale, readiness, retention, and family member well-being, are reported elsewhere (Ender 1996; Segal, Reed, and Rohall 1998). The OPT larger study provided us with an opportunity to partition out a sub-sample and explore the transfer of information.

Samples

The samples consisted of soldiers (N=366) and spouses of soldiers (N=89). The 10th Mountain Division is comprised of a total soldier population of approximately 10,000. Approximately 50 percent of the soldiers are married. The research team requested that a sampling frame of 500 (5 percent) soldiers and 250 (5 percent) spouses be made available to volunteer to participate in the communication study. The soldier sample response rate was 73 percent (n=366). The low response rate for spouses (36 percent; n=89) was the result of a snowstorm and subsequent closing of the military installation during the two days of data collection. No effort was made to link married couples and couples may not be represented in the samples.

Soldiers

The sample of soldiers (N=366) includes 292 men and 42 women (two did not provide gender) ranging in age from 19 to 50 with mean, median, and modal ages of 26, 24, and 22 respectively. Most are enlisted soldiers (98 percent; n=352). Forty-nine percent (n=174) of the soldiers were married at the time of the survey and thirty-nine percent (n=141) have one or more children (n=64). Most (67 percent; n=239) lived on Fort Drum. Eighteen percent (n=64) are from career military families.

The racial/ethnic breakdown includes Native Americans/ Alaskan Natives (3.9 percent; n=14), Asian American/Filipino (4.5 percent; n=16), Black/African American (23.1 percent; n=83), Hispanic/Spanish (10.3 percent; n=37), Other (3.9 percent; n=14), and White/Caucasian (54.3 percent; n=195). The educational background of the soldiers included 56.3 percent (n=198) with high school diplomas or less, 25 percent (n=128) with some college or vocational training, and 7.2 percent (n=26) with baccalaureate, post- undergraduate, or advanced college degrees. The majority of those from the sample (90 percent) were veterans of at least one major military deployment during their years of service.

Spouses of Soldiers

A separate, soldier's spouse survey included 87 women and 2 men ranging in age from 19 to 47 with mean and medium ages of 27 and a modal age of 22. The vast majority of the spouses reporting their spouse's rank were enlisted (84 percent; n=58). Seventy-six percent (n=61) of the spouses reported having one or more children and 17 percent (n=14) were from career military families.

The racial/ethnic breakdown included Native Americans/ Alaskan Natives (3.8 percent; n=3), Asian American/Filipino (3.8 percent; n=3), Black/African American (10.1 percent; n=8), Hispanic/Spanish (3.8 percent; n=3), Other (2.5 percent; n=2), and White/Caucasian (75.9 percent; n=60). The educational background of the spouse sample included 41.3 percent (n=33) with high school diplomas or less, 43.8 percent (n=35) with some college or vocational training, and 15.5 percent (n=12) with baccalaureates, post-undergraduate, or advanced college degrees.

269

In terms of population representation, junior enlisted and senior officer spouses were overrepresented in the sample and non-commissioned and junior officers' spouses were underrepresented in proportion to the total population on the base. Overall, and similar to the soldier sample, the social characteristics of the sample are in relative proportion to their representation in the Army in general.

Procedures

Both soldiers and the spouses of soldiers were surveyed and interviewed at Fort Drum, New York. The surveys were in pencil and paper format and required the shading of bubbles on scantron sheets for the forced response items, and writing directly on the questionnaire for the open-ended responses. A survey instrument of seventy items queried soldiers and spouses about separation during the next military deployment. They were asked to rank how effective seven different modes of communication might be during a *future* military deployment for the ten types of communication activities.

Measures

The Media Appropriateness Scale (MAS) (Rice 1993) described earlier is modified for use in a work-family context for face validity purposes. In the present study, communication activities were adopted from the organization context, modified, renamed, and introduced into a unique work and family context. We adopted items to represent the socio-emotional demands of work-family separation. The items were chosen with agreement among key informants that they would represent family communication during a separation. The MAS scale is renamed the Media Effectiveness Scale (MES) with the term "effectiveness" substituted for "appropriateness" in the instructions. Socio-emotional communication activities are (1) sharing feelings; (2) reducing feelings of separation; (3) showing support; (4) staying in touch; and (5) resolving disagreements and somewhat more instrumental communication activities including (6) exchanging time-sensitive information; (7) making decisions; (8) exchanging very personal information; (9) exchanging general information; and (10) asking questions. These activities were explored and compared across seven modes of communication: (1) face-to-face; (2) mail; (3) email; (4) FAX; (5) audio tapes; (6) videotapes; and (7) and telephones.[6]

The qualitative results are from open-ended items on the questionnaire survey. The responses refer to their actual reflections on their most recent deployment. Three general questions were asked: (1) communication media used and why; (2) communication not used and why; and (3) any additional comments related to communication media.

Results

Table 1 displays the rank of the seven modes of communication from the highest to lowest means on social presence effectiveness scores for both soldiers and spouses. The mean is based on ten activities with each mode of communication in a future military deployment. The telephone has the highest overall mean effectiveness rank for all communication activi-

---

New Direction 9.4

Email and FAX are ranked lowest in effectiveness.

---

ties. Face-to-face communication is second, followed by regular mail. The two two-way modes of communication rank
highest in social presence and mail ranks highest among the
remaining one-way modes. As one soldier wrote, reflecting on
his actual experience with communication media, "I used
phones because, other than mail, it was the most effective
means." A female spouse talked of her experiences: "We used
letters because they were a good source of reinforcement when
you were lonely." Another spouse explained her use of the
phone:

> I communicated with my husband during the deploy-
> ment to Haiti very well, but we pay for the phone. We
> communicate a lot because I was in stress before he
> left. I lost a baby. When he went to Somalia, I had lost
> one too. I didn't receive any support.

Email and FAX are ranked lowest in effectiveness.
Spouses and soldiers had virtually identical responses. A
female spouse said "I live off the post so email was not readily available." A soldier said "I never used e-mail or FAX
because everyone would read it first."

**Table 1. Soldiers' and Spouses' Mean Ranking of the
Seven Communication Media**

Mode of Communication	Means	
	Soldier	Spouses
Telephone	3.0	3.1
Face-to-Face	2.7	2.8
Regular Mail	2.5	2.6
Audio Tape	2.3	2.3
Video Tape	2.3	2.1
E-mail	1.9	2.1
FAX	1.9	1.8

Soldiers

Table 2 shows the means for each mode of communication by communication activity for the soldiers. For soldiers, the most effective mode for staying in touch would be the telephone (mean of 3.1) while for making decisions (3.0) and resolving disagreements (2.9) it would be slightly less effective. For example, reflecting on a real situation, one soldier wrote of his Haiti experience, "I used mail and telephone to communicate with home because I would like to tell my parents the news of the day as soon as possible. I would write my friends because they don't need to know all that quickly." Another soldier wrote, "I mostly used the phone system, they were very effective in maintaining communication with the home-front."

In comparison, face-to-face communication for soldiers is similar to the results received from spouses (see below) and is reported as being most effective for showing support (2.9) and staying in touch (2.8) in a future military deployment. Face-to-face communication is rated by soldiers to be most ineffective (the lowest mean) for exchanging very personal

Table 2. Soldiers' Mean Level of Effectiveness of Seven Communication Media for Each Mean of Ten Communication Activities

	Touch	Sepa	Supp	Quest	Inform	Pers	Time	Feel	Deci	Disa
1	3.1 Phone	3.0 Phone	3.0 Phone	3.1 Phone	3.1 Phone	3.0 Phone	3.0 Phone	3.0 Phone	3.0 Phone	2.9 Phone
2	2.9 Mail	2.7 Face	2.9 Face	2.7 Face	2.7 Face	2.7 Mail	2.7 Face	2.8 Face	2.7 Face	2.6 Face
3	2.8 Face	2.6 Video	2.8 Mail	2.4 Mail	2.7 Mail	2.6 Face	2.2 FAX	2.7 Mail	2.3 Mail	2.0 Mail
4	2.7 Video	2.6 Mail	2.7 Video	2.3 Video	2.4 Video	2.2 Audio	2.0 Email	2.5 Audio	2.1 Video	1.9 Audio
5	2.6 Audio	2.5 Audio	2.7 Audio	2.2 Audio	2.1 Audio	2.1 Video	1.9 Video	2.5 Video	2.0 Audio	1.9 Video
6	2.1 Email	2.0 Email	2.1 Email	2.0 Email	2.1 FAX	1.7 Email	1.8 Mail	1.9 Email	1.9 Email	1.7 Email
7	2.0 FAX	1.9 FAX	2.0 FAX	2.0 FAX	2.0 Email	1.7 FAX	1.5 Audio	1.7 FAX	1.8 FAX	1.6 FAX

Note: Touch= Staying in Touch; Sepa= Reducing feeling of separation; Supp= Showing support; Quest= Asking questions; Inform= Exchanging general information; Pers= Exchanging personal information; Time= Exchanging time-sensitive information; Feel= Sharing feelings; Deci= Making decisions; and Disa= Resolving disagreements.

information (2.6). Soldiers indicated that, on average, mail would be the most socially effective for staying in touch (2.9) and showing support (2.8). As one soldier noted from personal experience, "I used mail because that way I could get mail every day and it kind of lets you know someone is still thinking about you." Mail would be most ineffective for exchanging time-sensitive information (1.8) and resolving disagreements (2.0). One soldier wrote, "I think if you stuck a message in a bottle and stuck it in the ocean it would have gotten there sooner than our mail system."

For newer information technology such as email, FAX, video, and audio, showing support (Supp) and staying in touch (Touch) have the highest mean scores. A soldier wrote, "The FAX is too impersonal, the telephone lacks privacy, and I was unaware of the email distribution program." The highest mean score for a facsimile (FAX) is sharing time-sensitive information (2.2) while it is much lower for the other one-way communication media. As one soldier stressed, "FAX is used least, unless it is during tax time, there is no real need for it." Speed is clearly the defining feature of the FAX.

Spouses of Soldiers

Table 3 provides an overall comparison of the seven communication media and the ten communication activities for spouses of soldiers. Telephones (Phone) have the highest social effectiveness mean for asking questions (3.4). A spouse of a veteran shared the following thought: "with telephones you could get a better feeling for how they were faring." The lowest mean score is for resolving disagreements (3.0). Face-to-face communication would be the most effective for showing support (3.1) and keeping in touch (3.1) and the most ineffective for exchanging very personal information (2.4).

274

Table 3. Spouses' Mean Level of Effectiveness of Seven Communication Media for Each Mean of Ten Communication Activities

	Touch	Sepa	Supp	Quest	Info	Pers	Time	Feel	Deci	Disa
1	3.2 Phone	3.1 Phone	3.2 Phone	3.4 Phone	3.2 Phone	3.1 Phone	3.2 Phone	3.3 Phone	3.1 Phone	3.0 Phone
2	3.1 Mail	2.9 Face	3.1 Face	2.9 Face	2.9 Mail	2.8 Mail	2.6 Face	2.9 Mail	2.8 Face	2.4 Face
3	3.1 Face	2.6 Video	3.1 Mail	2.4 Mail	2.8 Face	2.4 Face	2.3 FAX	2.8 Face	2.3 Mail	1.9 Mail
4	2.7 Audio	2.5 Mail	2.9 Video	2.3 Email	2.6 Audio	2.2 Audio	2.1 Email	2.7 Audio	1.9 Email	1.8 Audio
5	2.7 Video	2.5 Audio	2.7 Audio	2.2 Audio	2.1 Email	1.6 Video	1.7 Mail	2.2 Video	1.8 Audio	1.6 Email
6	2.4 Email	2.2 Email	2.4 Email	2.0 Video	2.3 Video	1.5 Email	1.7 Audio	1.9 Email	1.6 FAX	1.4 Video
7	2.0 FAX	1.7 FAX	1.9 FAX	1.9 FAX	2.1 FAX	1.4 FAX	1.5 Video	1.6 FAX	1.6 Video	1.3 FAX

Comparing mail (Mail) and face-to-face (Face) communication shows that spouses believe, on average, the mail would be most effective for both showing support and staying in touch (3.1). One wife explained "we used the mail and the telephone the most. The mail gave us a forum for more personal communication but the phone is great for getting timely information and boosting his morale." Another spouse described her communication activities:

> We wrote letters daily...and spoke on the telephone daily. We used letters because they were a good source of reinforcement when you were lonely. Anytime of the day or night you could take out a letter and read how your spouse was thinking of you. We used the telephone to hear how we loved and missed each other. There is no better reinforcement than verbal when your spouse is away.

Mail, according to spouses, would be the most ineffective for resolving disagreements (1.2) and for making decisions (1.9). Video would be the most effective for showing support (2.8) and keeping in touch (2.7). Audio-tapes would be similar to video as most effective for keeping in touch (2.7) and showing support (2.7) and least effective (1.7) for the sharing time-sensitive information. Email would be most effective for staying in touch (2.4) and exchanging very personal information (2.4). As one spouse wrote, "email makes it easy to stay in touch." Resolving disagreements (1.5) and sharing feelings (1.6) have the lowest mean scores. For the FAX, the highest mean is for exchanging time-sensitive information (2.3). As one wife wrote, "A FAX sounds as stupid as email—they are too business like and impersonal. However, I do concede the modes are extremely fast."

Difference of means tests were conducted for the communication media and compared a number of independent variables including military rank, race/ethnicity, education, gender, marital status, number of children, and parents' careers and features of the MES.

Military Rank: For face-to-face conversation, spouses of officers reported higher effectiveness of face-to-face conversation for keeping in touch and showing support than spouses of enlisted soldiers [Fs(1, 66) = 4.88 and 5.25, respectively, $p < .05$] and reported higher effectiveness of mail for sharing time sensitive information and making decisions than spouses of enlisted soldiers [Fs(1, 64 and 66 respectively) = 6.24 and 5.40 respectively, $p < .05$].

Officers reported higher effectiveness of face-to-face conversation for making decisions than enlisted soldiers [F(1, 353) = 4.62, $p < .05$].

More spouses of officers indicated that audio tapes would be effective for both making decisions and resolving disagreements than spouses of enlisted soldiers [Fs(1, Ns = 66) = 10.51 and 12.55 respectively, $p < .01$ respectively] and reported audio tapes effective for asking questions than enlisted soldiers [F(1, N = 67) = 4.656, $p < .05$].

Army officers reported video as more effective for resolving disagreements and sharing feelings [$Fs(1$, Ns = 77 and 66 respectively) = 9.907 and 8.612 respectively, $p < .01$ and .05 respectively]; asking questions and sharing personal information [$Fs(1$, Ns = 77 and 66 respectively) = 6.463 and 6.557 respectively, $p < .05$]; and sharing time-sensitive information [$F(1$, N = 66) = 5.256, $p < .05$] than enlisted soldiers.

Spouses of officers reported the use of email to resolve disagreements more effective than did spouses of enlisted soldiers [$F(1$, N = 65) = 5.18, $p < .05$].

Enlisted soldiers rated keeping in touch, reducing feelings of separation, and sharing very personal information via email more effective than officers [$Fs(1$, Ns = 353, 354, and 354 respectively) = 5.284, 4.088, and 7.8442 respectively, $p <$ .05, 05 and .01 respectively].

Race/ethnicity: Minority soldiers reported higher levels of effectiveness of mail to resolve disagreements than white soldiers [$F(1, 356) = 5.67$, $p < .05$] and spouses of color reported audio tapes more effective for sharing feelings than whites [$F(1$, N = 78) = 4.166, $p < .05$]. Minority soldiers reported video as more effective for sharing time-sensitive and personal information [$Fs(1$, Ns = 77) = 6.364 and 9.213 respectively, $p < .05$ and .01 respectively] and asking questions and making decisions than whites [$Fs(1$, Ns = 77) = 4.913 and 6.149 respectively, $p < .05$].

Finally, minority (excluding Hispanics) soldiers were more likely to identify resolving disagreements and reducing feelings of separation via FAX as effective, than white soldiers [$Fs(1$, Ns = 358) = 5.832 and 4.312 respectively, $p < .05$].

Education: Spouses with at least some college education or more reported higher effectiveness of face-to-face conversation for sharing personal information than spouses with a high school diploma or less [$F(1, 62) = 6.64$, $p < .05$].

Soldiers with at least some college education reported significantly higher levels of effectiveness of mail to reduce feelings of separation [$F(1, 342) = 7.29, p < .01$]; show support [$F(1, 342) = 6.99, p < .01$]; asking questions [$F(1, 342) = 6.70, p < .05$]; exchange general information [$F(1, 342) = 7.94, p < .01$]; share personal information [$F(1, 342) = 4.06, p < .05$]; and share feelings [$F(1, 342) = 11.83, p < .001$] than soldiers with a high school diploma or less.

Soldiers with some college education or more reported audio tapes having a higher effectiveness for reducing feelings separation, showing support, and keeping in touch than soldiers with a high school education or less [$Fs(1$, Ns $= 342$, 342, and 343 respectively) $= 10.158, 3.85, 6.249$ respectively, $p < .01, .05$, and $.05$ respectively]. Soldiers with at least some college were more likely to rate reducing feelings of separation via email more effective than soldiers with a high school diploma or less [$F(1$, N $= 344) = 5.063, p < .05$].

Gender: Male soldiers rated asking questions via video tape higher than female soldiers [$F(1$, N $= 333) = 4.0367, p < .05$].

Marital Status: Married soldiers reported significantly higher levels of effectiveness of mail to reduce feelings of separation, and the sharing of general and personal information than single soldiers [$Fs(1, 355) = 5.52, 4.36$, and 13.47 respectively, $p < .05, .05$, and $.001$ respectively].

Married soldiers reported significantly higher telephone effectiveness for keeping in touch and reducing feelings of separation [$Fs(1$, Ns $= 356) = 5.666$ and 7.491 respectively, $p < .05$]; sharing personal information and making decisions [$Fs(1$, Ns $= 356) = 5.177$ and 4.426 respectively, $p < .05$] and the sharing of time sensitive information [$F(1$, N $= 357) = 9.666, p <$ and $.01$] than single soldiers.

Finally, married soldiers rated sharing very personal information via email more effective than non-married soldiers [F(1, N = 356) = 6.373, p < .05].

Number of Children: Spouses with children reported higher effectiveness of mail for making decisions and resolving disagreements than spouses without children [Fs(1, 78) = 4.13 and 4.36 respectively, p < .05].

Parents' Career: Soldiers from non-career military backgrounds reported higher effectiveness of face-to-face conversation for asking questions and resolving disagreements than soldiers from career military families [Fs(1, 347) = 5.76 and 5.27 respectively, p < .05]. Spouses not from career military families of orientation reported significantly higher effectiveness of mail for making decisions and resolving disagreements than their peers with military career backgrounds [Fs(1, 77) = 4.36 and 5.46 respectively, p < .05].

Soldiers from non-career military backgrounds reported significantly higher levels of effectiveness of mail to reduce separation of a deployment [F(1, 347) = 7.08, p < .01]; show support [F(1, 347) = 10.08, p < .01]; exchange general and personal information [Fs(1, 347) = 8.92 and 6.67 respectively, p < .01 and .05 respectively]; share feelings [F(1, 347) = 8.51, p < .01]; and resolve disagreements than their military background peers [F(1, 347) = 4.75, p < .05].

Finally, soldiers from non-career military backgrounds seemed more likely to report videotapes as effective in exchanging general information and asking questions, showing support, and keeping in touch than their peers raised in military career families. [Fs(1, Ns = 348 and 349 respectively) = 5.608 and 5.022 respectively, p < .05 and Fs(1, Ns = 349 and 346 respectively) = 5.0748 and 6.098 respectively, p < .05, respectively].

Discussion

The integration of the univariate results across the seven communication media and ten interpersonal communication activities can now be discussed. First, soldiers and spouses do distinguish between kinds of communication media and the utility of specific devices for effective communication for specific activities. Second, soldiers and spouses report virtually identical effectiveness ratings of seven communication media used for interpersonal communication activities. In their reporting, both groups anticipate that military forward deployments are separations requiring the soldiers be removed from their families and communities. Both prefer the telephone as a two-way medium for communicating across the distance during a future deployment. Choosing the telephone ranks highest and is contemporaneous for both soldiers and spouses for effectively performing all ten communication activities. However, if telephones are unavailable, face-to-face communication, the only other real-time mode of communication of the seven, would be the next most effective at meeting their communication needs. The two modes are both real-time and traditionally provide the highest degree of social presence.

It remains unclear what, exactly, face-to-face communication means to soldiers and spouses. Soldiers and spouses of soldiers appear to be saying that if they cannot communi-

---

New Direction 9.5

Soldiers and spouses of soldiers appear to be saying that if they cannot communicate via the telephone, they want to wait and communicate face-to-face.

---

cate via the telephone, they want to wait and communicate face-to-face. No reference to face-to-face communication is recorded in the open-ended results. The results from each group may be suggesting the soldier and spouse should meet half-way between the home and war-front, similar to the way U.S. soldiers met their spouses in Hawaii during the Vietnam War. Alternative explanations are that the spouse should either deploy with the soldier to or near the operation location, the soldier shouldn't deploy at all, or more realistically, soldiers receive periodic "environmental leave" similar to the two-week vacation home U.S. soldiers received while in Iraq in 2004. We know that telephone communication is desired soon after a deployment (Schumm et al. 2004); however, in the absence of electronic media, how long will spouses wait for face-to-face communication?

Regarding the five remaining one-way modes of communication, mail ranks after face-to-face communication as the next most effective mode. Overall, mail is the third most effective mode of communication. Mail is ranked lower than third in only two communication activities—reducing the feelings of separation and sharing time sensitive information. Spouses find FAX and email more effective for sharing time sensitive information, and video tape VHS more effective for reducing the feelings of separation. Soldiers include video as a more effective mode for sharing time sensitive information. Otherwise, mail, a one-way mode and one of the oldest and most traditional forms of long distance communication media available, satisfies their communication needs.

While mail is a one-way mode, it does share a number of logistical characteristics with telephony and face-to-face communication. First, mail is familiar. Similar to the telephone and face-to-face interaction, mail is a traditional mode of communication. Virtually every user of mail and telephones was socialized using these media in the civilian society. They trust mail; it has a significant tradition as the primary mode of communication during war (Litoff and Smith 1990; 1991). Second, both mail and telephones have universal access. Third, mail, telephones, and face-to-face communication are relatively private. Email, FAX, and audio and video-tapes could provide privacy. However, non-sealed, hardcopy email and FAX messages, in the military context reported in this study, exchange a number of hands prior to their final destination (Ender 1997).

The MES results can also be discussed by communication activity rather than by communication media and provide insight to the kinds of activities that might most be preferred and performed by both soldiers and spouses via communication media. Both staying-in-touch and showing support are the highest on effectiveness related to communication media while resolving disagreements via communication media scores the lowest mean. The results confirm a long-standing tradition to communicate emotionally uplifting and positive information to support the soldier on the war-front (Litoff and Smith, 1990; 1991).

In terms of divergence between groups, some results are notable. On the MES, spouses with higher status discriminate between one-way and two-way types of communication media. Spouses of officers and/or those spouses with some college or more appear to prefer the traditional face-to-face and snail mail for socio-emotional communication activities (e.g., sharing feelings and keeping in touch). The one-way modes of email, audio and video-tapes, and snail mail meet their instrumental needs (e.g., asking questions and resolving disagreements). Racial/ethnic minorities, in contrast to Whites, prefer the one-way, audio-visual communication media for communicating activities. The spouse socialized in a military family and with children would prefer one-way modes for resolving disagreements and making decisions.

282

For soldiers, there is greater divergence among specific subgroups than for spouses. As a group, soldiers with some college education are more likely than the less educated groups to report one-way communication as effective as two-way communication for communication activities. Married and non-career military background soldiers are more likely than the single and careered military background soldier to report one way communication as effective as two-way communication media for communication activities.

The results are interesting as they confirm and further support a 50-year-old research finding that the American soldier is concerned about the home-front (Shils and Janowitz 1948). Today, soldiers are concerned about the home-front and they have a plethora of media to help them act on their concerns. Traditionally, the home-front has been responsible for supporting the troops. The findings of the MES suggest that the behavior is complemented by soldiers keeping in touch and showing support for their spouse, significant others, and/or family members during dangerous, life-threatening missions. This phenomenon seems directly related to the availability of communication media in war zones and may be paralleling real-time mass media use as well (Ender 1996). On the other hand, there are differences between how, and what, spouses and soldiers want to communicate.

Implications for Social Presence Theory

The early social presence research used primarily white-collar, organizational workers and contexts to study social presence. Given the increasingly large demand of telecommuting work and the diffusion of communication media in the larger society, this study sought to expand the idea of social presence beyond the work world. Given the major demands of the military lifestyle, the work and family domains were a worthwhile place to explore such concepts.

In general, the consistent rating of the ten communication activities between soldiers and spouses in the present study lends a degree of reliability to the scale for indicating the degree of effectiveness of specific types of communication media in a military work and family context. The two communication media reported most effective are the two-way modes of telephone and face-to-face. Overall, the results both confirm and contradict the findings of earlier research. In his review of the literature, Rice (1993) provided a ranking of different media across eight different studies in organization contexts. The results of the present study confirm the findings of that research suggesting that the more stimulus conveying communication media score higher overall (Rice 1987, 1993).

Finally, there is support in a military context for the three-fold paradigmatic convergence of media communication —telephone, computer, and television (Adler 1995). Communication media are ubiquitous in the military and show evidence of converging into a single medium. This provides evidence that the military family context reflects the uses in the larger society. The results also suggest that families and soldiers distinguish between communication media for their communication needs. Moreover, the seemingly homogenous and traditional military family is fragmenting and segmenting somewhat along race and class lines, similar to the larger society in general (Schement 1995).

Conclusion

Information technology has become ubiquitous in American households. The revolution of communication media has also affected the military and appears to upset the insulating space between soldiering and the military family. This study explored future uses of communication media via the Media Effectiveness Scale while confirming the historical findings in a work and family context. The pattern for the future suggests soldiers and their significant others would prefer to continue to use two-way, stimulus-rich communication media. On the other hand, they will continue to rely on the traditional modes of letter writing and perhaps even prefer them for some communication activities (such as showing support), and yet desire others for specific communication media attributes, such as speed. Moreover, the uses of communication media will likely continue to reflect those of the larger society during peacetime but become somewhat more acute during times of military separations such as advanced training exercises, military engagements other than war, and war.

A key to understanding the military family is to recognize that soldiers and their spouses are socialized in a society that is rich in communication media and is rapidly moving into the information age where they will come to expect access to communication media devices in their new military and family roles. Consequently, social concern about families and communication media and the ability to establish new ways of interaction and the ability to reduce social separation should be of greater interest to not only peace and war researchers, but family and information society scholars as well.

Finally, communication studies, in general, appear to offer new vistas of analysis for military sociologists. As noted earlier, the link between communication studies and military sociology is historical and substantive. Recent research has linked war, communication, technology, and informatics (Levidow and Robins 1989; Roach 1993; Ydén 2005). We have documented the relationship between soldier and family communication as well (Ender 1996; Ender and Segal 1996;

Schumm et al. 2004). In addition to computers and other communication devices, there are other areas worthy of inquiry and include, but are not limited to, the following:

- Organization Communication: Institutional and organizational research on the rhetorical norms and communication practices within the military or between the military and other organizations such as NGOs and the mass media;
- Communication Education and Training Technologies: The uses and gratifications of communication media to educate and train military personnel especially the use of simulations (*Communication News* 2003);
- Diversity and Communication: The role of differing communication patterns among the various groups within and outside the military, such as different genders and ethnicities but inclusive of different cultures, age, religious, and sexual orientations;
- Film and Audience Studies: The role of film and other devices at the intersection of the armed forces and society (Ender forthcoming; Harper 2003);
- Language, Linguistics, and Rhetoric: The analysis of language and the origin of language in a military context (Dowd 2000);
- Mass Media and the Military: The relationship between television, print media, and electronic media reporting of the military including embedded reporting (Cooper 2003; Dauber 2003; Murray 2001).

SUMMARY

Social presence theory is used to compare future uses of communication media among U.S. army soldiers (N=366) and spouses (N=89). Future uses of seven communication media to communicate ten activities are explored through closed survey questions. Actual uses are solicited through open-ended questions. Social presence theory is moderately supported in a military work and family context. Two-way communication media (for example, telephones and face-to-face) are highest in social presence, overall, for communicating during the imposed family separation. One-way communication media (for example, mail, email, and video tapes) are lower in social presence. Divergent and convergent uses of information technology and the role in soldier-family separation are discussed. On a broader level, communication studies offer new approaches for military sociologists in studying military communities.

KEY TERMS AND CONCEPTS

<table>
<tr><td>• Communication media</td><td>• Spill over hypothesis</td></tr>
<tr><td>• Military family</td><td>• Work and family</td></tr>
<tr><td>• Separations</td><td>• Privacy issues</td></tr>
<tr><td>• Social presence</td><td></td></tr>
</table>

STUDY AND DISCUSSION QUESTIONS

1. Summarize the research literature on communication and military families. Define social presence theory.

2. Identify and describe the two population samples and the two types of methods used in the present study.

3. Describe the results on adults from military versus non-military family backgrounds.

4. Formulate some explanations to account for the differences.

5. Design a research project examining the intersection of military sociology and communication studies.

NOTES

1. An earlier version of this paper received the Elise M. Boulding Student Paper Award of the Peace, War, and Social Conflict Section of the American Sociological Association. The author wishes to thank Wendelin Hume, David Segal, Mady Segal, Jay Stanley, Clifford Staples, Eric Ouellet, and Kathleen Tiemann for their assistance on previous versions of this chapter. This research was supported in part by the U.S. Army Research Institute for the Behavioral and Social Sciences under Contract No. DASW 01-95-K-0005. Some early travel funding was provided by the Peace Studies Program, University of North Dakota in Grand Forks. The views expressed by the author are not necessarily those of the United States Military Academy, the Army Research Institute, the Department of the Army, or the Department of Defense.

2. Following the advent of the All-Volunteer Force (AVF) in 1973 the demographic composition of the Armed Forces also changed. An increase in married soldiers, women, ethnic minorities, male and female single parents, and dual-career service couples in the military precipitated an increased concern with the implications of military families for retention and operational readiness (Segal and Harris 1993).

3. V-mail was a process of photographing letters in the U.S., mailing the negatives overseas, printing the photograph-letters, and delivering them to soldiers. The process reduced an 8 ½ by 11-inch letter to a 4 by 5 ½ inch photograph/open-letter. The micro-filming process did make communication more efficient by reducing the bulk of letters.

4. Operation Uphold Democracy (OUD) was an interventionary, nation-building effort in Haiti organized to restore democracy following the departure of a military ruler. On September 19, 1994, following political negotiations, U.S. soldiers from the 10th Mountain Division, Fort Drum, New York came ashore on Haiti from U.S. naval vessels and were ordered to "be a presence" during the political transition and the restoration of civil order. The mission ended, for the 10th Mountain Division, in December 1994.

5. The rationale for *future military deployments* rather than a retrospective study rested on sample size. We wanted to maximize participation and thought it better to include all soldiers and spouses and compare results.

6. The item values are scored 0 for "Very Ineffective," 1 for "Ineffective," 2 for "Equally Effective and Ineffective," 3 for "Effective," and 4 for "Very Effective." Means were computed for each medium in each group.

REFERENCES

Adler, R. P. 1995. "Introduction." In *Crossroads on the Information Highway: Convergence and Diversity in Communication Technologies,* edited by R. P. Adler. Queenstown: Aspen Institute Wye River Conference Center.

Bell, D. B. 1991. "The Impact of Operation Desert Shield/ Storm on Army Families: A Summary of Findings to Date." *Proceedings of the 53rd Annual Conference of the National Council on Family Relations.* Denver, CO.

Bell, D. B., M. L. Stevens, and M. W. Segal. 1996. *How to Support Families During Overseas Deployments: A Sourcebook for Service Providers* (Research Report 1687). Alexandria: U.S. Army Research Institute for the Behavioral and Social Sciences.

Bell, D. B., J. Teitelbaum, and W. R. Schumm. 1996. "Keeping the Home Fires Burning: Family Support Issues." *Military Review* 76(2):80-84.

Bowen, G. L. and D. K. Orthner, eds. 1989. *The Organization Family: Work and Family Linkages in the U.S. Military.* New York: Praeger.

Campbell, D. 1984. *Women at War with America: Private Lives in a Patriotic Era.* Cambridge: Harvard University Press.

Cohen, A. A. and J. Dotan. 1976. "Communication in the Family as a Function of Stress during War and Peace." *Journal of Marriage and Family* (February):141-148.

Collins, R. 1989. "Sociological Theory, Disaster Research and War." Pp. 365-385 in *Social Structure and Disaster,* edited by G. A. Kreps. Newark: Deleware Press.

Communication News. 2003. "West Point Unwired." *Communication News* 40(6):14-18.

Cooper, S. D. 2003. "Press Controls in Wartime: The Legal, Historical, and Institutional Context." *American Communication Journal* 6(4). An on-line journal available at: http://www.acjournal.org/index.htm.

Coser, L. A., ed. 1974. *Greedy Institutions: Patterns of Undivided Commitment.* New York: Free Press.

Dauber, Cori. 2003. "Image as Argument: The Impact of Mogadishu on U.S. Military Intervention." *Armed Forces and Society* 27(2):205-230.

Dowd, J. J. 2000. "Hard Jobs and Good Ambition: U.S. Army Generals and the Rhetoric of Modesty." *Symbolic Interactionism* 23(2):183-205.

Ender, M. G. 1996. "Soldiering Toward the Information Superhighway: Old and New Communication Media Use During Military Operations in the Post-Cold War Era." Unpublished doctoral dissertation, Department of Sociology, University of Maryland, College Park.

_____. 1997. "E-mail to Somalia: New Communication Media between Home and War Fronts." Pp. 27-52 in *Mapping Cyberspace: Social Research on the Electronic Frontier*, edited by J. Behar. Oakdale: Dowling College Press.

_____. forthcoming. "Military Brats: Film Representations of Children from Military Families." *Armed Forces and Society.*

Ender, M. G. and D. R. Segal. 1996. "E(V)-mail to the Foxhole: Soldier Isolation, (Tele)communication, and Force-Projection Operations." *Journal of Political and Military Sociology* 24:83-104.

_____. 1998. "Cyber-Soldiering: Race, Class, Gender and New Media Use in the Military." Pp. 65-82 in *Cyberghetto or Cybertopia?: Race, Class, and Gender on the Internet*, edited by B. Ebo. Westport: Greenwood.

Fischer, C. S. 1992. *America Calling: A Social History of the Telephone to 1940*. Berkeley: University of California Press.

Fulk, J., J. Schmitz, and C. W. Steinfield. 1990. "A Social Influence Model of Technology Use." Pp. 117-140 in *Organizations and Communication Technology*, edited by J. Fulk and C. W. Steinfield. Newbury Park: Sage.

Harper, H. 2001. "The Military and Society: Reaching and Reflecting Audiences in Fiction and Film." *Armed Forces and Society* 27(2):231-248.

Hill, R. 1949. *Families under Stress: Adjustment to the Crisis of War Separation and Reunion*. New York: Harper.

Hunter, E. J. 1982. *Families under the Flag: A Review of Military Family Literature*. New York: Praeger.

Hunter, E. J. and D. S. Nice. 1978. *Children of Military Families: A Part and yet Apart*. Washington: Superintendent of Documents, U.S. Government Printing Office [008—4—00181-4].

Kanter, Rosebeth Moss. 1977. *Work and Family in the United States: A Critical Review and Agenda for Research and Policy.* New York: Russell Sage Foundation.

Kaslow, F. W., ed. 1993. *The Military Family in Peace and War.* New York: Springer.

Kraut, R. E. 1989. "Telecommuting: The Trade-offs of Home Work." *Journal of Communication* 39(3):19-47.

Levidow, L. and K. Robins, eds. 1989. *Cyborg Worlds: The Military Information Society.* London: Free Association Books.

Litoff, J. B. and D. C. Smith. 1990. "'Will he get my letter?' Popular Portrayals of Mail and Morale during World War II." *Journal of Popular Culture* 23(4):21-43.

_____. 1991. *Since You Went Away: World War II Letters from American Women on the Home Front.* New York: Oxford University Press.

McCubbin, H., et al., eds. 1974. *Family Separation and Reunion.* Washington: U.S. Government Printing Office. [Cat. No. D-206.21: 74-70].

McLuhan, M. 1964. *Understanding Media: The Extensions of Man.* New York: McGraw-Hill.

Miller, T. E. 1995. "New Markets for Information." *American Demographics* (April):46-54.

Morris, M. and C. Ogan. 1996. "The Internet as Mass Medium." *Journal of Communication* 46(1):39-50.

Murray, G. 2001. *Together or Separate?: Newspaper Coverage of Gender Integrated Training.* Patrick Air Force Base: Defense Equal Opportunity Management Institute.

Powell, C. L. 1995. *My American Journey.* New York: Random House.

Reymers, K. 1998. "Telecommuting: On the Re-integration of Work and Family." *Red Feather Journal of Graduate Sociology* 2.

Rice, R. E. 1987. "Computer-Mediated Communication and Organizational Innovation." *Journal of Communication* 37(4):65-94.

———. 1993. "Media Appropriateness: Using Social Presence Theory to Compare Traditional and New Organizational Media." *Human Communication Research* 19(4):451-484.

Roach, C., ed. 1993. *Communication and Culture in War and Peace.* Newbury Park: Sage. '

Sanchez, J. 1987. *Telecommuting: A Selective Annotated Bibliography.* Montecello: Vance Bibliographies.

Schement, J. R. 1995. "Divergence amid Convergence: The Evolving Information Environment of the Home." Pp. 135-160 in *Crossroads on the Information Highway: Convergence and Diversity in Communication Technologies,* edited by R. P. Adler. Queenstown: Aspen Institute Wye River Conference Center.

Schepp, B. 1990. *The Telecommunicator's Handbook: How to Work for a Salary—without ever leaving your House.* NY: Pharos Books.

Schumm, W. R., et al. 2004. "Expectations, Use, and Evaluations of Communications Media among Deployed Peacekeepers." *Armed Forces and Society,* 30(4):649-662.

Schumm, W. R., et al. 1999. "The Desert FAX: A Research Note on Calling Home from Somalia." *Armed Forces and Society* 25(3):509-521.

Schwarzkopf, H. N. 1992. *It doesn't take a Hero: General H. Norman Schwarzkopf, the Autobiography.* NY: Bantam Books.

Segal, D. R., B. J. Reed, and D. E. Rohall. 1998. "Constabulary Attitudes of National Guard and Regular Soldiers in the U.S. Army." *Armed Forces and Society* 24(1):535-548.

Segal, M. W. 1986. "The Military and the Family as Greedy Institutions." *Armed Forces and Society* 13(1):9-38.

———. 1989. "The Nature of Work and Family Linkages: A Theoretical Perspective." Pp. 3-36 in *The Organization Family: Work and Family in the U.S. Military*, edited by G. L. Bowen and K. Orthner. New York: Praeger.

Segal, M. W. and J. J. Harris. 1993. *What We Know about Army Families* (Special Report 21). Alexandria: U.S. Army Research Institute for the Behavioral and Social Sciences.

Shils, E. A. and M. Janowitz. 1948. "Cohesion and Disintegration in the Wehrmacht in World War II." *Public Opinion Quarterly* 12:280-292.

Siebold, Guy L. 2001. "Core Issues and Theory in Military Sociology." *Journal of Political and Military Sociology* 29(1):140-159.

Silverstone, R. 1993. "Time, Information, and Communication Technologies and the Household." *Time and Society* 2(3):283-311.

Short, J., E. Williams, and B. Christie. 1976. *The Social Psychology of Telecommunication*. London: John Wiley and Sons.

Stanley, J., D. R. Segal, and J. C. Laughton. 1990. "Grassroots Family Action and Military Policy Responses." *Marriage and Family Review* 15(3-4):207-223.

United States Post Office Department. 1991. *Annual Report of the Postmaster General*. Washington: U.S. Post Office Department.

Wartella, Ellen and Nancy Jennings. 2001. "New Members of the Family: The Digital Revolution in the Home." *Journal of Family Communication* 1(1):59-69.

Wellman, B. 1997. "The Road to Utopia and Dystopia on the Information Highway." *Contemporary Sociology* 26(4):445-449.

294

Wellman, B., et al. 1996. "Computer Networks as Social Networks: Collaborative Work, Telework and Virtual Community." *Annual Review of Sociology*: 213-238.

Williams, F. and R. E. Rice. 1983. "Communication Research and New Media Technologies." Pp. 200-224 in *Communication Yearbook 7,* edited by R. N. Bostrom. Beverly Hills: Sage.

Williams Jr., R. M. and M. B. Smith. 1949. "General Characteristics of Ground Combat." Pp. 59-104 in *The American Soldier: Combat and its Aftermath*, Vol. II, edited by S. A. Stouffer et al. Princeton: Princeton University Press.

Ydén, K., ed. 2005. *Directions in Military Organizing.* Stockholm: NorstedtsTryckeri.

Chapter 10

THEORIZING
THE EMBODIED VETERAN
IN TIMES OF HARDSHIP [1]

Paul Higate
University of Bristol
Bristol, United Kingdom

LEARNING OBJECTIVES

After reading this chapter, you should be able to

- demonstrate an awareness of the embodiment of social practice;
- reflect on the sentience of the physical body;
- discuss some of the ways in which physical capital is developed in the military more generally;
- recognize the methodological difficulties in researching the body;
- understand that human agents may be largely unaware of the influence of their physical capital in shaping current and future horizons of action.

*Army life is sort of embedded into you...you don't real-
ize that it is a totally different style of living, breathing,
eating. (Brian 1996)*

It has recently been argued that a disproportionate number
of the single homeless population have a background in
the armed forces, and that this can be explained by ex-
servicemen's[2] vulnerability to the effects of "military
institutionalization." In these popular understandings, the long-
term influence of military socialization is claimed to limit the
development of a range of skills vital for reintegration into
civilian life (Jolly 1996; Randall and Brown 1994). Given that
formerly "mapped out life trajectories have now to be
selected" across an increasing range of areas (Campbell
1996:163), these single, ex-servicemen may be disadvantaged
as a consequence of the extra demands created by the "do-it-
yourself biography" (Beck and Beck-Gernsheim 1996). For
example, single ex-servicemen who lived on base may remain
dependent on paternalistic military structures, as the institution had assumed total responsibility for housing them in
barrack blocks (Beevor 1991; Jessup 1996). These conditions
contrast sharply with the insecure employment and housing
markets in civilian life, perhaps compounding the factors
underlying the emergence of homelessness for ex-servicemen
both in the UK and in other advanced economies. Research in
the U.S., for example, has demonstrated links between veteran
status and housing/employment insecurity (see Rosenheck and
Fontana 1994; Rosenheck and Koegel 1994; Wenzel et al. 1993).

It is surprising that military sociologists have largely
failed to examine a concept that many would argue is of great
significance to both military experience and civilian life: institutionalization (Higate 2001). Clues to this neglect can be
found in the dominant influences shaping military sociology,

in which interpretive approaches have been underdeveloped and scarcely utilized. Drawing on Morris Janowitz, for example, Lester Kurtz (1992) has argued that sociologists, generally, have shown little interest in war and peace, with military research tending to be dominated by applied psychological or "scientific" approaches. Thus, military sociology's location on the periphery of the discipline has left it relatively isolated from theoretical elaboration seen in other subfields of sociology, particularly within the context of qualitative approaches.

Another possible explanation for the relatively limited methodological and epistemological toolkit of military sociologists, might lie in the somewhat narrow social profiles of those with an interest in this sub-discipline. These predominantly U.S.-based white men, it is argued, contain a disproportionate number of veterans among their ranks (Caforio 2003). Their approaches to research seem to have been skewed toward an empirical focus by military agendas, with "most social science investigations of war and peace...designed...to make the armed forces more efficient and effective" (Kurtz 1992:64). In this way, research has been oriented toward the engineering rather than the enlightenment model of sociology. Here, interpretive approaches are less obviously quantifiable into "hard" and "scientific" data, and, perhaps accorded only marginal importance by the military as end-user of research.

New Direction 10.1

Sociologists have shown little interest in war and peace, with military research tending to be dominated by applied psychological or "scientific" approaches.

298

Background to Study

The starting point for the current study[3] was the research carried out by Anderson, Kemp, and Quilgars (1993), Gunner and Knott (1997), and Randall and Brown (1994), who suggest that up to one in four of the single homeless population has completed full-time military service.[4] In these reports, however, the links between military service and homelessness are framed causally, with little reflection on the contestability of the categories "military service" or "homeless." The authors overstate the strength of the relationship between military service and homelessness, as they fail to explore the significance of inter- and intraservice difference. In so doing, the varied experiences of military occupations that could range from the bureaucratic, office-bound, *Royal Air Force* Personnel Administrator to the *Army* Infantryman (who may have spent much of his career patrolling the hazardous streets of Northern Ireland or Kosovo), are conflated. However, though the diverse military does not have a "universalizing" effect on its members (Beevor 1991; Edmonds 1988; Morgan 1987; Royle 1997), nevertheless, the available evidence does suggest that the links between military service and homelessness are sufficiently robust[5] to warrant further consideration.

Study Design and Methodology

The current small-scale study was designed to minimize—as far as was practically possible—the differences between participant experiences of the military. To these ends, sixteen of the seventeen participants (details of which can be found in the appendix) served within the non-commissioned ranks of the British Army for a duration of time between one and

299

twelve years.[6] One of them had attained the rank of Sergeant, though primarily they constituted a mix of Privates, Lance Corporals, and Corporals on discharge. This junior rank profile mirrored earlier research in which, aside from casual anecdote, there was no evidence for ex-officers or commissioned status amongst this element of the homeless population. This means that all had experienced similar (if not identical) basic training and broader career regimes, within a comparable cultural milieu.[7] These ex-servicemen were subject to semi-structured interviews between 1996 and 1997 in six major cities in Britain, which lasted between 1 and 2 hours. Interviews were broad in scope and, as research progressed, quickly centered on the most physically testing manifestation of homelessness—rough sleeping—which was used as the working definition throughout the study.[8] The term rough sleeping refers quite literally to the experience of sleeping outdoors in shop doorways, in garbage skips, and the like, and has also been referred to as rooflessness (Pleace et al. 1997:4). The participants' experience of rough sleeping was mixed. A number had slept rough only once, while others had slept rough episodically, and one ex-soldier reported sleeping rough "habitually." These experiences mirror the categories developed by Pleace (1998) in his three stage typology of rough sleeping. More importantly, the sample was recruited on the basis that they had slept rough within five years of discharge from the Army, as a way in which to limit the influence of civilian experience. Surprisingly, the influence of the civilian environment had been largely ignored in earlier evidence, with a number of ex-servicemen experiencing difficulty ten or more years after discharge from the armed forces.

The recurrence of the rough sleeping theme appeared to be linked in complex ways to the participant group's shared knowledge of outdoor survival techniques and high levels of fitness fostered through the demands of Army-regulation physical tests, measured both "in the field," and in the gym. The accounts of military training and rough sleeping were surprisingly consistent and were framed in terms of a masculinized "pseudo-challenge" (Higate 1997). This consistency in data may have reflected the extent to which physical performance in the Army is relatively less open to subversion[9] than other dimensions of this occupation. While individuals routinely resist the inculcation of military values and attitudes—even during the intensive phase of infantry training (Hockey 1986)—timed runs, or "beastings," and the successful completion of assault courses are crucial to the unquestionable development of "quantifiable" physical capital. In pursuing this "embodied line of enquiry" (Scott and Morgan 1993), I hoped to highlight one of the more pervasive themes to emerge from Army life and make sense of the emergence and sustaining of the physically challenging experience of rough sleeping. The findings from the current study should be seen within the context of the limited number of participants and, for this reason, attention is focused on the validity of the analysis, rather than its overall representativeness (Mitchell 1983:187–211).

The empirical material presented below was derived from ten of the seventeen participants, and combines the themes of military-masculine gender ideology with their

---

New Direction 10.2

Accounts of military training and rough sleeping are surprisingly consistent and are framed in terms of a masculinized "pseudo-challenge."

301

corporeal groundings. Precursors to this combination of empirical and theoretical materials are to be found in Connell's (1995) discussion of men's bodies and Bourke's (1999) historical account of soldiers maimed in World War I. Although Connell's focus on the "middle-class included body" is enlightening, it is worthwhile illuminating the experiences of the socially *excluded*, particularly those that sleep rough. Within the context of this chapter, consideration is given to the unintended consequences of military survival training. Here, I focus on the ways in which physical resilience to testing conditions—developed in the army—may play a role in the emergence of rough sleeping for a number of ex-servicemen. Elsewhere, and within the context of other data derived from the same study, I have sought to use the theme of gender as an analytical focus for investigating the high mobility of the homeless population (Higate 2000).

From Bodies to Data

A smoothly functioning body rarely invokes its owner's interests (Scott and Morgan 1993:86) as all tasks demanded of it are performed successfully. Yet, its antithesis, the "disabled body," has been shown to dwell largely within the *discursive* or monitored consciousness of the "masculine" self (Bourke 1999; Connell 1995:54). In these cases, reflection on bodily performance and the perception of others (who possess bodies that *conform* to "normal" functioning and appearance) resonates throughout the sense-of-self in terms of felt, and expressed, "physical deviance." While a number of the participants in the current study displayed the deleterious effects of long-term alcohol use, thereby bringing their body into the discursively monitored realm through poor health, the majority of them were, nevertheless, untroubled by their bodily

302

states. For this reason, attempts to elicit information around the role of the body within the context of physical hardship had to be approached tangentially, such that participant accounts concerning bodily-reflexive practice (Connell 1995) could be transformed into "expressible" and "substantive" material (Scott and Morgan 1993:135-139; Watson 1998:165). The alternative approach—asking explicit questions about the body—may have provided participants with "mental maps" (Connerton 1989) with which to inadvertently exaggerate the role of the frequently "unacknowledged" physical body (Higate 1998:181).

These methodological considerations influenced the interview content that explored factors focused on the lack of attention to physical selves. Here, exercise, diet, and accounts of resilience in tough conditions, signaled the unspoken centrality of the participant's bodies against the backdrop of masculinized identity.[10]

Institutionalization

Individuals who have fostered complexes of routine (within temporally patterned institutional structures) are vulnerable to processes of institutionalization (Goffman 1961). Unconscious and routine action, also called habit, can be conceptualized as "unreflective accommodation" that proceeds through the "practical consciousness" (Cohen and Taylor 1992). Actors, while not articulating "the conditions of their own action" (Giddens 1984:375), nevertheless, remain attentive at a non-verbal level. Human agents could not possibly "go on," unless they relegated reflection on action to these non-monitored realms (Campbell 1996). Some suggest that the intensity of these processes is of central significance within the total institutional context of the military (Goffman 1961; Jolly 1996).

303

Here, immersion into a pervasive series of both basic and continuation training regimes produces individuals capable of taking the lives of others (Morgan 1994).

Not surprisingly, a number of service people may experience difficulty in re-adapting to a civilian environment in which, for some, these "skills" represent negative capital as some anecdotal evidence involving "anomic" and "culture shocked" ex-servicemen would suggest. A change of circumstances in which habit loses its significance (for example, military practice in a civilian context) could serve to limit the freedom of the human agent. Thus, deeply ingrained habit could become "dysfunctional" (Campbell 1996:159; La Plante 1992:43). Theoretical concern regarding these unspoken dimensions of human agency offers an insight into the longer-term influence of the habitualized institutional setting. This, indeed, may pivot centrally on the fostering of habit, grounded—in the current study—in the *masculine* self. As Jenkins (1992:179) asserts more generally:

> Conscious and unconscious mental processes lie at opposite ends of a continuum...in between is an area which is, as yet, little considered by sociologists...inasmuch as it is the domain of habit it is of great sociological importance...this may be where much socialisation put down [its] strongest roots...it is also likely to be the source of the potency of the processes of institutionalisation.

Though ex-soldiers are likely to be geographically dispersed after discharge, as they return to place of origin or seek paid employment, they will often possess behavioral residue as a consequence of immersion into the Army habitus. Ways of moving, the presentation of the "smart" self, and so

304

forth, refer to the control of, and attention to, the bodily dimension. A heightened awareness of the military-civilian transition brings these issues into sharp focus, as the comments of an Army psychiatrist illustrate through reference to the "demobbed" World War II ex-serviceman:

> We see them here and there already in our streets, those straight, bronzed figures, moving with a precision that no civilian suit can disguise. (Turner and Rennell 1995:40)

However, it is important to differentiate between "habituation" and "institutionalization," as Jenkins (1996:132) states "*collective* habit is a form of institutionalisation...habit is often the individual expression of institutionalised patterns" (emphasis added). In this respect, understanding what links "institutionalized" with "ex-serviceman," comes inappropriately close (Edmonds 1988) to the allied notion of the "squaddie" as a stereotyped "unthinking automaton" (Stone 1996:101). Comments concerning institutionalization are heuristic in intent and can be linked most directly to combatant rather than non-combatant roles; the differences between which come into sharpest focus within the context of peace-keeping duties[11] (Olsson 1999). Explorations of these collective habits might turn more directly to a consideration of their "absently present" bodily foundations (Shilling 1993).

Embodying Institutionalization

In recent years, considerations of the embodied dimensions of human agency have moved into a more central sociological position (Featherstone, Hepworth, and Turner 1991; Nettleton and Watson 1998; Shilling 1991, 1993, 1997; Scott and Morgan 1993; Turner 1996). The importance of the body within human agency is acknowledged by Shilling (1997:746):

> Socialisation needs analysing in terms of the partial social shaping of *embodied dispositions* as well as in terms of the partial internalisation of mental views and attitudes. (Emphasis added)

Bodies are vulnerable to transformation through their owner's actions, which are typically mediated by broader social forces through dieting, physical exercise, and a whole range of other activities that develop particular aspects of physical "capital" (Featherstone et al. 1991; Shilling 1991). Here, the consequence of bodily practice aimed toward specific outcomes swiftly enters corporeal repertoires. While not directly invoking the physical realm, the following comments are salient in this context:

> Every single deliberate, freely-chosen...action contains the potential to become the first step in the construction of an unconsidered and automatic, habitual routine of conduct...all actions will necessarily decay over time into conditioned behaviours. (Campbell 1996:163)

Shilling's notion of "disposition" is suggestive of the durability of bodily transformation and, in turn, the long-term legacy of collectively habituated practice within particular relationships of dependency—these practices may result in the production of "institutionalized selves." However, in using these concepts, it is clear that we are *all* dependent on a stock of routine bodily practices that proceed on an "habitual basis" (Campbell 1996:163), though relatively few of these practices are grounded in aggressively masculinized settings in which body *potentialities* (for example, the ability, ultimately, to fight and kill) are of central concern.

Military bodies are located within tightly ordered institutional and bureaucratic orders (Scott and Morgan 1993:16). They represent "irreducible elements" (Freund 1990; Williams 1998) of spatially bounded social fabrics characterized by organizationally idiosyncratic "somatic hierarchies." Within the Army, this hierarchy is headed by a broadly consensual hegemonic masculinity that prescribes "templates of embodiment" against which both servicemen and servicewomen might be appraised. These constitute a social order that resonates through bodily practice and sense of self. As Connell states more broadly:

> Body reflexive practices...are not internal to the individual. They involve social relations and symbolism: they may well involve large-scale institutions... Through body reflexive practices, more than individual lives are formed: a social world is formed. (Connell 1995:64)

With these conceptual comments in mind, I intend next to map out the somatic terrain of the Army substantively, with a focus on its repercussions for sense of self, rooted in *trans-*

New Direction 10.3

Military bodies are located within tightly ordered institutional and bureaucratic orders (Scott and Morgan 1993:16).

formed physical disposition and gender ideology, which is brought about by basic and continuation training. Contributions from both Crossley (1995) and Wacquant (1995) are emphasized as they point to the significance of the *sentient* body.

Producing the Military Self

Military socialization is aimed at creating a range of bodily capitals among its constituent members that broadly cluster around the importance of the hyper-masculine "soldier" (Foucault 1977; Higate 2003; Mansfield and McGinn 1993; Willetts 1990). Those that concern us here are linked to individuals most likely to endure front-line combat. In these instances, efficient cardio-vascular systems, strength, agility, and overall tolerance to hardship, represent the particular attributes toward which military basic and continuation training is oriented (Hockey 1986). Army Infantrymen, Paratroopers, the *Royal Air Force Regiment* and the Special Forces, exemplify well-developed capitals attuned to tough physical exigency. These somatic processes are embedded in masculinized gender ideologies that—in parallel to the context-contingent legitimacy of bodily capitals—vary within, and between, the three military services and occupations (Barrett 1996; Bourke 1999). Morgan explains these ideologies at a higher level of abstraction, highlighting more universal military experiences:

> Being able to take it like a man was, and continues to be, part of the military experience with its particular emphasis on a whole range of deprivations from harsh and sometimes all-embracing disciplines to cold water, hard beds and lack of sleep. (Morgan 1990:23)

308

The body-man-warrior nexus (Morgan 1990), pivots centrally on the production of masculinized bodily disposition, on a range of fronts. These processes capitalize on the complex interplay between bodies, their internal functioning, and their environments, mediated by discourses of agent interpretation (Featherstone and Hepworth 1998). Within the military context, interaction between biochemical endorphins and tough training exercises are interpreted *beneficially* by soldiers in consequence of institutional belief systems. The "no pain/no gain" ethos pervades rationalizations for training up to limits that occasionally result in the death of hopeful recruits, as McCallion (1995) has demonstrated within the extreme *Special Air Service* (SAS) "Selection" process. The linkage (some might say) of excessive physical exercise to a sense of masculinized status is central. Considering Connell's (1995) notion of "circuits and staging posts" concerning the body, masculinities, and sexuality, it is suggested that "body-military culture-masculinity" represents a bodily disposition crucial to a sense of gendered soldierly confidence. Comments describing the socialization of boxers have sharp resonance with those immersed in the military life:

> The boxer's body is simultaneously his means of production, the raw materials he and his trainer have to work with, and on...*Bodily capital and bodily labour are thus linked by a recursive relation* which makes them closely dependent on one another. (Wacquant 1995:67; emphasis added)

A closely linked circuit could concern a high tolerance to alcohol. It is similarly recognizable, by both somatic and cognitive components, developed in line with gender ideologies linked to "proper" men "being able to hold their drink"

(Morgan 1987). The deep roots of gender in robust bodily integrity, sketched here, add to the critique of "dualist legacies of the past," in which body and mind has been reified (Williams 1998:125). Thus, somatic potential and a sense of the masculinized self may converge seamlessly on the site of identity, within the context of Army life.

Soon after enlistment, successful recruits actively, though unconsciously, wring a transformed sense of self from the harsh and frequently protracted period of Army socialization (Hockey 1986). They are assimilated into "culturally patterned institutional gender orders" (Barrett 1996:130) that recursively colonize the practical and non-conscious realms. Regimental histories, stories of combat, and all manner of extreme situations, serve as readily accessible discursive resources, through which masculinized ontological security is fostered. Servicemen come to have a sense of self and of belonging in a newly ordered world, the material foundations of which are nested in the physical self. Not unlike boxers, basic military training

> reorganizes the entire corporeal field...bringing to prominence certain organs and abilities and making others recede, transforming not only the physique...but also (his) *"body sense,"* the consciousness he has of his organism and, through this changed body, of the world around him. (Wacquant 1995:73; emphasis added)

Thus, the mind is inseparable from the body and they exist as "reversible aspects of a single fabric" (1995:47). The ways of being-in-the-world directly concern practical achievements experienced through the corporeal dimension or the "body-subject" (1995:47, 53). A prime example suggestive of long-term bodily habituation would be the ex-soldier sponta-

310

New Direction 10.4

Bodily transformations vary in their extent and range, with Army training likely to produce the durable shift in the sense of body and self, thereby shaping future horizons of action.

---

neously diving for cover in the presence of an unseen backfiring vehicle.[12] Here, the body responds in a conditioned way, demonstrating how individuals can become "corporeally predisposed towards certain actions rather than others" (Shilling 1997:746). Although these more obviously *conditioned* responses operate at the non-verbal level, tolerances to extremes of cold, heat, and general physical exigency also become deposited into the bodily repertoire, and may remain obstinate. More broadly, bodies "remember"; and this is demonstrated by the research that explores experiences of "bodily memories of the warmth and comfort" of the family (Morgan 1996:122) and post-traumatic stress disorder (Grillon, Southwick, and Charney 1996; Van der Kolk 1994). A mundane example of the sentient body within the context of what we might call the "somatic memory," is the experience of feeling the cold more intensely upon returning to a chilly British winter from a hot foreign clime. Hence, bodily transformations vary in their extent and range, with Army training likely to produce the durable shift in the sense of body and self, thereby shaping future horizons of action.

Physical Continuities—Out of the Military and into Civilian Life

The inclusion of the empirical material from the current study is included in this and the following sections. It is intended to

311

illustrate the ways in which trajectories in civilian life may be partially influenced by the mix of military-masculine gender ideology and physical capital developed in the Army. With little in the way of white-collar, transferable skills, many ex-combat soldiers are drawn to those occupations where "tough" physical capital may be financially recognized. Among the participants in the current study, these included the fishing, construction, and security industries—the latter exemplified by "bouncers" in clubs and pubs. A typical comment came from "Mick," who echoed the common reference to paid employment of this sort: "I mean, in the building trade, the fitness I got in the Army has helped me" (Mick 1996) "Rolly" explained what he did soon after discharge:

> Long line fishing...you need to be fit...and window cleaning. Of course you're out all year round (in this work) no matter what the weather. (Rolly 1996)

The restructuring of capitalist societies, however, has resulted in a sharp reduction in paid work that demands machismo and high levels of physical capital (Connell 1995; Turner 1996). This is an issue of particular importance for men (typically), whose status is negotiated through the deployment of "hard" physical capitals (Seidler 1997). The "traditional" masculinized body's declining significance in the contemporary work place (Cockburn 1983), may invoke a sense of anxiety around masculinized identities that must be continually attended to and improved (Kerfoot and Knights 1993).[13] In these circumstances, ex-soldiers might be drawn to a pseudo-militarized habitus, through which familiar gender ideologies are rekindled. Of particular note are the uniformed services (prison and police) or, more dramatically, employment as a mercenary. A significant percentage may even attempt to re-enlist in the military. While the links between labor market transformations and rough sleeping are extremely complex, nevertheless the participants in this study had all experienced redundancy in occupations that had relied on their physical strength and/or working outdoors. Alternative opportunities for employment (many of which were located within the service sector) tended not to be present in the ex-servicemen's thinking. Occupations that could be perceived as feminized and sedentary were unable to provide the "man of action imagery" that might be associated with more physical employment (Higate 1998).

Testing the Body—Rough Sleeping *

The corporeal self represents a barometer of the conditions in which it functions. Clearly, rough sleeping in poor weather conditions makes excessive demands on the physical resources, which is illustrated more generally by the health of "the homeless." However, it is important to acknowledge the complexities of the health/homelessness relationship:

> The physical health...of single homeless people was found to be considerably worse than that of the general population. While it is difficult to know the direction of cause and effect between homelessness and poor health, the findings...nevertheless confirm that there is a strong relationship between the two. (Bines 1997:146)

Hunger and cold almost certainly accompany the experience of rough sleeping. Carlen's (1996) accounts of youth homelessness detail the daily struggles of keeping body and mind together. Narrative extracts from the young homeless

313

people in her study made frequent reference to "starvation" and "freezing to death" (Carlen 1996). In contrast to this, the physical states of rough sleeping soldiers remained relatively robust and their descriptions of it somewhat matter-of-fact. Indeed, the participants tended to distinguish themselves from the wider rough sleeping "civilian" population. Widespread sentiments drawn from the present study acknowledge the issues of both preparation and the "ability to cope" in the face of oppressive conditions. The following explanations were offered by "Benny" and "Dougy":

> A lot of people have an argument and just walk off from where they are. They don't think about what they are going to do the next day. They'll sleep in a bus shelter for the night. But the next day when they wake up, they've got nothing, no sleeping bag; then they start to panic. But if you think it all out, what you're going to do first; then you can survive. (Benny 1996)

> Some of these people, they just can't cope...it's a terrible thing. But if you've been in the Army, self-discipline is drummed straight into you...It can be pouring but you know the score - you know what to do. Rather than sitting there soaking wet, get yourself in a nook and cranny somewhere - you'd be dry in the morning. (Dougy 1996)

"Paul," appearing to speak on behalf of absent colleagues, described the way in which Army survival training helped during rough sleeping:

> What we're saying is that you've had it rough at times in the military. You know, when you've been on exercise, you're living in jungle somewhere for 5 weeks

and you're just living on compo [military] rations…it
does make you…aware. (Paul 1996)

Paul's account signals an awareness of the physical
hardship of field exercises. In these contexts, the Army "buddy
system," which relies on close interdependence, requires individual soldiers take responsibility for ensuring their physical
selves are ready for operations. Failure to tend to blisters, for
example, amounts to the undermining of self *and* team cohesion.

Ex-soldiers appeared to be hit hard by bodily attenua-
tion, when it became clear that it would impinge on the
liberating potential associated with a fit and strong body. The
reasons for this might be, first, that failing bodies undermine
the integrity of the hyper-masculine self in which this identity
is deeply embedded, as we saw earlier. Second, poor physical-
ity restricts opportunities to travel around the country, which
represents continuity with military experience (Jolly 1992;
Randall and Brown 1994) that had been facilitated through
rough sleeping.

"Benchmark Experience"—Rough Sleeping

For a number of participants, the first instance of rough sleeping represented something of a watershed in their experience
of civilian life. However, once they realized that sleeping
outside was manageable and somewhat familiar, future
prospects of sleeping rough seemed less threatening and less
alien. Ex-soldiers regarded their first episode of rough sleeping (normally on exercise in the army) as a physical
rite-of-passage—these usually came in the form of military
"field-craft" exercises. In addition, two participants described
experiences of rough sleeping *prior* to enlistment and, indeed,
these influenced the decision to "join up" (Higate 1997).

315

Interestingly, the high profile Army campaign conducted in Britain during the latter months of 1997 to recruit for the Armed Services from "hostels for the homeless" pointed to the value of the "independent survival skills" of this group as useful for military life. However, in the following extracts, the spotlight is shifted to initial experiences of what we might term "military rough sleeping." "Ziggy," who slept rough shortly after discharge from the Army, talked about the experience: "to tell you the truth (rough sleeping) didn't bother me...I just looked at it like doing a fieldcraft exercise...something like that" (Ziggy 1996). "John" echoed this apparent indifference:

> When it came to...sleeping rough, I just used to think "well, I've done this in the Army, it's no big thing." In a way (Army life) helped because you used to do the old training exercises, where you went out...I got a sleeping bag, so it wasn't too bad...yeah...it sort of— how can I put it—it prepares you for anything...you know if you have to sleep out. (John 1996)

"Benny's" approach was similar:

> I found it easier to do what (we'd) been doing—on exercise all the time...sleeping rough, it was just an extension of that...I was quite at home with it...I went to Newbury...I moved down there with the tree protestors...you've done it all before...so it's not new to you. (Benny 1996)

These extracts signal a continuity between military and civilian experience and, indeed, Benny's account invokes the notion of "home" while sleeping out, demonstrating the

316

concept's variability on the one hand (Somerville 1992:530) and, on the other, the ways in which "'home' and 'homelessness' serve to define each other at a phenomenological level" (Wardhaugh 1999:91). When combined with discursive knowledge linked to food and diet, and the utility of equipment that might facilitate sleeping out, these potentialities resonated throughout the "option" to sleep rough. However, to assert that these individuals discursively formulated a "strategy" to join the ranks of the homeless would be, in the words of Morgan (1989:29), to "surrender too much to the forward march of rational calculation." The genesis of rough sleeping in these examples is to be found in the shifting intersections of housing/labor market asymmetries and the resilience of a masculinized physical capital.

Fuelling the Body-Food

Though food and diet are subject to a panoply of cultural mediators (Lupton 1996; Morgan 1996), their centrality to continued physical functioning is, nevertheless, worthy of reiteration, particularly within the context of literature exploring the "causes" of homelessness. Ex-soldiers from the study expressed a range of insights into food/body interaction and narrative accounts ranged in breadth and insight. For example, in relation to the knowledge fostered during Army training, "Wicksy" explained that he knew "what to eat, and what's good to eat, and what can help you in the cold weather...I was taught chocolate was good for you in cold weather" (Wicksy 1996).

And "Lenny," who had recently moved into a hostel after being discharged from the Canadian Army, followed by rough sleeping in Manchester, talked at length about the physical body and the overconsumption of food and obesity:

317

Loads of extra weight creates tension on your heart...blood system, arteries, respiratory system, liver, kidneys, brain...an unfit body (is linked) with your mind because it effects the ability to make decisions...because your brain is an organ...If your internal system is not functioning 100 percent or near that, then obviously your brain is going to function at a nominally deficient capacity...as opposed to somebody who is 100 percent physically fit,...his brain is working to its maximum ability. (Lenny 1996)

"Mick" expressed the importance of a diet that contains water, high fiber, and carbohydrates. Knowledge about food and the experience of hunger more generally entered tacit bodily repertoires during military service. From this a stoically unspoken tolerance appeared to develop. While it could be argued that familiarity with a nutritious (military) diet would *problematize* situations in which it remained elusive (for example, during the experience of rough sleeping), it appeared that, for the participants, procurement, preparation, and consumption represented *continuity* with their military experience, a situation we would likely find throughout the military. Within the Army, the traditional association between food preparation and women is loosened considerably. As David Morgan (1996) has suggested, traditional social relations and knowledge concerning food has tended to turn on the involvement of women:

Food preparation also represents divisions in terms of knowledge. This knowledge may be about particular cooking techniques, about dietary needs, about the combination of various textures...Sources of this knowledge may be informally passed down from mother to daughter. (Morgan 1996:159)

318

Tolerances to hunger and awareness of diet, grounded within the masculinized ideology of self-sufficiency and independence, served as well-developed coping behaviors, within limited conditions of possibility, in the civilian environment (Higate 1997). Unintentionally, these physical dispositions—knowing and learning to "put up" with a degree of hunger—together with knowledge linked to maintaining bodily integrity, acted to *demystify* the rigors of rough sleeping, thereby contributing to the likelihood of both its emergence and continuance over time. Here, institutionalization is conceptualized in a more sophisticated and dynamic sense, through a range of discursive and practical consciousness-pathways, of which the masculinized sentient body is one.

Bodily Limits

Though a number of ex-soldiers might be relatively well-adapted and prepared for the experience of rough sleeping; nonetheless, the lengthy exposure to conditions of cold and hardship has limits. In addition, heavy and sustained use of alcohol can inflict long-term damage on the body (Bines 1997; Keyes and Kennedy 1992) leading to—as participants in this study reported—nervous system damage, weight loss, and serious stomach ulcers. Furthermore, *perceptions* of inequality, and the stigmatization that characterizes the lives of rough sleepers (Carlen 1996; Snow and Anderson 1987), may be manifested through the psychosocial pathway contributing, in the long-term, to ill-health (Wilkinson 1996; Williams 1998; Keyes and Kennedy 1992). Paradoxically, these physical "warning signals" were either ignored' or, more dangerously, were compounded by further use of both licit and illicit drugs as a way in which to appease this sense of bodily detrition and its corollary erosion of masculinized identity. One way in

319

PAUL HIGATE

New Direction 10.5

The themes of violence, alcohol, and pride offered
Ken a possible escape from his experience of social
distress during his fleeting rough sleeping episodes. He
could distance himself from the personal responsibility
of suicide by the ultimate "test" at the hands of unknown,
violent men.

which the body was implicitly "attacked," mediated by both
alcohol and violence, is described by "Ken," a keen supporter
of the Scottish football club *Rangers*. In this account, he
describes the ways in which he would court violence by
frequenting the public bars of staunch rivals, *Celtic*:

> I would be getting myself into situations (like) walking
> into places...and causing trouble...Basically, I was
> looking to kill myself...but not actually doing it...I
> wanted to die...but I didn't want my kids to think I
> committed suicide and taken the easy option...So, I
> would walk into a pub full of *Celtic* supporters, and I
> would walk in singing "the Sash" (normally sung by
> supporters of *Ranger's* football club). I would get
> beat...I ended up in the hospital with my arm broke, my
> leg broke, my skull fractured...I mean, I wasn't doing it
> consciously; subconsciously I was doing things like
> this. (Ken 1996)

Here, the body's fragility is conjoined with activities
that are typically associated with masculinized performance
(Barrett 1996). The themes of violence, alcohol, and pride
offered Ken a possible escape from his experience of social

320

distress during his fleeting rough sleeping episodes. He could distance himself from the personal responsibility of suicide by the ultimate "test" at the hands of unknown, violent men. This ex-soldier expressed bitterness that he was not "finished off." After hospitalization, he continued with these somewhat ritualistic and potentially lethal activities. Here, the themes of the body's failure to mirror the desires of its owner relate closely to its extreme assailment. Connell (1995:97-98) describes this linkage:

> Not only are men's bodies diverse and changing, they can be positively recalcitrant. Ways are proposed for bodies to participate in social life, and the bodies often refuse...The body is virtually assaulted in the name of masculinity and achievement.

However the men in this study "used" their physical resource, it was necessarily a "site of final truth." Here, academic commentators Sue Scott and David Morgan (1993) highlight the body's limits; at some point it will cease functioning altogether. Through time, a less chaotic relationship with the (albeit insecure) elements of the housing market was engendered through the "recalcitrant body." In this way, the following comment by Seidler, is somewhat ironical, as "revenge of the body" within the context of the present study indicates tentative and somewhat reluctant moves *into* more stable tenure, away *from* the challenge, risk, and "freedom" of rough sleeping.[11] Seidler (1997:21), writing in the first person, states that (men's) bodies are

> Despised and often punished for letting us down when we need them most. For our bodies as machines have become property that is at our disposal. Our freedom

321

supposedly lies in being able to do with them whatever we will. If they let us down we can feel they deserve to be punished. But the body has its own way of getting its revenge.

In the final analysis, the truth of the somatic dimension of human agency concerns its inevitable, and final, exhaustion. Within the context of homeless individuals, death through "natural causes" occurred more broadly ten years earlier than for members of the housed population (Keyes and Kennedy 1992:10-11).

Conclusion

Comments in this paper reflect the resilience of human agency during times of mental and physical hardship. In this way, the physical dimensions of human agency that have been taken for granted should warn against the conflation of "choice" with "rough sleeping." Thus, individuals unwittingly assign social meanings and identities to their physical selves and, in doing so, are "more than mere products of society" (Shilling 1997:737). Rather, they are active survivors that exploit bodily capital attuned to the experience of rough sleeping. The unintended consequence of familiarity with survival techniques, a key element of Army training, serves to shape the conditions of possibility that form an important component in the emergence of the most deviant of identities—rough sleeper.

In this paper, I have explored the experience of rough sleeping among a number of individuals whose biographies are linked through their immersion in a highly physical or embodied environment, and there has been an attempt to reframe what is meant when the notion of "institutionalization" is used. The resonance of these arguments is likely to transcend the illustrative, though somewhat limited, case of the ex-soldier in the current study, and may provide useful points of departure for considering the experience of rough sleeping in a more general sense. However, in this paper, particular attention has been paid to both the gendered and bodily dimensions, as they offer, hitherto unconsidered ways in which to conceptualize how a number of individuals are able to sustain themselves during physically demanding situations. The skills that broadly differentiate these individuals from other members of the transitory rough sleeping population are linked to Army experience in which bodies are disposed to overcome tough physical exigency.

In addition, knowledge diet and the maintenance of the physical body are woven into a masculinized ideology of fierce pride and independence, within limited conditions of housing and labor market opportunities. The idea of "standing on one's own two feet" and a kind of stoicism, crystallized in the phrase "soldiering on," serve as ready vocabularies of motive. Over time, these individuals may "take pride in," and become "psychologically attached to" (Carlen 1996:79) experiences that become assimilated into their identity as highly resourceful men enduring a degree of alienation in an unfamiliar, civilian environment. In foregrounding the somatic dimensions of human agency, there has been an attempt to transcend crude duality. According to Carlen (1996:9),

> Just as the concepts of homelessness and the homeless should not be conflated, neither are the sociological dualities of agency/structure...very useful in analysing the extremely complex and contradictory meanings conferred on the term homelessness by those who either experience or witness it.

323

While some in the settled population may remain intrigued by homelessness on account of its liberation from the consumptive norms of society and, therefore, its promise of "existential simplicity" (Wardhaugh 1999:91-92), others are likely to be surprised at the apparent *impossibility* of sleeping outside in freezing conditions. Here, an understanding of "resilient bodies" served to lessen the enormity of the imaginative leap required for those unfamiliar with such physically testing situations.

SUMMARY

The training of combat troops is oriented at producing high levels of physical fitness and strength. In order to be effective "in the field," soldiers must be tolerant of deprivations ranging from extremes of temperatures through to resilience in the face of "sleeping out" in uncomfortable conditions. This ability to survive and fight effectively could persist in civilian life in terms of both the transformed physical capital on which it depends, and the associated knowledge-including the importance of food and diet-vital for sustenance of the body in times of hardship. In this chapter I argued that the ex-soldier's resilient body represents a useful point of departure in attempting to account for the disproportionate number of ex-servicemen among the single homeless population, within the context of limited conditions of possibility. This line of inquiry could be particularly appropriate within the context of rough sleeping, an experience characterized by some continuity with life as a combat soldier.

KEY TERMS AND CONCEPTS

- Physical capital
- Embodiment
- Institutionalization
- Conditions of possibility
- Sociology of the body
- Somatic disposition
- Rough sleeping

STUDY AND DISCUSSION QUESTIONS

1. What methodological considerations might you include when devising a study to explore the embodied dimensions of social practice?

2. In the modern military, the physical fitness of personnel is becoming less important as technology assumes a more prominent role. Discuss.

3. Women could never serve in the combat arms as they are physically inferior to men. Discuss.

4. The masculine culture of the military is unlikely to change. Discuss.

NOTES

1. Elements of this article are reprinted with permission from the journal *Housing Theory and Society,* published by Taylor and Francis Group of Publishers.
2. In the study of Anderson et al. (1993), 1346 single homeless individuals were interviewed and only one woman reported that she had completed full-time military service. A similar picture emerged from the work of Gunner and

Knott (1997) and Randall and Brown (1994). This likely reflects the low number of women in the British military (Dandeker 1994) along with their scant visibility among the homeless population more generally (Wardhaugh 1999; Watson 1999). For practical reasons, the current study focused on the links between military service and ex-service*men*. In the text, and where appropriate, more general descriptions, including "service people," "service person," or "service personnel," are used.

3. The research project from which this paper has been drawn was funded by the ESRC, No R00429534145. All participant names used in this paper are pseudonyms.

4. The Anderson et al. study included those who had completed service in the Merchant Navy, but excluded National Servicemen who had been conscripted between 1945 and 1963.

5. In addition to the three reports outlined here, a good deal of anecdotal evidence points to the links between military service and homelessness for a number of ex-soldiers.

6. Jolly (1996) suggests that there is unlikely to be a straightforward relationship between length of military service and the effects it has on service people. Indeed, in her research in which 62 ex-service people were interviewed about their transition from military to civilian life, no such link between length of service and degree of institutionalization could be detected. For this reason, a focus on length of service is likely to explain less than is popularly thought within the context of homeless individuals with a military background.

7. The Army has remained relatively unchanged throughout the second half of this century, until the mid-1980s when political and other pressures may have influenced its traditional character. However, participants in this study tended

326

to have enlisted from the late 1960s through to the mid-1980s, before these transformations occurred. It is important to remember that the Army, within the context of a rapidly changing "host society," displays remarkable cultural continuity (Beevor 1991).

8. How "rough" is rough sleeping? For individuals who have extensive familiarity with sleeping outdoors, together with a well-developed awareness of survival techniques, the experience may be less traumatic than is popularly thought.

9. While this is the case, scope does exist for subverting these physical requirements, particularly in the context of war where Bourke (1999) reveals the extremely well-developed strategies of "malingering" used by soldiers to avoid various duties. In the training phase, however, tests have to be passed, and aside from the (unlikely) use of drugs or, for example, short-cuts on timed runs, there is little opportunity to resist such mechanisms of physical appraisal.

10. We should be aware of the context in which these comments were elicited. Indeed, "within gender" interviews between men (McKeganey and Bloor 1991) are often pervaded by "face saving work." Here, putting on a "brave face" and reluctance to admit defeat while enduring difficulty bolsters masculine identity (Owen 1996) leading to the articulation of a somewhat blasé or bravado account of events. These comments may have particular force within the context of ex-servicemen whose military experiences are grounded in a gender ideology in which "failure" (through homelessness) might be conflated with "weakness," resulting in an undermining of masculinized identity.

11. Studies of peacekeeping operations have found that troops trained for combat are more disposed to the use of force to

resolve conflict than other service personnel trained in "support roles." It seems likely that combat training produces effects relatively resistant to change (Olsson 1999). One explanation might be traced to the centrality of the sentient body to achieving these more aggressive "hands-on" aims most obvious during preparation for direct physical confrontation with the enemy.

12. In a parallel sense, Campbell (1996:167) describes the old soldier "who cannot stop himself saluting if anyone shouts 'Attention!'" Campbell's observation is drawn from comments by James (1890:114).

13. There may be some interesting links here between the acquisition of masculine identity and crime (Hearn 1998) where the tough and resilient bodies are deployed in violence, vandalism, and the use of drugs and alcohol.

REFERENCES

Anderson, I., P. Kemp, and D. Guilgars. 1993. *Single Homeless People*. London: HMSO.

Barrett, F. J. 1996. "The Organizational Construction of Hegemonic Masculinity: The Case of the U.S. Navy." *Genderwork and Organization* 3(3):129-142.

Beck, U. and A. Beck-Gernsheim. 1996. "Individualization and Precarious Freedoms: Perspectives and Controversies of a Subject-Oriented Sociology." In *Detraditionalization*, edited by P. Heelas, S. Lash, and P. Morris. London: Blackwell.

Beevor, A. 1991. *Inside the British Army*. London: Corgi Books.

Bines, W. 1997. "Health of Single Homeless People." In *Homelessness and Social Policy,* edited by R. Burrows, N. Pleace, and D. Quilgars. London: Routledge.

Bourke, J. 1999. *Dismembering the Male. Men's Bodies, Britain and the Great War*. London: Reaktion Books.

Caforio, G. 2003. *Handbook of the Sociology of the Military*. Amsterdam: Kluwer Academic/Plenum Publishers.

Campbell, C. 1996. "Detraditionalization, Character and the Limits to Agency." In *Detraditionalization,* edited by P. Heelas, S. Lash, and P. Morris. Oxford: Blackwell.

Carlen, P. 1996. *Jigsaw: A Political Criminology of Youth Homelessness*. Open University Press: Buckingham.

Cockburn, C. 1983. *Brothers, Male Dominance and Technological Change.* London: Pluto.

Cohen, S. and L. Taylor. 1992. *Escape Attempts.* London: Routledge.

Connell, B. 1995. *Masculinities.* Cambridge: Polity Press.

Connerton, P. 1989. *How Societies Remember.* Cambridge: Cambridge University Press.

Crossley, N. 1995. "Merleau-Ponty, the Elusive Body and Carnal Sociology." *Body and Society* 1:43-63.

Dandeker, C. 1994. "New Times for the Military: Some Sociological Remarks on the Changing Role and Structure of the Armed Forces of the Advanced Societies." *British Journal of Sociology* 45(4):637-654.

Edmonds, M. 1988. *Armed Forces and Society*. Leicester: Leicester University Press.

Featherstone, M. and M. Hepworth. 1998. "The Male Menopause, Lay Accounts and The Cultural Reconstruction of Midlife." In *The Body in Everyday Life,* edited by S. Nettleton and J. Watson. London: Routledge.

Featherstone, M., M. Hepworth, and B. S. Turner. 1991. *The Body: Social Processes and Cultural Theory.* London: Sage.

Foucault, M. 1977. *Discipline and Punish.* London: Penguin.

Freund, P. 1990. "The Expressive Body: A Common Ground for the Sociology of Emotions and Health and Illness." *Sociology of Health and Illness* 12:452-457.

Giddens, A. 1984. *The Constitution of Society.* Cambridge: Polity Press.

Goffman, E. 1961. *Asylums.* Garden City, New York: Doubleday Anchor.

Grillon, C., S. M. Southwick, and D. S. Charney. 1996. "The Psychobiological Basis of Post-Traumatic Stress Disorder." *Molecular Psychiatry* 1(4):278-297.

Gunner, G and H. Knott. 1997. *Homeless on Civvy Street.* London: Ex-Service Action Group.

Hearn, J. 1998. "Troubled Masculinities: Young Men." In *Men, Gender Divisions and Welfare,* edited by J. Popay, J. Hearn, and J. Edwards. London: Routledge.

Higate, P. 1997. "Soldiering On? Theorising Homelessness Amongst Ex-Servicemen." In *Homelessness and Social Policy*, edited by R. Burrows, N. Pleace, and D. Quilgars. London: Routledge.

_____. 1998. "The Body Resists: Everyday Clerking and Unmilitary Practice." In *The Body in Everyday Life,* edited by S. Nettleton and J. Watson. London: Routledge.

_____. 2000. "Ex-Servicemen on the Road: Travel and Homelessness." *The Sociological Review* 48(3):331-348.

_____. 2001. "Theorizing Military-Civilian Continuity." *Armed Forces and Society* 27(3): 443-460.

_____, ed. 2003. *Military Masculinities: Identity and the State.* New York: Greenwood.

Hockey, J. 1986. *Squaddies: Portrait of a Subculture.* Exeter: Exeter University Press.

James, W. 1950. *Principles of Psychology.* New York: Dover.

Jenkins, R. 1992. *Pierre Bourdieu.* London: Routledge.

_____. 1996. *Social Identity.* London: Routledge.

Jessup, C. 1996. *Breaking Ranks—Social Change in Military Communities.* London: Brassey's.

Jolly, R. 1992. *Military Man, Family Man—Crown Property?* London: Brassey's

_____. 1996. *Changing Step: From Military to Civilian Life, People in Transition.* London: Brassey's.

Kerfoot, D and D. Knights. 1993. "Management Masculinity and Manipulation: From Paternalism to Corporate Strategy in Financial Services in Britain." *Journal of Management Studies* 30(4):659-667.

Keyes, S. and M. Kennedy. 1992. *Sick to Death of Homelessness.* London: CRISIS.

Kurtz, Lester R. 1992. "War and Peace on the Sociological Agenda." Pp. 61-98 in *Sociology and its Publics,* edited by Terence C. Halliday and Morris Janowitz. Chicago: University of Chicago Press.

La Plante, L. 1992. *Civvies.* London: BCA.

Lupton, D. 1996. *Food, the Body and the Self.* London: Sage.

Mansfield, A. and B. McGinn. 1993. "Pumping Irony: The Muscular and the Feminine." In *Body Matters: Essays on the Sociology of the Body,* edited by S. Scott and D. H. J. Morgan. London: Falmer Press.

McCallion, H. 1995. *Killing Zone.* London: Bloomsbury.

McKeganey, N. and M. Bloor. 1991. "Spotting the Invisible Man: The Influence of Male Gender on Fieldwork Relations." *British Journal of Sociology* 42(2):195-210.

Mitchell, J. C. 1983. "Case and Situation Analysis." *American Journal of Sociology* 31:187-211.

Morgan, D. H. J. 1987. "'It Will Make a Man of You'. Notes on National Service, Masculinity and Autobiography." *Studies in Sexual Politics* No. 17, Department of Sociology: University of Manchester.

_____. 1989. "Strategies and Sociologists: A Comment on Crow." *Sociology* 23(1):25-29.

_____. 1990. "No More Heroes?" In *The State, Private Life and Political Change,* edited by L. Jamieson and H. Corr. Basingstoke: Macmillan.

_____. 1994. "Theater of War: Combat, the Military and Masculinities." In *Theorizing Masculinities,* edited by H. Brod and M. Kaufman. London: Sage.

_____. 1996. *Family Connections.* Polity Press: Cambridge.

Nettleton, S. and J. Watson. 1998. *The Body in Everyday Life.* London: Routledge.

O'Brien, S. 1993. "Morale and the Inner Life in the Armed Forces." *Therapeutic Communities* 14(4):285-295.

Olsson, L. 1999. *Gendering UN Peacekeeping.* Uppsala University: Department of Peace and Conflict Research.

Owen, D. 1996. "Men, Emotions and the Research Process: The Role of Interviews in Sensitive Areas." In *Qualitative Research: The Emotional Dimension,* edited by K. Carter and S. Delamont. Aldershot: Avebury.

Pleace, N., R. Burrows, and D. Quilgars. 1997. "Homelessness in Contemporary Britain. Conceptualisation and Measurement." In *Homelessness and Social Policy,* edited by R. Burrows, N. Pleace, and D. Quilgars. London: Routledge.

Pleace, N. 1998. "Single Homelessness as Social Exclusion: The Unique and the Extreme." *Journal of Social Policy and Administration* 1:46-59.

Randall, G. and S. Brown. 1994. *Falling Out: A Research Study of Homeless Ex-Service People.* London: CRISIS.

Rosenheck, R and A. Fontana. 1994 "A Model of Homelessness among Male Veterans of the War Generation." *American Journal of Psychiatry* 151(3):421-427.

Rosenheck, R. and P. Koegel. 1993. "Charateristics of Veterans and Non-Veterans in Three Samples of

332

Homeless Men." *Hospital and Community Psychiatry* 44(9):858-863.

Royle, T. 1997. *The Best Years of Their Lives*. London: John Murray.

Scott, S. and D. H. J. Morgan, eds. 1993. *Body Matters: Essays on the Sociology of the Body*. London: Taylor and Francis.

Seidler, V. 1997. *Embodying Masculinities*. London: Sage.

Shilling, C. 1991. "Educating the Body: Physical Capital and the Production of Social Inequalities." *Sociology* 25:653-672.

_____. 1993. *The Body and Social Theory*. London: Sage.

_____. 1997. "The Undersocialised Concept of the Embodied Agent in Modern Sociology." *Sociology* 31:737-754.

Snow, D. A. and L. Anderson. 1987. "Identity Work among the Homeless: The Verbal Construction and Avowal of Personal Identities." *American Journal of Sociology* 92:1136-1171.

Somerville, P. 1992. "Homelessness and the Meaning of Home: Rooflessness or Rootlessness." *Journal of International Regional and Urban Studies* 16(4):529-539.

Stone, C. J. 1996. *Fierce Dancing*. London: Faber & Faber.

Turner, B. S. 1996. *The Body and Society*. London: Sage.

Turner, B. and T. Rennell. 1995. *When Daddy Came Home*. London: Hutchinson.

Van Der Kolk, A. B. 1994. "The Body Keeps the Score: Memory and the Evolving Psychobiology of Post-Traumatic Stress." *Harvard Review of Psychiatry* 1(5):253-265.

Wacquant, L. 1995. "Pugs at Work: Bodily Capital and Bodily Labour among Professional Boxers." *Body and Society* 1:65-79.

Wardhaugh, J. 1999. "The Unaccommodated Woman: Home, Homelessness and Identity." *The Sociological Review* 47(1):91-109.

Watson, J. 1998. "Running Around Like a Lunatic: Colin's Body." In *The Body in Everyday Life*, edited by S. Nettleton and J. Watson. London: Routledge.

Watson, S. 1999. "A Home is Where the Heart is." In *Homelessness: Exploring the New Terrain*, edited by P. Kennett and A. Marsh. University of Bristol: The Policy Press.

Williams, S. 1998. "'Capitalising' on Emotions? Rethinking the Inequalities in Health Debate." *Sociology* 32(1):121-139.

Wilkinson, R. 1996. *Unhealthy Societies: The Afflictions of Inequality*. London: Routledge.

INTERVIEWS

Benny. 1996. Interviewed by the author. York, 21 November.

Brian 1996. Interviewed by author. London, 13 July.

Dougy. 1996. Interviewed by author. Glasgow, 23 July.

John. 1996. Interviewed by author. London, 14 September.

Ken. 1996. Interviewed by author. Glasgow, 12 December.

Lenny. 1996. Interviewed by author. London, 5 May.

Mick, 1996. Interviewed by author. Leeds, 12 August.

Paul. 1996. Interviewed by author. Leeds, 7 September.

Rolly. 1996. Interviewed by author. Manchester, 18 November.

Wicksy. 1996. Interviewed by author. York, 30 April.

Ziggy. 1996. Interviewed by author. York, 21 April.

334

INDEX

A

Abrahamsson, B., 14, 31, 184, 201
Adler, A.B., 235, 252
Adler, R.P., 256, 284, 289, 293
Afghanistan War, 79
Afghanistan, 17, 43, 46, 49, 196
Air Force, 183, 214-215, 219, 222
America's Army, 50-51, 57, 59
Anderson, L., 299, 319, 325-326, 328, 333
Anderson, R.J., 95-96, 132
Andreev, G., 81, 85-86
Anthropology, 28, 36
Armed Forces Entertainment, 46, 49
Armor, D., 62, 86
Army Sport Clubs, 41-42
Army, 210, 214-217, 219-222, 224, 227, 229
Aron, R., 8, 31
Athletes, 40-45, 56-57
Austerity, 134, 136, 141, 144-145, 149, 151-152
Austria, 189

B

Bach, T., 142, 157
Bader, W., 7
Balbier, U., 41, 57
Bald, D., 138-141, 154, 157
Banal Militarism, 37, 53-56
Barrett, F.J., 308, 310, 320, 328
Bartone, P.T., 235, 252
Bartov, O., 25, 31
Bauer, M., 43, 57
Bavaria, 135
Bavelier, D., 49, 58
Beck, U., 297, 328
Becker, S., 42, 45, 57

C

Ender, M.G., 28,255-256, 261, 264-265, 268, 282-283, 285-286, 290-291
England, 168, 174, 178-179, 189, 200, 205
Entropic Emotions, 231, 234, 236-237, 239, 241-242, 245, 248-249
Ethics, 136, 151-153
Ethnomethodology, 130
Europe, 62, 79
European Union, 194
Eyre, D.P., 8, 35

F

Featherstone, M., 305-306, 309, 329
Finkelstein, J., 186, 203
Finland, 189
Fischer, C.S., 256, 291
Fontana, A., 297, 332
Foucault, M., 308, 329
France, 27-28, 34, 36, 73, 148, 174, 178, 189, 205, 209-211, 213, 216, 219, 227, 229
Franks, D., 232, 252-254
French Armed Forces, 210, 226-227
French Ministry of Defense, 217
French Ministry of National Defense, 216
Frerk, C., 140, 158
Freund, P., 307, 329
Fulk, J., 259, 291

G

Gabriel, R., 236-238, 252
Garb, M., 14, 33
Garfinkle, H., 16, 33
German Armed Forces, 40-43, 45-47, 56, 135-136, 141, 152
German Army, 25, 27, 45-46, 48
German Department of Defense, 40-41
German Federal Armed Forces, 40, 57

Kemper, T.D., 252-253
Kennedy, M., 319, 322, 331
Kerfoot, D., 312, 331
Kertzer, D.I., 239, 253
Kestnbaum, M., 246, 252
Keyes, S., 319, 322, 331
Kleinheyer, A., 42, 58
Klinkert, W., 183-184, 203-205
Knights, D., 312, 331
Knott, H., 299, 326, 330
Koegel, P., 297, 332
Konopliev, V., 76, 79, 88
Korf, N., 62, 66, 78, 88
Korobejnikov, M., 79, 91
Korte, H., 171, 204
Kosovo, 17, 299
Kovaliev, V., 79, 88
Kraut, R.E., 256, 292
Krieken, R., 165, 171, 204
Krippendorff, E., 54, 58
Kruijf, F., 192-193, 204
Kuhlmann, J., 39, 58
Kuipers, G., 185, 204
Kümmel, G., 38-39, 59
Kurtz, L., 158-159, 298, 331
Kutz, M., 139, 159

L

La Plante, L., 304, 331
Lammers, C.J., 172, 204
Lardenoye, F., 192-193, 204
Lasswell, H., 151, 160
Latour, B., 16, 22, 34
Laughton, J.C., 263, 294
Leer, G., 65-66, 88
Levidow, L., 261, 285, 292

Nuciari, M., 6, 9, 13, 32, 35
Nvidia, 51, 59

O

O'Connell, R.L., 236, 254
Oberuchev, K., 62, 67, 88
Obraztsov, I., 26, 61-62, 68, 81, 85, 89, 91
Ogan, C., 261, 292
Olsson, L., 305, 328, 332
Olympics, 41-42
Organized Sports, 37, 56
Organized Violence, 1, 18, 23, 25, 30-31, 36
Orthner, D.K., 290, 294
Ouellet, E., 1
Owen, D., 327, 332
Oxford, R.L., 95, 133

P

Parker, I., 11, 35
Parsons, T., 165-166
Passeron, J.C., 185, 201
Patriarchy, 10
Patriotism, 19
Peacekeeping, 6, 20, 24, 35, 101, 131, 195, 197, 257, 305, 327, 332
Perinbanayagam, R.S., 233, 254
Persian Gulf War, 265
Pleace, N., 300, 328, 330, 332
Plessner, H., 135, 161
Poland, 79
Political Sociology, 2, 6, 24, 35
Portugal, 189
Post-Traumatic Stress, 231, 238, 248
Powell, C.L., 265, 292
Praetorian Guards, 2
Prisoners of War, 262

Sredin, G., 79, 91
Stalin Purges, 64, 72
Stalin, J., 64, 68, 70-72, 74, 79
Stalinism, 64
Stanley, J., 263, 288, 294
Steinfield, C.W., 259, 291
Steinmetz, R.S., 62, 91
Stolk, V., 171, 203
Stone, C.J., 305, 333
Suid, L.H., 45, 59
Svechin, A., 70, 91
Sweden, 189
Switzerland, 189

T

Tabunov, N.D., 78, 91
Taylor, L., 303, 325, 329
Teitler, G., 172-173, 206
Television, 256, 259, 284, 286
Thiéblemont, A., 16, 36
Thomas, T., 47, 55, 57, 59
Tilly, C., 167, 207
Tjushkevich, S., 79, 92
Toffler, A., 236, 254
Toffler, H., 236, 254
Tulder, J.J.M., 201, 207
Turkey, 189
Turner, B., 305, 312, 329, 333

U

U.S. Armed Forces, 38, 50
U.S. Army, 257, 286, 288-290, 293-294
U.S. Military, 238, 263, 290, 294
U.S. Soldiers, 281, 289
United Kingdom, 28, 170-171, 189, 195, 296

Printed in the United States
26218LVS00003B/43-84